THE IUVENILIA OF MARC-ANTOINE MURET

THE IUVENILIA OF MARC-ANTOINE MURET

With a translation, introduction, notes, and commentary by

Kirk M. Summers

The Ohio State University Press
Columbus

Copyright © 2006 by The Ohio State University.
All rights reserved.

Library of Congress Cataloging-in-Publication Data
Muret, Marc-Antoine, 1526–1585.
[Juvenalia. English & Latin]
The Iuvenilia of Marc-Antoine Muret / [translation, introduction, notes, and commentary by] Kirk M. Summers.
p. cm.
Latin text with English translation; notes and commentary in English.
Includes bibliographical references and index.
ISBN-13: 978-0-8142-1037-6 (cloth : alk. paper)
ISBN-10: 0-8142-1037-6 (cloth : alk. paper)
ISBN-13: 978-0-8142-9114-6 (cd-rom)
ISBN-10: 0-8142-9114-7 (cd-rom)
1. Muret, Marc-Antoine, 1526–1585—Translations into English. I. Summers, Kirk M., 1961– II. Title.
PA8555.M5A2 2006
871'.04—dc22
                    2006014409

Paper (ISBN: 978-0-8142-5758-6)

Cover design by Dan O'Dair
Text set in Adobe Garamond

CONTENTS

Preface and Acknowledgments	vii
Introduction	xiii
Bibliography	xxvii
Major Editions of the *Iuvenilia*	xxxi
Orthography and Punctuation	xxxiv
Identifiable Names of Muret's Contemporaries Appearing in the Text	xxxvi
Meters	xlvi
Liminary Poems: The Poems of Introduction	1
Muret's Praefatio to Jean de Brinon	9
Elegies	17
Commentary on the Elegies	41
Satires	53
Commentary on the Satires	63
Epigrams	67
Commentary on the Epigrams	137
Epistles	175
Commentary on the Epistles	183
Odes	187
Commentary on the Odes	203
Index	211

PREFACE AND ACKNOWLEDGMENTS

Before he produced editions of Catullus and Tacitus, wrote a commentary on Ronsard, or delivered orations as a diplomat of the Vatican, Marc-Antoine Muret (1526–1585) composed Latin elegies, poetic epistles, satires, odes, and epigrams. These *nugae*, or "trifles," as such pieces are often called, he published in a volume simply entitled *Iuvenilia*, along with the play *Iulius Caesar*. The latter I have not included in the present volume for reasons explained below. The rest, however, were in want of a modern edition, in particular, one that collated the first edition with subsequent printings to reconstruct the author's original manuscript as sent to the publisher. Here, of course, I am treading on dangerous ground, for, one might ask, what if the first printer reproduced Muret's manuscript exactly as he found it? And surely Muret himself proofed the galleys, as we would term them, before the press run. Even so, I have seen numerous first editions of neo-Latin poetry with errata sheets attached to the end, corrections that soon found their way into succeeding editions. Muret's *Iuvenilia* did not have such an errata sheet, perhaps as a result of the troubles he was then finding himself in at Paris, troubles that soon landed him in prison. Later editions do show a few variations, however, but without explanation as to their source. Are these conjectures that clean up some obvious problems, or are they derived from corrections found in the margins of Muret's own copy? At any rate, the changes are few, so that it was an easy enough task to bring all the editions together to make some gentle corrections to the first edition as it was printed. In essence, then, what the reader will find here is the Paris edition of 1552 with a few alterations that are duly documented by an apparatus criticus.

An important backdrop to this book has been Virginie Leroux's 2000 dissertation, directed by René Martin at Paris III and entitled *Les* Iuvenilia *de Marc-Antoine Muret (1552): édition, traduction, commentaire*. Currently, Dr. Leroux is revising this dissertation for publication with Librairie Droz in Geneva. One may reasonably question why, in light of that pending edition, my own edition is even needed. There is more than one justification. Dr. Leroux is not translating into English, but into French, and while admirably she translates much more precisely and carefully than Moret did four hundred years ago, the problem remains: the *Iuvenilia* has never been turned into English for English readers. Additionally, a second commentary will benefit

vii

everyone. Although from the beginning I corresponded with Dr. Leroux and saw bits and pieces of her commentary along the way, I only saw a complete copy of her dissertation *after* I had finished the task to which I had committed myself. In other words, we wrote our commentaries independently of one another, thus offering the reader two distinct perspectives to compare. In the end, however, I did obtain a copy of her dissertation and could myself compare my ideas with hers. In cases where I have added her observations to my own finished work, I have duly given her the credit in the text. This is particularly true, or frequent, I should say, when it comes to the identification of some obscure individuals named in the text. The reader will notice as well that Leroux emphasizes what I do not, and vice versa, that we often diverge in our approach to the text and reach differing interpretive conclusions. I consider this a bonus, a beginning of the attempt to come to grips with what Muret meant and wanted to convey, if indeed he even wanted to convey only one thing. No one scholar can hold all the keys in this regard.

With this said, I think the incredulous reader will still want to see some examples of how and where Leroux and I diverge. One obvious example occurs in regard to *epig.* 15. In lines 3–4 of that poem, Leroux gives the following text and translation:

> Pande, agedum, lasciva. Quid, o, quidnam oculis illud,
> Quo mea versantur corda, supercilium?

> Allons, coquine, laisse-les voir. Pourquoi, o pourquoi sur tes yeux,
> ce sourcil provoqunt les tourments de mon coeur?

She notes, with apparent puzzlement, that Charles Dejob in his biography on Muret has translated these lines as follows: "Pourquoi, o pourquoi cacher ce sourcil dont les mouvements agitent mon coeur!" The key lies in Dejob's word *cacher*. What, in Muret's lines, does this word translate? In fact, an error was introduced by Leroux herself when she accidentally replaced Muret's *occulis* with her own *oculis,* and then found herself without a main verb. Thus in English this is to be rendered as follows:

> Come, open them, naughty girl. Why are you hiding that
> brow, wherein my heart dwells?

Perhaps it is not fair to ferret out mistakes that may not make it into the published edition. The first epigram addressed to Julius Caesar Scaliger permits us to trace real differences in our approaches, both in the translation and in the commentary. The first two lines read as follows:

Preface and Acknowledgments   ix

> In tenues numeros, primi monumenta furoris,
> Quo mea non simplex corda subegit Amor . . .

Leroux translates these lines in this way:

> Sur mes modestes vers, témoignages de la première passion
> par laquelle le perfide Amour assujettit mon coeur . . .

The *perfide* stands as her rendering of the rather odd *non simplex* describing *Amor,* and, long before I saw Leroux's choice, my own inclination was to translate it with some English equivalent to *perfide* too. But when I encountered a similar phrase at *epig.* 32.3, I began to doubt my own translation. There Muret writes *geminus Cupido,* which led me to think of Eros and Anteros, as well as Ovid's phrase, *geminorum mater Amorum* (*Fast.* 4.1). This *geminus,* then, seems to stand behind *non simplex* as the positive expression, or, if you will, the obverse of the litotes. In fact, we find in the ancient writers mention of, not just two Erotes, but many, sometimes even thousands (e.g., Prop. 2.2). Thus I have opted to translate *non simplex Amor* as "the band of Erotes," which is an option that Leroux herself entertains as a possibility in her commentary: "Ou 'où des Amours multiples ont entrainé mon coeur.'"

At the end of the same poem, Muret concludes with the following line:

> Dux olim, et princeps: nunc mihi paene Deus.

The translation is obvious, and on that Dr. Leroux and I do not disagree. In the commentary, however, we take a different approach. She believes that Muret is playing on the identification of *dux* Julius Caesar and Julius Caesar Scaliger. The idea is interesting, since it can be said of the former that he was a general, a ruler, and then, in his apotheosis as a comet, a god. Yet, nothing else in the epigram itself leads us to think of Julius Caesar. To the contrary, if Muret were introducing Julius Caesar here, he would at the same time be insulting Scaliger, since he would be attaching honor to him that he had only earned through his namesake, not by virtue of his own accomplishments. Further, in no other epigram of Muret that is addressed to Scaliger do we discern even the remotest hint of a play on the name of the Roman leader. It is more pertinent, therefore, to ask by what accomplishments Scaliger himself has earned the titles *dux, princeps,* and *Deus.* Indeed, Scaliger does claim to belong to a family who ruled for a time over Verona (*princeps*), and he did serve as an officer in the Battle of Ravenna (*dux*). That he deserved the title *Deus,* Muret asserts over and over again in other epigrams.

Many more examples of our divergences could be mentioned. In *epig.* 2, the phrase in line 7, *aeterna damnentur ut omnia nocte,* is handled by Leroux in this way: "sinon, qu'ils soient, comme tout, condamnés à une nuit sans fin." But since here we are dealing with a hyperbaton not uncommon to poetry, this should be taken as a purpose clause correlated to the one in line 5 (*Ut tibi si . . .*). Both are introduced by the *iussa subire* in line 4. Therefore, I have translated the line, "[but if not,] that they might all be condemned to an eternal night of death." In *epig.* 22, Leroux and I have a different interpretation of the ending. The reader can decide whether her explanation of *philosomphos* as "one who absorbs without understanding," or my own as "lover of void." I frankly do not think the poem suggests that Caliantheus has absorbed the material but merely failed to understand it. Rather, he loves the empty show. For *epig.* 25, I believe that the reader will look for some comment on the pun with which the poem ends: *Quod se frugibus unicus repertis, / Multa pascere glande perseverat.* Leroux points to the parallel in Cicero's *Orator,* from which Muret definitely borrowed: *Quae est autem in hominibus tanta perversitas, ut inventis frugibus glande vescantur?* But how does this borrowing explain the pun? No comment is offered. Given the portrayal of the subject of this epigram elsewhere in Muret's poetry, however, we should not be surprised that this is actually a tasteless sexual metaphor, drawn from Mart. 12.75.3: *pastas glande natis habet Secundus.*

This is not meant to be a review of Leroux's dissertation. Her work is thoroughly researched and dense, and will provide the scholarly reader with a wealth of information. Instead, I mean to justify the present volume in light of her work by demonstrating that they are not a duplication of one another.

The same can be said for the German translation and "edition" of D. Schmitz published in 1995, but for a radically different reason. Leroux herself has dismissed Schmitz's work as flawed in many ways, and with her I must concur. The translations frequently do not reflect the Latin; the commentary is superficial and full of gaffes; and the text depends on only one later edition, that of Frotscher. For this reason, I have almost never referred to it (Leroux does, at times, but he is hardly worth refuting), even though I have read it through.

Now another decision must be defended, namely, why I did not include the play *Julius Caesar* along with the poems, even though it was part of the first edition. In the final analysis, my rationale boils down to the fact that I have no compelling interest in theater during this period and no special background in it to allow me to make a useful contribution. The reader would gain more by going to the editions of Blanchard (1995) and Lemarque (1998) listed in the bibliography. Both have translations and the former includes a commentary. Much is to be gained also from reading Bloemendal's article in

Recreating Ancient History. Anything that I could produce here would simply be redundant and derivative.

My aim with this edition is to supply a reliable text and up-to-date translation of Muret's poetry for the nonspecialist. In the term "nonspecialist" I include a) those who study the Renaissance but whose proficiency in Latin is weak or nonexistent, and b) classical scholars who are interested in the *Nachleben* of ancient literature but who lack experience in reading neo-Latin texts. The commentary is meant to aid in the interpretation of the poems *particularly* in light of classical literature, though ample attention is given throughout to Muret's contemporaries writing in Latin. The commentary is tied to the Latin text instead of the English text because, more often than not, it is the precise provenance and meaning of some Latin phrase that is in view. I have not wanted the critical apparatus to become cumbersome and unwieldy, filled with tangential bits of information, since the state of the text does not require it. For this reason I have not included obvious misprints from the various editions, nor have I detailed punctuation and orthographic variances. For example, it is not necessary in the preface to note that the 1579 edition has *Comes hortari* when the 1553 has *Comes valde hortari*. Nor is it necessary to linger over the almost endless permutations of punctuation that exhibit themselves throughout the various editions. Conventions change, so that what once made sense in the context of the Renaissance is largely useless to us today. In fact, in this edition I have updated the punctuation within the Latin text itself to reflect modern norms. On both issues of punctuation and orthography I have explained my *modus operandi* in more detail below in "Orthography and Punctuation."

Finally, I want to acknowledge the generous help I received from a number of sources. As always, the Newberry Library of Chicago is a gold mine of information and hard-to-find texts. I am grateful to the staff there who went out of their way to accommodate me and help me track down *minutiae* hidden away in corners of the library. Also, my thanks go out to Bruce Swann, Special Collections and Classics librarian at the University of Illinois at Urbana-Champaign, who assisted me in certain quests for documents and data along the way. And, to be sure, I have relied heavily on the comments and advice of the anonymous referees for The Ohio State University Press and owe them a debt of gratitude for steering me in the right direction many times over.

INTRODUCTION

Marc-Antoine Muret (1526–1585) exemplifies the essence of French Renaissance humanism. A master of Latin and student of Classical antiquity, he not only engaged in the recovery and exposition of ancient texts, he also actively employed the old genres and skills in the contemporary ecclesiastical and public spheres. He wrote Latin poetry, both sacred and profane, delivered public orations in Latin, and lectured in various schools throughout France and Italy on authors as diverse as Catullus and Tacitus and on topics as varied as Greek philosophy and Roman law. His list of friends, acquaintances, teachers, and students reads like a *Who's Who* of the period. He twice received counsel from the elder Scaliger at Agen and at Poitiers participated in a poetry contest judged by Jean Salmon Macrin. At Limoges, he knew Jean Dorat and Joachim du Bellay. Pierre Ronsard and Montaigne attended his lectures at various times, and Ronsard corresponded with him throughout his life. Denys Lambin, the great commentator of Lucretius, befriended him until their odd falling out in 1559. At Paris, he crossed paths with George Buchanan, Claude Goudimel, François le Duchat, Étienne Jodelle, and other well-known poets, printers, musicians, and intellectuals active there. At Venice he knew Paulus Manutius, who helped him to publish some of his books. Through his association with Ippolito d'Este, Cardinal of Ferrara, Muret came to the circle of Pope Pius V. And like many humanists of the day, he faced the turmoil that was fueled when classical world views clashed with Christian piety. Charged with heresy and sodomy, he was nearly burned at the stake while at Toulouse. Lambin, his old friend, would later accuse him of plagiarism for his *Variae Lectiones*. At Rome he was forbidden to lecture on certain subjects, such as Law and Plato. Despite the scandal and turbulence, in 1576 he received his Holy Orders, a humanist turned minister of the Church, and in that capacity he spent the rest of his life.

Muret's outlook and style, his way of reading ancient texts and putting them into practice, the odd *contaminatio* of Christian piety and classicizing humanism, the almost religious enthusiasm for learning and living, mark him as fairly typical among intellectual elites of the period. For him, antiquity not only provided the tools for rhetoric and elegant expression, but was the means to explore ethical questions as well, on a level rivaling that of the Scriptures. In an oration delivered in 1573 as his inaugural lecture on Plato, for example, Muret expresses the hope that God will favor his examination of the civic *summum bonum* in Plato's *Republic* and the individual *summum bonum* in Cicero's *De finibus,* an enterprise that he describes as *utilis* and *honestum.* To this he adds a remarkable assertion about the capacity of ancient learning to guide human lives:

> Primum igitur istis Graecae linguae osoribus ita responsum volo, omnem elegantem doctrinam, omnem cognitionem dignam hominis ingenui studio, uno verbo, quicquid usquam est politiorum disciplinarum, nullis aliis, quam Graecorum libris ac literis, contineri.[1]

> First, I wish to respond to those who hate the Greek language by saying this: Every elegant doctrine, all knowledge worthy to be studied by a freeborn man; in short, whatever at all belongs to the polite disciplines, is contained nowhere else but in the books and literature of the Greeks.

All knowledge (*omnem cognitionem*) worth pursuing? It is no wonder that Muret fell into disfavor with the Church from time to time. In October of 1554, shortly after the publication of the *Iuvenilia,* Muret was in Venice extolling the same humanist manifesto in another public oration, this time in praise of classical literature. Arguing that literature is a necessary precursor to virtue and the foundation of a flourishing State, he speaks of its ability to entice readers with its pleasurable form to fill themselves with healthy precepts:

> ... non tantum bene dicendi, verum etiam bene vivendi commonstrant vias: excitant in animis nostris igniculos gloriae: quantus sit in virtute splendor, quanta in vitiis deformitas, edocent: quae qui semel bene penitus imbiberint, ii nunquam non postea et vitii turpitudinem omni studio refugient, et officii honestatisque rationem rebus aliis omnibus anteponent.[2]

> They show us the paths, not only of speaking well, but also of living well. They quicken in our souls flashes of glory. They teach how much splendor lies in virtue, how much ugliness in vice. Whoever imbibes their doctrines deeply and completely will ever after flee from the shamefulness of vice and place above all a devotion to duty and goodness.

---

1. *Mureti opera* (Ruhnken), I: 236.
2. Ibid., I: 18.

The path to living well starts with the ancient authors, who ignite "flashes of glory" in our souls. Literature, he adds, has its own kind of *voluptas* and *oblectatio*. It imitates the alluring power of Venus and Cupid, the most powerful of the gods, to draw the reader away from sensual temptations into the vestal world of Minerva, just as once Orpheus used his enchanting songs to turn the Argonauts from the delicate songs of the Sirens back to the thoughts of virtue. The artifice of literature, therefore, its rhetoric and charms, the sounds and fabulous nature of it, merely counter the artifice of sensuality, fighting fire with fire, as we say.

Thus we have a guide for understanding the *Iuvenilia* here at hand. Although we cannot deny that this poetry reflects the typical schoolboy exercises deemed necessary for teaching style, Muret never condones literature for the sake of literature, delight for the sake of delight. Instead, the present work was born out of his humanist convictions that literature should ennoble the human spirit and "inflame the soul with a zeal for excellence."[3] If that does not seem the case at first glance, we can blame it on the competition with Venus.

Muret and his work must be put into a historical context. He was born on April 12, 1526, in the town that bears his name near Limoges. We do not know enough about his early years or his intellectual formation, except that much of what he knew was self-taught, as he was "stimulated to study by domestic examples."[4] The fields of philosophy and jurisprudence drew him from the earliest age, but it was in rhetoric that the young Muret naturally excelled, so much so that Montaigne would later call him "le meilleur orateur du temps."[5] Much doubt has been cast on the traditional chronologies of Muret's early years, at least up until 1547, when we can definitely place him in Bordeaux. In general, the biographers have tended to reconstruct the humanist's early years as follows: We first find him already a professor in 1544 in the college of Auch at age eighteen, where he composed the Latin tragedy *Julius Caesar,* a production of which Montaigne himself supposedly played a part in later at Bordeaux. Then, after a brief teaching stint at Villeneuve-d'Agen in 1545, and possibly a short excursion to Paris, he made his way to Poitiers to teach in the college of Sainte-Marthe there. Finally, in 1547 he

---

3. Ibid.: " . . . aut animum praeclararum rerum studio accendere . . ." Muret's practical prescription for the training of the youth as expressed in his *De via ac ratione tradendarum disciplinarum* (*On Instructional Methodology*) has been analyzed and put into historical context by P. Sharratt (see bibliography). He observes that Muret believed "the teacher of literature should strive for encyclopedic knowledge," and resisted the segregating of disciplines. He also sees in Muret an insistence on the usefulness of the study of literature for creating well-informed, moral leaders.

4. According to his 2nd discourse, 1554.

5. Essay 1, 26.

went to Bordeaux, with the recommendation of Julius-Caesar Scaliger, where he spent the next four years teaching at Collège de Guyenne,[6] until he left in 1551 for Paris.

R. Trinquet has cast serious doubt on this canonical early chronology.[7] All of it appears to stem from a mistake that Joseph Scaliger, the son of Julius-Caesar Scaliger, made in a polemical work published in 1608 at Leiden. In that work, *Confutatio stultissimae Burdonum fabulae*, Scaliger explicitly asserts that at age eighteen Muret was teaching Cicero and Terence at the college in Auch. But he appears to have made a mistake in his old age, by transcribing the date M.D.XL.V.IIII as M.D.XL.IIII from the first edition of the *Julius Caesar*, an edition that is now completely lost to us. From that mistake, he began to calculate the age of Muret to fit other events of his early days. In reality, Muret likely spent only part of 1547 and 1548 at Bordeaux, not four years, during which time he tutored Montaigne, and afterwards went to Auch (for the first time) to teach for about three years. While there, he published his *Julius Caesar* (1549), along with some eclogues for the Cardinal d'Armagnac.[8]

At any rate, in 1551 we find Muret in Paris delivering lectures at the Collège du Cardinal Lemoine and the Collège de Boncourt. In 1552 Muret lectured on Catullus to a large audience that included several members of the Pléiade, in particular his friend Ronsard. We can only assume that the commentary on Catullus that Muret produced "in three months" in Italy the following year, after a request by Paulus Manutius, reflects fairly closely the content and style of the lectures. M. Morrison has shown that Ronsard assimilated much material from those lectures and applied them to his own practice of poetry. Clearly, Ronsard knew Catullus well before hearing Muret's lectures, but without a doubt Muret's lectures brought Catullus into vogue.[9]

---

6. Gaullieur (see. bibliography below), 230, suggests that certain personality traits, exhibited very noticeably by him while teaching at Bordeaux, eventually brought about his downfall: "Dové de beaucoup d'esprit naturel, il avait la répartie fort vive, et lorsque les écoliers troublaient ses leçons pars leurs propos ou leurs polissonneries, il avait l'art de leur imposer silence par quelque mot piquant. Cette promptitude à décocher des traits lui fit, dit-on, beaucoup d'ennemis."

7. R. Trinquet, "Recherches chronologiques," 272ff.

8. The play was probably written in 1547 (see Blänsdorf), then reworked by Grévin in 1560. Jeffrey Foster's edition of Grévin's play (Paris, 1974) includes the Latin text of Muret's *Caesar* on pp. 103–23. Muret was the first to show the murder of Julius Caesar on the stage. The chorus of his play concentrates, however, not so much on the pros or cons of monarchy, but on the constant cycle of power reversals, or action and reaction, at work in the politics of any given State.

9. M. Morrison, "Ronsard and Catullus," 246; cf. also J. Gaisser, "Catullus," 261.

INTRODUCTION   xvii

The commentary demonstrates his sensitivity to the text both as a humanist scholar and as a poet. Unlike most other commentators of the time, he occasionally offers aesthetic judgments on Catullus' poetry (we are told that poem 68 is the most beautiful elegy in the Latin language, primarily on account of its Alexandrian technique), mulls over the choice of vocabulary, and discusses how the meter serves to produce a certain effect. But Muret may have done the most for Catullus' text by not flinching or allegorizing when he came to difficult passages. On Catullus 16 (*pedicabo et irrumabo* . . .), for example, Muret is matter-of-fact in his interpretation of the poet's most strikingly obscene lines:

> Furius et Aurelius de Catullo, tanquam effeminato, et impudico, ob mollitiem carminum, senserant. id nunc eis irascitur, negatque, poetarum mores e scriptis spectari oportere. eadem excusatione utitur Ovidius,
>
> Crede mihi, distant mores a carmine nostri.
> Vita verecunda est, Musa iocosa mihi.

et Martialis,

> Lasciva est nobis pagina, vita proba est.
>
> et notum est illud in Voconium,
> Lascivus versu, mente pudicus eras.
>
> Furius and Aurelius had felt that Catullus was effeminate and unchaste, because of the softness of his poems. He is angry at them about that, and denies that one can learn the poet's mores in his writings. Ovid used the same defense: "Believe me, my mores are different from my poetry. My life is modest, my Muse is jocular." And Martial: "My page is wanton, my life is good." And that well-known line about Voconius: "You were wanton in verse, chaste in mind." [Apuleius, *Apol.* 11.3, quoted from Hadrian]

This comment, though far too brief for the demands of the passage (he only comments on *male marem* from the rest of the poem), is fairly remarkable in its historical context, not so much for what he *does* do, but for what he *does not* do.

As he typically does, Muret begins with a summary of the gist of the poem and then follows up with a few explanatory notes on individual phrases or words. One looks in vain here and elsewhere in the commentary for the "flashes of glory" that he promised to ignite when he lectured to the Venetians on the value of classical literature. The fact that the obscenities in poem 16 are read as an integral part of the poem and not glossed over with the forced moralizing that characterizes his predecessor, Pierio Valeriano, who lectured on Catullus at the University of Rome in the 1520s, suggests that Muret was more interested in technical matters of philology and exegesis than in ethical precepts. It had been Valeriano's view that the interpreter should edify and instruct his students in matters of virtue through the use of the ancient texts, and furthermore that (and this was typical of the period as well) he should teach his students to draw from authors such as Catullus stylistic tools to imitate in their own writing.[10] Given the oration about morality in ancient literature, one would assume that Muret would applaud Valeriano and want to imitate his style of commentary. He does not. On close inspection, however, Muret is not being inconsistent with his oration, since there we see that the "flashes of glory" stem, not so much from the teacher drawing lessons willy-nilly from a text, but from a direct contact with the text on the part of the reader. His commentary, in fact, assumes that the ability of the classics to edify goes hand in hand with a correct reading and comprehension of the text. That explains why, throughout, Muret is genuinely interested in textual matters and significant philological concerns, and though he often errs, he does strive to explicate a passage as a whole unit rather than as a set of individual words that serve as a conduit for digressions.

Muret's gaffe in accepting and commenting on the reading *mane mane* at Catullus 10.27 (from Guarino's version) has been the subject of some ridicule.[11] But one derives a better feel for what Muret was doing by looking at the first few comments on the very same poem:

> *Varus.*] Quinctilium Varum Cremonensem dicit, hominem belli, pacisque artibus clarissimum, qui postea in Germania cum tribus legionibus caesus est. *Ut mihi tum repente visum est,*] quantum ego ex primo illo aspectu iudicare potui. *Bithynia,*] ex qua ego haud ita pridem redieram, cum praetore Memmio illuc profectus. *nec praetoribus.*] puto locum hunc non vacare mendo. neque enim plures praetores in unam provinciam mittebantur. fortasse legendum sit, *quaestoribus. Cur quisquam caput unctius referret,*] cur quisquam, propter lucrum in provincia factum, quidquam adiiceret ad solitum victus cultusque splendorem. Olim elegantiores homines odoratis unguentis caput perfundere solebant. Horatius:
>
> —*coronatus nitenteis Malobatro Syrio capillos.*

---

10. Gaisser, *Catullus*, 116–18.
11. Ibid., 158.

Martialis,

Si sapis, Assyrio semper tibi crinis amomo splendeat.

Plautus Casina,

—*unde hic, amabo, unguenta olent? St. oh, peri.*
Manufesto miser teneor. cesso caput pallio obtegere?

Varus.] He is talking about Quinctilius Varus Cremonensis, a man renowned in the arts of war and peace, who later was cut down in Germany together with three legions. *Ut mihi tum repente visum est,*] as much as I could judge from that first glance. *Bithynia,*] from which I just barely returned, having gone there with the praetor Memmius. *nec praetoribus.*] I think this passage needs correcting, because they did not used to send more than one praetor into a province. Perhaps he wrote *questoribus. Cur quisquam caput unctius referret,*] Why anyone, because of the profit made in the province, should enhance his lifestyle or his appearance. Once the elegant people used to pour sweet-smelling unquents on their head. Horace: "crowned on their glistening hair with Syrian malobathrum." Martial: "If you are smart, you hair will always shine with Assyrian balsam." Plautus in his *Casina:* "Whence here this strong scent of unguents, pray tell?" Stalino: "Oh dear, I'm undone. Wretch that I am, I'm caught in the act. Am I going to quit rubbing my head with my cloak?"

Obviously, Muret has confused his Varuses, and I know of no modern editor who has accepted his conjecture *quaestoribus.* Even so, he has offered some useful parallels for the phrase *caput unctius* and provided a basic explanation of it. He goes on in the commentary to highlight *beatiorum* in line 17 (he does not entertain the reading *beatiorem*), and then gloss it with several Latin and Greek passages to show that it means "rich."

Right or wrong, Muret was teaching Catullus to a packed house and enthusiastic crowds in Paris. DeJob, citing the description of Benci, describes a scene where every nook and cranny was filled with students waiting to hear him, and that the teacher himself had to climb to his chair on the shoulders of the audience. Perhaps even the king and the queen came to hear him lecture.[12] But

---

12. Lazeri (Ruhnken IV: 525) reports this anecdote from Benci's funeral oration, and though Scaliger had scoffed at it, he gives it some measure of credence.

Muret's glory in Paris was not long-lived. At the very height of his success, when he was preparing the publication of the *Iuvenilia* and a commentary on the *Amours* of Ronsard, he was accused of "penchants antiphysiques," which one may presume means he took too much interest in some of his young male students. He was locked in the Chatelet de Paris, where he would have starved himself to death out of despair rather than face an ignominious execution, if not for the intervention of his friends.

After being freed from that prison, Muret fled to Toulouse. There, while beginning to teach on Roman law, he was accused of not having desisted from his former sodomy, this time carrying on, so the charge went, illicit relations with a young boy in his tutorship, by the name Luc-Menge Fremiot (sometimes called "Memmius"). This is the same youth whose two poems appear in editions of the *Iuvenilia* itself, and to whom Muret dedicated with great affection his translation of the *Topica* of Aristotle in 1554.[13] There he speaks of their "common disgrace," but without admitting to the crime. In fact, Muret's accusers charged him with both sodomy and heresy—they had concluded he was a Huguenot, perhaps because of his association with Buchanan—and the judges condemned him to be burned at the stake. In the end, they could only burn him (and Fremiot) in effigy. Again with the help of friends, Muret was able to escape, and this time he sought asylum in Italy. In the course of that journey he fell gravely ill while in North Italy (Lombardy). An anecdote has come down that the doctors who were assigned to attend to him thought, because of his tattered clothes (a disguise?), that he was a vagrant. One spoke to the other, "faciamus experimentum in anima vili," at which point Muret startled them by replying in elegant Latin, "Vilem animam appellas pro qua Christus non dedignatus est mori," thus escaping once again from imminent torture.[14]

After this harrowing incident, Muret found himself in Venice (at least by May 1554), where he made important contacts. Here he immediately met Paulus Manutius (Paolo Manuzio, 1512–1574), the youngest son of Aldo, who founded the famous press that bears his name. We learn from the preface of Muret's commentary on Catullus that Manutius shared the enthusiasm for Catullus and encouraged Muret to publish his lecture notes as soon as possible. After some reluctance and brief hesitation, Muret produced them in less than three months: "hoc tamen, quidquid est, trium mensium, aliquanto etiam minore, spatio absolverim."

---

13. He also composed the poem, "In imaginem M. A. Mureti e vivo expressam," which appears in some of Ronsard's editions of poetry.

14. Told by his contemporary Colletet (see bibliography below) and reported by DeJob, 60.

Venice was a tolerant and liberal place at the time, and so would not have been completely inimical to accepting someone suspected of protestant leanings. Even so, Muret's hasty retreat from France had not allowed him to obtain the letters of recommendation or introduction that were normally expected in this era. Thus, when he tried to obtain a public teaching post, he met with some obstacles and resistance. The position itself, which normally would not be open to foreigners in any case, appears to have been a chair of humanities, one of six created by an ordinance of a special council in 1551 to serve inhabitants in some of the more distant quarters of the city.[15] Thanks, however, to the intervention and support of a certain Girolamo Ferri, a member of the commission of public instruction, Muret was allowed to stand for the examination required of candidates who had no previous record of accomplishment (or in Muret's case, no evidence or letters). For the most part, the examination required that Muret compose and deliver a discourse in Latin. The oration delivered appears to be *De laudibus literarum*,[16] and, not surprisingly, one finds there sundry niceties about the value of an education along with much laud and tribute to the Venetians themselves. At any rate, the outcome is clear: Muret held the professorship of humanities from 1555 to 1558.

To this period of his life belongs many of Muret's publications in the press of Manutius. The Catullus commentary in 1554, already mentioned, was followed up with another edition that included the texts of Tibullus and Propertius as well (1558). In rapid succession he published editions of Horace and Terence with notes (1555), three orations on the study of literature (1555), annotated editions of the *Catilinarians* (1556) and the first book of the *Tusculan Disputations* (1557). It was in Venice too that Muret made the acquaintance of Denys Lambin, who was in Italy in the service of Cardinal de Tournon. Lambin came from Rome just to see Muret and Manutius and to discuss scholarly matters. A frank and open friendship developed between them, and Lambin felt comfortable sharing with Muret details about the edition of Horace that he was working on.

In 1557 Ippolito d'Este, Cardinal of Ferrara, began to gather to his patronage several French and Italian savants. Through his agent, Pierre Morin, he negotiated with Muret under what conditions he might be willing to connect himself with him at Ferrara. But Morin was soon to withdraw the offer, when the old charges of indiscretion again surfaced, this time from none other than de Tournon. In early 1558, under obscure circumstances, Muret left Venice and moved to Padua to take up private tutorials there in the houses of the nobility, while the negotiations with

---

15. This is the view of DeJob, 81.
16. Ruhnken, I, 16–24 (Oratio II, October, 1554, at Venice, excerpts of which are quoted above).

the cardinal, though now strained, continued. It would be late 1558, however, after Ippolito's envoy, the abbot Nichette, interviewed him, and after Lambin and others spoke successfully on his behalf with de Tournon, before he would finally enter the service of the cardinal and come to live in his household.

During his time at Padua, Muret continued to teach and to publish. In 1558 he came out with the first book of the *Variae Lectiones,* a random collection of observations on a variety of texts. This work, which was the most important achievement of Muret's career to that point, unfortunately sparked a feud with Lambin. In all sincerity Muret had sent a copy of the *Variae* to Lambin, pointing out to him that he had mentioned him in several places. Lambin, however, responded in a rather harsh letter with charges of plagiarism and broken confidence. He claimed that the scholia on Horace were stolen from an edition of Horace that he himself was working on and had shared with Muret out of friendship. Within two years after this incident, the rupture between the two old friends was complete. After a trip to Rome at the death of Pope Paul IV, Muret had followed Ippolito to France, with some trepidation, to participate in the Colloquy of Poissy. Ostensibly he was there to keep Antoine de Bourbon in the Catholic fold and to resist the Calvinists (Bèze would always hold a grudge against Muret for his role),[17] but he may have seen this trip as an opportunity to clear his name with his detractors and to meet some old friends. Among these friends, or so he thought, was Lambin. After what appears to have been a cordial meeting, something changed. For reasons that cannot really be explained, Lambin handed over the intimate correspondence between himself and Muret, from their time together in Italy, to Gryphius at Lyons, which the latter published at his press (1561). These letters included not only the charges of plagiarism, but also the details of the charges leveled against Muret during the negotiations with Ippolito. For this cruelty and indiscretion that ultimately lowered his public stature, Muret was never able to forgive Lambin.

In 1563 Muret followed Cardinal Ippolito from France and returned to Rome. Shortly after his arrival, Pope Pius IV appointed Muret professor of Moral Philosophy at the University of Rome (the Studium Sapientiae) with, it is assumed, the consent of Ippolito. This marks the beginning of an entirely new era of Muret's life, one in which he began to take on an international reputation as a first-rate savant, able to marry eloquence and philosophy in the way Ramus was advocating at the University of Paris. His course on Aristotle's *Nicomachean Ethics*

---

17. In the 1597 and 1599 (p. 74v) editions of his poetry, Bèze included a scathing epitaph directed at Muret, in which he calls him a *monstrum* and a *cinaedus,* who died in a city (Rome) worthy of his impiety.

that he taught from 1563–1567 drew eager listeners and met with great success. It also solidified his fame as an orator. In 1566 and 1567 he was asked to deliver eulogies to Pope Pius V on behalf of Alphonse II d'Estes, Charles IX, and Sigismond of Poland. In 1571 Muret proclaimed a panegyric on the victory of Lepante and earned the title "Roman citizen." The next year he delivered a funeral oration for Pope Pius V in which he praised him for his harsh dealings with "heretics." Ippolito, meanwhile, for whom he still worked, continued to entrust his secretary more and more with important ecclesiastical and personal matters on an international scale.

It was during this time that Muret turned to the study of law. He began teaching the *Pandects,* not with the usual methodology of the day, but more along the lines of his contemporary, the French jurist Jacques Cujas (1522–1590), who interpreted the ancient legal texts with philological tools adapted from the humanists along with a sensitivity to historical development. For the Romans, this was an innovation, though they could look to Alciati for a similar approach, and they dubbed the critical technique practiced by Muret the "French method of teaching" (*mos docendi gallicus*).

By 1572 Muret faced several new challenges for his career. His unorthodox teaching style and the fame that he was winning from it brought suspicions of general unorthodoxy upon him from jealous peers. Muret had further alienated many of them by his malicious and ironic way of dealing with them. But if there was one area in which Muret was careful, it was in regard to his finances. Perceiving that the end was near for his beloved protector Ippolito d'Este,[18] and not knowing what would be his condition after Ippolito's death, he agreed to step down from the teaching of law, but only after negotiating a significant pay raise. Again Muret found himself teaching literature, or more specifically, rhetoric, a subject with which the cardinals thought he could do the least harm to the students if indeed he was less than orthodox. The cardinals, to judge from Muret's letters at the time, believed that he was inviting too much free critical thinking among his listeners. Therefore, it was his *un*dogmatic teaching style and his willingness to examine a text without the prejudice of authority that distressed them most.

It would not be long before they had another cause for concern. Muret did not stick to his subject, but quickly and somewhat surreptitiously exchanged the teaching of rhetoric for the teaching of philosophy. He began with Cicero's philosophical works, in particular the *De republica,* which he coupled with a study of Plato's

---

18. Ippolito did indeed die at the end of 1572, but his heir, Louis d'Este, retained Muret in his house, though in a somewhat diminished status.

Republic. His introduction of Plato into the curriculum and the fact that he was using the Athenian philosopher to comment on the Roman author excited his listeners greatly. This proved too much for the cardinals, however. Muret was hardly trained in theological matters, but here he was quoting the Church Fathers constantly and colliding with matters of theology under the guise of philosophical inquiry. In 1575 they forbade him to teach Greek philosophy, and Muret obeyed.

At the very moment that the cardinals were trying to corral Muret to where he could do the least harm, he was, in fact, on the road to spiritual transformation. Many factors appear to have been at work to bring about the change: In the midst of a rather tumultuous life, he had surrounded himself with students and protectors whose piety had begun to make an impression upon him. In 1575 he published a volume of religious poems and hymns glorifying various saints and feast days of the Church.[19] The titles of the poems themselves indicate his religious preoccupations: *In die ascensionis; In Festo corporis Christi; In die Paschae; Commune angelorum; Ad beatissimam virginem, Dei matrem, quae religiosissime colitur in aede Lauretana;* and so on. Many of them echo relevant parts of the mass, which, as his student Benci reports, Muret loved so that often he was induced to tears while celebrating it. In 1576 Muret received Holy Orders.

Over the next few years Muret continued to teach as he had always done, and even had the opportunity at one point to return to Greek when he gave lessons on Aristotle's *Rhetoric*. Offers for new teaching posts came from Poland and Padua, but the Romans always met the new offers with a pay raise of their own, and so Muret stayed at the Studium Sapientiae. Even so, we see him these days complaining to his many correspondents in both France and Italy that his students were abandoning the study of literature for the study of medicine and law. Wearied from the constant struggle and eager to devote himself to his writing, Muret implored the pope to allow him to retire, which the pope granted in November of 1584. Within a year (June of 1585) Muret was dead. His library passed to the Jesuits in Rome, a group where he had found many friends in his latter days, and from there in great part to the Library of Victor-Emmanuel (that is, la Biblioteca Nazionale Centrale di Roma), where it remains today.[20]

---

19. The poems were published at the Aldine Press in Venice as part of a volume of Muret's collected prose and poetry (Renouard 219: 11); the first separate edition came out of Robert Estienne's Paris press in 1576.

20. Pierre de Nolhac, "La bibliothèque d'un humaniste au XVIe siècle: Catalogue des livres annoté par Muret," *Mélanges d'Archéologie et d'Histoire* (published by the French Academy of Rome), 3 (1883): 202–38. Also see Paolo Renzi, *I libri del mestiere. La 'Bibliotheca Mureti' del Collegio Romano* (Florence, 1994) [a critical edition of MS Vaticano-latino 11562, a catalogue of Muret's books in the library of the Jesuit Roman College from 1606 to 1782].

Muret almost never mentioned his juvenile poetry again after its publication, though it continued to draw some notice. Baluze (see bibliography under "Boys") judged Muret and Dorat to be the best poets to come out of Limoges and cites Scaevola Sammarthanus as saying Muret is "as much like Catullus as Catullus is like himself." True, Muret picks up some of the vocabulary, meters, and themes of Catullus in his epigrams, but that's a far cry from being an *alter Catullus*. The epigrams alone look back, not just to Catullus, but to Martial, Ausonius, Italian poets Pontano and Poliziano, Secundus, Bourbon, and Bèze. The elegies and satires imitate Ovid and Juvenal respectively, the odes Horace, but usually with the later influences mixed in as well. In fact, imitation in Muret is never without contamination from a variety of sources. For example, in some poems one finds hints of the influence of the emblematic tradition, if not the hieroglyphic mysticism of Horapollo. Such cabalistic imagery stands behind the following lines in Muret's ode to Claudius Voesius:

> Non sic timenda est, in Libyae iugis
> Quae, matre rupta, vipera nascitur.

The "vipera ex utero matris rupto erumpens" was a frequent image among the writers of emblems. They used it sometimes as a metaphor for internal dissension, to talk about punishment and vengeance, or to warn against pernicious talkativeness. It is the last use that Muret borrows as he writes to Voesius about the dangers of hidden calumny. In *epig.* 8 Muret turns to the emblematic imagery of the *Herculeus lapillus* to describe the enticing charm of Marguerite's tongue. Indeed, just how much of a role the emblematic and hieroglyphic traditions play in Renaissance poetry is a worthy study in and of itself.

The Iuvenilia

I have already written in some detail elsewhere about the origins of the title of Muret's poetry (see bibliography below). The appellation itself, *iuvenilia*, does not seem to have been used in its Latin form as a title before Muret, but even so, the word has a long history in poetry. We find in Latin elegiac and epigrammatic poetry, from Roman times to the Renaissance, constant reference to the "poetry of youth," often standing in contrast to a kind of poetry suitable to be written in old age. The poets characterize the latter poetry as serious, moral, and austere, touching on wars and politics and patriotism. The former is filled with passion and exuberance, concerned not with weighty national issues, but with jokes and laughter and erotic affairs. Muret may have had in mind the title of Marot's work, *L'Adolescence clementine* (1532) which itself looks to Petrarch's phrase *giovenile errore* in the first poem of the *Canzoniere*. It is clear, though, that Muret perceives *iuvenilia* to be a generic term, and not simply a reference to the period of his life when he composed the poems. In other words, the title was meant to clue the reader to what *kind* of poetry to expect in the volume.

The genres included in the volume—elegies, satires, epistles, epigrams, and odes—all have classical antecedents and a long *Nachleben*. For his models in composing these, Muret had many places to which he could turn. He was certainly aware of the Italian neo-Latinists and their way of handling these genres. He also knew the efforts of his fellow countrymen to write in the vernacular. He chose, however, to follow the lead of writers such as Nicolas Bourbon and Théodore de Bèze, who strove to imitate the classical authors directly, with minimal interference from medieval and Italian innovations. Bèze, for example, compiles a list of the ancient authors he was imitating with each genre, with no mention of later influences. In fact, the only elements within his poems that do not hark back directly to antiquity are references to the Church (in particular, criticism of the hypocrisy within the hierarchy), to current events (battles, strange portents, politics, etc.), and to friends. All these elements are found in Muret as well. What is especially striking, however, is the desire for generic purity. Muret's poems, as do those of Bourbon and Bèze, reveal a particular reading of the genres of antiquity that for us help to fill out the picture of their reception. What the nature of this reading is will best be learned from reading the poems themselves.

BIBLIOGRAPHY

Journal Abbreviations

AJP   *American Journal of Philology*
BHR   *Bibliothèque d'Humanisme et Renaissance*
BICS   *Bulletin of the Institute of Classical Studies*
CB   *Classical Bulletin*
CW   *Classical World*
PMLA *Proceedings of the Modern Language Association*

Adams, James N. *The Latin Sexual Vocabulary*. Baltimore, 1982.
Aldrich, R., and Garry Wotherspoon. *Who's Who in Gay and Lesbian History*. New York, 2001. The Muret entry by Giovanni Dall'Orto is on pp. 320–21.
Andersson, D. C. "Marc-Antoine Muret's Moral Philosophy: The Renaissance Contest of the Disciplines?" *BHR* 64 (2002): 669–78.
Bencius, Franciscus. "Oratio in funere M. Antonii Mureti." In *M. Antonii Mureti Scripta Selecta* (Heidelberg, 1809). Also, Benci, Francesco. *Oratio in funere M. Antonii Mureti . . . habita Romae in templo S. Trinitatis . . . XIV. kal. Quintil. MDLXXXV.* Rome, F. Zanettus, 1585, 15 p.
Bénétrix, P. *Un Collège de province pendant la Renaissance. Les origines du Collège d'Auch, 1540–1590*. Paris, 1908.
Blanchard, Pierre. *La tragédie de Iulius Caesar / Marc-Antoine de Muret; introd., commentaire, texte établi et traduit, notes et variantes*. Thonon-les-Bains, 1995.
Blänsdorf, Jürgen. "Die Verwandlung der senecanischen Tragödie in Marc-Antoine Murets 'Julius Caesar' und Jacques Grévins 'César.'" *IJCT* 1.2 (1994–1995): 58–74.
Bloemendal, Jan. "Tyrant or Stoic Hero? Marc-Antoine Muret's *Julius Caesar*, in *Recreating Ancient History. Episodes from the Greek and Roman Past in the Arts and Literatures of the Early Modern Period. Intersections.* Yearbook for Early Modern Studies 1, K. Enenkel, J. L. de Jong, J. De Landtsheer, eds. Leiden, Boston, Cologne, 2001, 303–318.

Boys, Émile du. *Les poètes Limousins jugé par Baluze.* Limoges, 1889. Publishes a letter of E. Baluze to Françoise d'Aguesseau in 1682.

Céard, Jean. "Muret commentateur des Amours de Ronsard,. In C. de Buzon and P. Martin, edd., *Les Amours, Leurs Commentaires.* Paris, 1999, 359–79. First published in 1990 in *Sur des vers de Ronsard,* 37–50.

Colletet, G. "Vie de Marc-Antoine Muret," ed. by Tamizey de Laroque in *Revue d'histoire littéraire de la France* 3 (1896): 270–85.

DeJob, Charles. *Marc-Antoine Muret: Un professeur Français en Italie dans la seconde moitié du XVIe siècle.* Paris, 1881. See the critical reviews of P. de Nolhac. *Revue critique,* 3 (1882): 483–88, and A. Desjardins. *Le Correspondant,* 91 (1882): 239–75.

Delage, Franck. "Un humaniste limousin du XVIe siècle, Marc-Antoine Muret." *Bull. Soc. Archéol. et hist. du Limousin* 55 (1905): 147–67.

———. *Marc-Antoine Muret, poète français.* 1910.

Foster, Jeffrey. *Cesar de Jacques Grevin.* A critical edition with introduction and notes; includes the text, in Latin, of Marc-Antoine Muret's *Julius Caesar,* pp. 103–23.

Gaisser, Julia Haig. *Catullus and His Renaissance Readers.* Oxford, 1993, esp. 146–92.

Gaullieur, E. *Histoire du collège de Guyenne.* Paris, 1874.

Ginsberg, Ellen S. "Change and Permanence in the French Renaissance: Muret and Ronsard." *Journal of Medieval and Renaissance Studies* 16 (1986): 91–102.

———. "Marc-Antoine de Muret: A Re-Evaluation," in *Acta Conventus Neo-Latini Guelpherbytani,* ed. M. Di Cesare, S. Revard, and F. Rädle. Binghamton, NY, 1988, 63–69.

Grévin, Jacques. *César,* critical ed. with intro. and notes by Jeffrey Foster. Paris, 1968. Includes Latin text of Marc-Antoine Muret's *Julius Caesar.*

Guglielminetti, Marziano. "Pour la défense de la poésie et du latin: Muret à Rome." In *Du Pó à la Garonne. Recherches sur les échanges culturels entre l'Italie et la France à la Renaissance,* in *Actes du Colloque International d'Agen (26–28 Sept. 1986),* ed. J. Cubelier de Beynac and M. Simonin. Agen, 1990, 115–25.

Hutton, James. *The Greek Anthology in France.* Ithaca, 1946.

IJsewijn, J. "Marcantonio Mureto." In *The World of Justus Lipsius: A Contribution towards His Intellectual Biography. Proceedings of a Colloquium Held under the Auspices of the Belgian Historical Insitute in Rome (May 22–24, 1997),* ed. M. Laureys. Brussels and Rome, 1998, 71–80.

Lebègue, R. *La Tragédie religieuse en France au XVIe siècle.* Paris, 1939.

Lamarque, Henri. "La première tragédie 'pretexte' de la Renaissance: Le Iulius Caesar de Marc-Antoine Muret." *Pallas* 49 (1998): 247–65. Includes the entire text of the play.

Laurens, Pierre. "Muret." In *Prosateurs latins en France au XVIe siècle*. Paris, 1987, 497–531.

———. *L'abeille dans l'ambre: Célébration de l'épigramme de l'époque alexandrine à la fin de la Renaissance*. Paris, 1989. Contains discussion of several of Muret's epigrams.

Macphail, Eric. "The Plot of History from Antiquity to the Renaissance." *Journal of the History of Ideas* 62 (2001): 1–16.

Ménage, Gilles. *Anti-Baillet*. La Haye, 1688. A critique of Adrien Baillet's *Jugemens des savans sur les principaux ouvrages des auteurs*, first published at Paris in 4 vols., 1685–1686. Ménage's work appears again as vol. 7 of a multi-volume edition of Baillet's *Jugemens des savans sur les principaux ouvrages des auteurs*, published in Amsterdam, 1725 (repr. Hildesheim, 1971). Page numbers in the text refer to the latter edition.

McFarlane, I. D. "George Buchanan and France." In *Studies in French Literature Presented to H. W. Lawton*, ed. J. C. Ireson, I. D. McFarlane, and Garnet Rees. Manchester and New York, 1968, 223–245.

Menager, D. "Marc-Antoine Muret à la recherche d'une patrie." In *La circulation des hommes et des oeuvres entre la France et l'Italie à l'époque de la Renaissance*. Paris, 1992.

Morrison, Mary. "Ronsard and Catullus: The Influence of the Teaching of Marc-Antoine Muret." *BHR* (1956): 240–74.

Mouchel, C. "*Muret (Marc-Antoine)*." In *Centuriae Latinae: Cent une figures humanistes de la Renaissance aux Lumières offertes à Jacques Chomarat*, ed. C. Nativel. Geneva, 1997, 575–79.

Muret, Marc-Antoine. *Commentaires au premier livre des* Amours *de Ronsard*. Geneva, 1985, esp. the introduction by Jacques Chomarat and Marie-Madeleine Fragonard.

Nolhac, Pierre de. *La bibliothèque d'un humaniste au XVIe siècle: catalogue des livres annotés par Muret*. Rome, 1883.

———. *Ronsard et l'Humanisme*. Paris, 1921, esp. 144–51.

Renzi, Paolo. *I libri del mestiere: La* Bibliotheca Mureti *del Collegio Romano*. Siena, 1993.

———, ed. *L'università e la sua storia. Origini, spazi istituzionali e pratiche didattiche dello Studium cittadino. Atti del Convegno di Studi (Arezzo, 15–16 novembre 1991)*. Siena, 1998. See esp. the editor's article, "Montaigne, Muret, Lipsio e il giuramento dei gladiatori."

Sabbadini, E. "Un umanista francese alla corte di Ippolito II d'Este: Marc-Antoine Muret." *Atti e Memorie della Società Tiburtina di storia ed arte* 60 (1988): 141–65.

Sharratt, Peter. "Marc-Antoine Muret: The Teaching of Literature and the Humanistic Tradition." *Acta Conventus Neo-Latini Torontonensis*, ed. A. Dazell, C. Fantazzi, and R. Schoeck. Binghamton, NY, 1991, 665–75.

Silver, I. "Marc-Antoine de Muret et Ronsard." In R. Antonioli, R. Aulotte, et al.,eds., *Lumières de la Pléiade*. Paris, 1966, 33–48.

Stachnine, Joann. "A Sixteenth-Century Latin Teacher [M. A. Muret] Talks on the Value of a Classical Education." *CJ* 25 (1969–1970): 258–60.

Summers, Kirk. "The Origins of the Title of Muret's *Iuvenilia*." *IJCT* 10 (2004): 407–15.

Trinquet, R. "Un maître de Montaigne: l'humaniste limousin Marc-Antoine Muret." *Bulletin de la Société des amis de Montaigne* (1966): 3–17. The same articles appears as "Recherches chronologiques sur la jeunesse de Marc-Antoine Muret," in *BHR* 27 (1965): 272–85.

Tunberg, Terence. "De Marco Antonio Mureto oratore et Gallo et Romano." *Humanistica Lovaniensia* 50 (2001): 303–327.

MAJOR EDITIONS OF THE *IUVENILIA*

1552: M. A. MURETI | IUVENILIA. *Elenchum sequens pagella continet.* 126 p., 8º, 168mm.[1] Inscribed: "ex officina viduae Maricii à Porta in clauso Brunello, ad d(ivi) Claudi insigne," i.e., published at the press of Catherine Lhéritier, widow of the printer Maurice Ier de la Porte, who died in 1548. Catherine ran the press until 1557. The house stood in the clos-Bruneau near the statue of Saint Claude. For his printer's mark he represented the philosopher Bias with the device: "Omnia mea mecum porto."[2] The date 1552 is given at the end of the preface.

1553: *Marci Antonii Mureti Iuvenilia* (Paris). A second edition, or rather a second printing, identical in every way with the previous edition.

1579: *Iuvenilia M. A. Mureti I. C. et Civis Romani* (Paris). Published at the press of M. Locqueneulx.

1590: *M. A. Mureti Iuvenilia* (Barth, Germany). Inscribed "ex officina principis." A second ed. in 1591. [non vidi]

---

1. The contents of the pages are as follows: 1: title page with liminary poem 2: elenchus (table of contents) 3–6: prefatory poems or poems of introduction 7–16: preface, dated "8 Calend. Decemb. 1552." 16: "personae dramatis" (a list of characters in the following tragedy) 17–40: the tragedy entitled "Julius Caesar" 41–56: elegies 57–62: satires 63–109: epigrams of Muret, ending with poem to Louis Valois, then closed with "epigrammatum finis" 109–110: two poems of Fremiot 111–115: epistles 116–126: odes 126: "Marci Antonii Mureti iuvenilium finis."

2. On this press and printer, see P. Renouard, *Répertoire des imprimeurs Parisiens libraires, fondeurs de caractères et correcteurs d'imprimerie* (Paris, 1965), 239; Roméo Arbour, *Dictionnaire des femmes libraires en France (1470–1870)* (Geneva, 2003), 321, s.v. La Porte, Maurice I de. For the printer's mark, see idem, *Les marques typographiques Parisiennes des XVe et XVIe siècles* (Paris, 1926), 182–183. The motto, which appears as emblem xxxvii in Alciato's collection (Lyons, 1550), is attributed to Bias of Priene in Ionia (fl. 6th century BCE), one of the so-called Seven Sages, and is drawn from Cic. *Par. Stoic.* 1.8–9.

1609: *Delitiae C. Poetarum Gallorum*, 3 vols. (Frankfurt). Muret's poems appear in vol. 2, 721–91. Additional poems, mostly from Muret's *Poemata varia*, are included up to p. 814. The *Institutio puerilis*, an instructional guide written to Muret's nephew, appears beginning on p. 801. The poems of Fremiot appear in vol. 2, 579–80, including one not in the 1553 ed. entitled, "In eiusdem imaginem." The latter was originally accompanied a woodcut of Muret himself in editions of his commentaries on Ronsard's *Amours*.

1682: *Poesies de Marc-Antoine Muret, mises en vers François, par M. P. Moret, controlleur général des finances de Montauban* (Paris). Published at the press of Christophe Journel. Moret omits the most lewd poems altogether.

1727: *M. Mureti opera* (Verona), 5 vols., finished in 1730. Published at the press of Albert Tumerman.

1757: *Marci Antonii Mureti Juvenilia* (Leiden). Bound together with other poets; an earlier version of the 1779 ed. described below, but without the appendix.

1779: *Amoenitates poeticae, sive Theodori Bezae, Marci-Antonii Mureti, et Joannis Secundi Juvenilia. Tum Jannis-Bonefonii Pancharis, Joachimi-Bellaii Amores, etc.* (Leiden). Published for sale through Joseph Barbou at Paris. Muret's poems appear on pp. 119–208. A fairly accurate reproduction of the text. Contains Muret's preface but not the *Caesar*. Two elegies ("Ad Neaeram puellam" and "Ad Fulviam puellam") plus an ode ("Ad Janum Tilium Paraeneticon") appear in an appendix (pp. 390–93) and are described as "quasi postliminio recuperatae." The second ode contains the note, "Haec edita primum in Editione Veronensi, nec usquam alias."

1789: *M. Antonii Mureti opera omnia*. Edition by David Ruhnken, 4 vols. (Leiden). Muret's *Iuvenilia* (with the *Caesar*) appears in vol. 1, 653–732. From the press of Samuel and John Luchtmans.

1834: *Opera omnia, ex mss. aucta et emendata, cum brevi annotatione Davidis Ruhnkenii, studiose ab se recognita, emendata et aucta, selectisque aliorum et suis adnotationibus instructa accurate edidit Carolus Henricus Frotscher* (Leipzig). The *Iuvenilia* appears in vol. 2, 235–304.

1879: *Prime armi dal latino di M. A. Mureto*. Edition and Italian translation by Vittorio Corbucci (Rome).

1995: *Marcus Antonius Muretus: Caesar. Juvenilia* (Frankfurt am Main). Edition, translation (German), introduction, and commentary by Dietmar Schmitz. Depends solely on Frotscher. Both the text and the translation contain numerous inaccuracies, while the commentary lacks basic information that the reader needs. Does not include Muret's preface.

2000: *Les* Iuvenilia *de Marc-Antoine Muret (1552): édition, traduction, commentaire.* Diss. by Virginie Leroux, Paris III.

ORTHOGRAPHY AND PUNCTUATION

The correct approach to the editing of Renaissance Latin texts is a subject of endless debate. Some scholars prefer that all spelling and punctuation be left as found in the original edition, arguing that, not only do the words themselves hold significance, but the way they appear on the page do as well. Others favor the adoption of modern conventions in printing to make the texts more accessible to a wider range of readers, both those who have been initiated into the Renaissance modes of writing and those who simply know their Cicero. I have opted for the latter approach, following, *mutatis mutandis,* the recommendations of a recent essay on the subject.[1] To do otherwise would require certain concessions of uniformity (for example, sometimes Muret writes *coelum,* sometimes *caelum*), logical punctuation (no standardized use of punctuation marks is in play during the Renaissance), and the meaning of "Renaissance" itself (what classical author would ever write *oci* for *oti?*). And what of diacritical marks? Should abbreviations be expanded? The fact is, no two texts of this period follow the same conventions, or at least no two publishing houses do. Even the early editions of the *Iuvenilia* themselves exhibit differences of orthography. So in the end, rather than championing an already confused state of affairs, the modern editor should go with what makes sense to the average modern reader. With that said, difficult choices still had to be made. It would have been convenient for the reader, for example, had I included quotation marks in the Latin text. Speakers change from time to time (dialogue is a hallmark of much of Roman poetry), and thus quotation marks would serve to guide the reader. Even so, I have opted out of using them for the simple reason that their presence in the text might delude the reader into thinking that they were part of the original instead of the result of an educated guess (similarly, no one would imagine adding italics to the Latin text). The reader will understand the interpretive nature of quotation marks, however, when they appear in the translation.

Below is a representative list of the orthographical changes I have made to the text. From this list, the reader should be able to extrapolate how the original text

---

1. Luc Deitz, "Editing Sixteenth-Century Latin Prose Texts: A Case Study and a Few General Observations," in Glenn W. Most, ed., *Editing Texts—Texte edieren* (Göttingen: Vandenhoeck & Ruprecht, 1998), 141–64.

appeared, if so desired. I have strayed once, though only slightly, from my own orthographic standards. In the case of *queis,* I have let the spelling stand rather than convert it to the somewhat confusing *quis.* I note that at times Teubner editions reflect this same editorial choice.

TEXT OF THE ORIGINAL 1552 ED.	CONVERTED FORM
Camoenae	Camenae
caussas	causas
coelum	caelum
coena	cena
disiicis	disicis
fathiscunt	fatiscunt
foemina	femina
fraenari	frenari
hulceros	ulceros
hyemis	hiemis
hymbre	imbre
imo	immo
iniiciens	iniciens
lacrymas	lacrimas
laeno	leno
letho	leto
litera	littera
littore	litore
Lycambaea	Lycambea
obscoenius	obscenius
oci	oti
ocieris	otieris
pene	paene

IDENTIFIABLE NAMES OF MURET'S CONTEMPORARIES APPEARING IN THE TEXT[1]

Alisius, Stephanus: Étienne Alis, from a politically prominent family of Bordeaux. Muret possibly held a tutorial in his house in early 1548 (?) before he left for Auch. Étienne wrote an introductory sonnet for Boaistuau's *Histoires prodigieuses* (1560), and so must have had some measure of success. See J. Chomarat, *Marc-Antoine Muret: Commentaires au premier livre des* Amours *de Ronsard* (Geneva, 1985), xxxii, n.16.

Alsinous, Comes: Nicolas Denisot (1515–1559), satellite to the members of the Pléiade from 1549 on, poet, painter, and musician. His occasional pseudonym, conte d'Alsinois (or comte d'Alsinoys in his 1545 work *Noelz*), was an anagram of his real name, and thus the source of the Latin variation. He is the source of the portrait of Ronsard published in the *Amours* (Ronsard calls him "Alsinois" in his odes). He contributed to the *Tombeau* of Marguerite de Navarre in 1551, and may have painted the portrait of the princess there. Two years later he published *Cantiques du premier avènement de Jésus-Christ, par le comte d'Alsinois*, in which the twelve Olympians hail the birth of Christ (Muret wrote introductory verse for this work). Henri II used him as a spy at Calais, under the pretext of teaching the governor's children, with the result that Denisot was instrumental in bringing about the recapture of that city in February of 1558. Also in 1558 he published a humanistic and Christian novel in five books under the pseudonym Theodose Valentinian, on which see Véronique Duché[-Gavet], "l'Amant resuscité de la mort d'amour, ou comment Nicolas Denisot a écrit son roman," *Nouvelle revue du XVIe siècle* 19.2 (2001): 33–48; and her edition of the work published in Geneva, 1998; there is also a study by Margaret Harris published in 1966. For general works on Denisot, see C. Jugé, *Nicolas Denisot du Mans (1515–1559)* (Le-Mans-Paris, 1907); J. C. Nash, "The Christian-Humanist Meditation on Man: Denisot, Montaigne, Rabelais, Ronsard, Scève," *BHR* 54 (1992): 353–71.

---

1. Dates of birth and death are given when known.

IDENTIFIABLE NAMES   xxxvii

Auratus: See under Jean Dorat.

Baïf, Jean Antoine de: a French poet (1532–1589) who studied under Dorat and joined him as a member of the Pléiade. His didactic and satirical *Mimes, enseignments et proverbes* (1576; modern edition: Geneva, 1992, ed. Jean Vignes, and idem, *Mots dorés pour un siècle de fer: les Mimes enseignemens et proverbes de Jean-Antoine de Baïf* [Paris. 1997]), won him some measure of fame. In 1570, Charles IX allowed Baïf and Joachim Thibault de Courville to found L'Académie de Poésie et de Musique, which worked for the revival of ancient music as a means to spiritual renewal. He also wrote Petrarchan sonnets and French versions of ancient plays. See Yvonne Roberts, *Jean-Antoine de Baïf and the Valois Court* (New York, 2000).

Bellay, Joachim du: 1525–1560, close friend of Ronsard and member of the Pléiade, he laid out the program for the group in his influential *La deffence et illustration de la langue françoyse* (1549; many modern editions). Otherwise he was best known for his *Olive* (1550; modern edition by E. Caldarini [Geneva, 1974]). See also V. L. Saulnier, *Du Bellay* (4th ed., Paris, 1968).

Bourg, Claude du: Leroux notes that he was a knight, Lord of Guerine, Counselor to the King, Secretary of Finances, Treasurer of France, and ambassador of Charles IX to the Turks. He wrote an Epistle on the interview between the Prince de Condé and the Cardinal de Lorraine that was printed in 1564. He died in 1562.

Brinon, Jean de: d. 1554, a Maecenas, of sorts, of poets and intellectuals in Paris, particularly members of the Pléiade or Brigade. Muret belonged to a circle of scholars who met in Brinon's house for discussion and at his Médan Castle for hunting parties and festivals (Ronsard recalls these *soirées* in his ode, "La chasse à Jean Brinon"). Many authors dedicated whole books (as Claude Goudimel, *Psaumes* 1551) and individual poems to him (see, e.g., Olivier de Magny, *Les Odes,* ed. Courbet (Paris, 1876), 1, 66. Cf. L. Sheler, "Jean de Brinon, bibliophile," *BHR* 11 (1949): 215–218; and I. D. McFarlane, "Ronsard's Poems to Jean Brinon," in *French Renaissance Studies in Honor of Isidore Silver,* ed. F. S. Brown (Kentucky Romance Quarterly Supplement to vol. 21, 1975), 53–67.

Cairiechius, François Laccius: The name suggests a Greek heritage, perhaps (Leroux considers Cairiechius to be a nickname meaning "l'homme providentiel"), but his precise identity is unclear.

Coletus Campanus, Claudius: Claude Colet de Rumilly en Champagne, author of *L'Oraison de mars aux dames de la Court . . . plus l'Épistre de l'amoureux de vertu* (Paris, 1544 and 1548, the latter revised and corrected, and adding several other minor pieces). He also translated the ninth book of the Spanish romance *Amadís de Gaula*. Étienne Jodelle addressed a poem to him ("Aux cendres de Claude Colet") that appears in the *Oxford Book of French Verse* (1908, 104).

Collaeus, Antoine: Leroux believes this individual could be Antoine Nicolay (d. 1597), about whom Scévole de Sainte-Marthe speaks in his *Gallorum doctrina illustrium* (Limoges, 1602). His grandfather, once chancellor of Naples, retired in Provence.

Condom, Rudolphe: Professor in the College of Auch where Muret taught. He is mentioned by Du Poey twice in his poem, *De collegio Auscitano carmen ad posteritatem*, Toulouse, 1551,11.83–84 and 245–48 (for the text see Bénétrix, 184–97): *Condomaeum addam qui non torpere tirones, / Coniungens graecis verba latina, sinet* ("I will add Condom who, by joining Latin words to Greek ones, does not allow his students to languish"), and *Grammatices prius, eloquii fundamina ponunt, / Qui pueros acri sedulitate docent. / Mureto, Lana, Lochiano, ubi Condomioque | Barreriano uti Rivalioque, potes* ("First they lay the foundations of grammar, then of eloquence, teaching the boys with great intensity").

Connanus, Franciscus: François de Connan, native of Paris, where he died in 1551. He studied at Orléans and Bourges under Pierre de l'Étoile and Alciato, and became one of the most distinguished jurists of his day. Muret refers to his *Commentaria iuris civilis* (Paris, 1538) in epig. 92. See further C. Bergfeld, *François Connan 1508–1551, ein Systematiker des römischen Rechts* (Cologne, 1968); E. G. Ehmke, "Gauls and Franks in 16th-Century French Historical Writing: The Theory of François Connan," *Proceedings of the Annual Meeting of the Western Society for French History* 6 (1978): 78–87.

Costecandus, Jean: The epigram of Muret incorrectly transmits the name as "Costecaudus," but the correct spelling is known from a dedication in Muret's 1551 *scholia* on Terence's *Andria* and *Eunuch*: "M. Antonius Muretus Ioanni Costecando suo, S. P. D." Writing the dedication from Paris in September 1551, as he notes, Muret speaks of private lessons he gave Jean the previous year (the text is given at Ruhnken, IV, xx). This is the clearest evidence that Muret is already in Paris at that time. Since Jean is described as "absent," one assumes that Muret taught him while at Bordeaux or early in his stay at Paris.

IDENTIFIABLE NAMES   xxxix

Cruselius, P.: or Pierre Crouzeil of Limoges, a doctor at Poitiers, who is supposedly responsible for some textual notes on the letters of Cicero to Atticus, which he shared with the Latinist Simon Dubois (or "Bosius"). The following odd tale of his role in the text of Cicero's letters is given by the *Encyclopaedia Britannica*, 11th ed., under the "Cicero" entry:

> A similar fate overtook three other MSS. containing the letters to Atticus, independent of the Veroitensis, viz, a mutilated MS. of Books i–vii. discovered by Cardinal Capra in 1409, a Lorsch MS. used by Cratander (C), and a French MS. (Z), generally termed Tornesianus from its owner, Jean de Tournes, a printer of Lyons probably identical with No. 492 in the old Cluny catalogue, used by Turnebus, Lambinus and Bosius. A strange mystification was practiced by the last named, a scholar of singular brilliancy, who claimed to have a mutilated MS. which he called his Decurtatus, bought from a common soldier who had obtained it from a sacked monastery; also to have been furnished by a friend, Pierre Crouzeil, a doctor of Limoges, with variants taken from an old MS. found at Noyon, and entered in the margin of a copy of the Lyons edition. The rough draft of his notes, however, upon books x.–xvi, which afterwards came into the hands of Baluze, is preserved in the Paris library (Lat. 8538 A), in which he continually ascribes different readings to these MSS., the alteration corresponding with a change in his own conjecture. It is, therefore, obvious that he invented the readings in order to strengthen his own corrections. The book, which he termed his Crusellinus, may well be his copy of the Lyons edition of f 545 (number 8665 in the sale-catalogue of Baluze), which is described as *cum notis et emendationibus MSS. inanu eiusdem Bosii.*

On this see also D. R. Shackleton Bailey, *Cicero's Letters to Atticus*, vol. 1 (Cambridge, 1965), 93–94. A hint of it is given at DeJob 10–11 and F. Arbellot and A. du Boys, *Biographie des hommes illustrés de l'ancienne province du Limousin* (Limoges, 1854), 166. The latter ends, "Muret, son contemporain, lui adresse la 7me élégie de ses *Juvenilia*. Crouzeil fleurissait vers l'an 1580, et a laissé plusieurs traités manuscrits de médicine, conservés dans le musée de Meynard Favellon."

Denisotus: See "Alsinous" above.

Dorat, Jean: 1508–1588, from Limoges, sometimes called Auratus or Daurat. He was the spiritual father to many of the French and neo-Latin poets. He was a tutor in the court of Francis I and "Poet Royal" under Charles IX. He did much to bring Greek literature into fashion in France, and his emendations on many of

Aeschylus' tragedies demonstrate his great Greek learning. He published his collection of Greek and Latin poetry, entitled *Poematia* at Paris in 1586 at the press of Guillaume Linocier.[2] Despite his influence, he was hesitant to publish his works. His very first work, *Sur la Cosmographie d'André Thevet,* appeared in 1575, when he was 67 years old. See esp. Henri Demay, *Jean Dorat (1508–1588): "L'Homère du Limousin," âme de la Pléiade, et poète des rois* (Paris, 1996), and Marie-Dominique Legrand, "*Honos alit artes*. Une pratique de l'éloge: les *Odes latines* de Dorat," *Nouvelle revue du XVIe siècle* 18 (2000): 37–53. The names of Muret and Dorat are brought together in a 1594 poem by their contemporary, Joachim Blanchon, appearing at the bottom of a map of Limousin (published as #35 in *Théâtre géographique du Royaume de France* [Paris, 1621]):

> Homère, Démosthène et Archimède ensemble,
> Lymoges a nourri où la vertu s'assemble;
> Muret, Dorat, Fayen, trois excellents esprits:
> Muret son Démosthène et Dorat son Homère;
> Fayen son Archimède ayant sa ville-mère.
> Sa province et son plan heureusement compris.

Flaminio, Marcantonio: Italian neo-Latin poet (1498–1550) of Serravalle. His life can conveniently be divided between a humanist phase, during which he produced love poetry (*Lusus pastorales,* 1515, part of a larger work, *Carminum libri V;* see the edition of M. Scorsone [Turin, 1992]) and associated with scholars, and a religious phase, during which he worked for the Church and wrote religious verse (*De rebus divinis carmina,* 1551). See C. Maddison, *Marcantonio Flaminio, Poet, Humanist and Reformer* (Chapel Hill, 1965).

Frémiot, Memmius: of Dijon, a student of Muret (see *epig.* 25, n. 7). The poems appearing in Gruter's *Delitiae* (vol. 2, 579–80) are simply those appearing here at the end of the epigrams with an additional poem on Muret's portrait. The latter is included in editions of Muret's commentary on Ronsard (see Jacques Chomarat, *Marc-Antoine Muret: Commentaires au premier livre des Amours de Ronsard* [Geneva, 1985], n.p., but immediately preceding Muret's preface).

Gouvéa, Antoine de: or Govéa, a celebrated Portuguese jurist and humanist

---

2. Long title: Joannis Aurati . . . *poematia, hoc est: Poematum libri quinque; Epigrammatum libri tres; Anagrammatum liber unus; Funerum liber unus; Odarum libri duo; Epithalamiorum liber unus; Eclogarum libri duo; Variarum rerum liber unus.*

(1505–1566), whom Muret probably met at Bordeaux. His brother André had served as director of that school for many years, but departed for Portugal in 1547 about the same time as Muret was beginning to make a name for himself there. Antoine's commentaries on civil law were influential well into the next century. Among other things, he published an edition of Terence's *Andria* at Lyons in 1541, to which Muret refers several times in his own work on the author; a commentary on Cicero's letters to Atticus in 1544, and his *Topica* in 1545; and *Opera iuris civilis* at Lyons in 1561. In epig. 2, Muret refers to his *Epigrammatum libri duo* (1539). Govéa's complete works were published by J. Van Vaassen in 1766. He died in Turin. See E. Caillemer, *Étude sur Antoine de Govéa (1505–1566)* (Paris, 1864); F. Mugnier, *A. Govéan, professeur de droit* (1901); Martha Katherine Zeeb, *The Latin Letters of Antonio de Gouvea* (Philadelphia, 1934).

Jodellus, Stephanus: Étienne Jodelle (1532–1573). A member of the Pléiade, in 1552 he wrote the first French tragedy, the lyrical *Cléopâtre captive,* which was presented in the court of King Henry II the following year at Rheims. He composed many other verses during his lifetime, which his friends, particularly Charles de la Mothe, collected and published as a single volume in 1574 (*Oeuvres poétiques*). Jodelle resisted the influence of pagan and Petrarchan themes in poetry, and for this reason was at times an independent spirit at odds with members of the Pléiade. See É. Jodelle, *Oeuvres complètes,* ed. E. Balmas, 2 vols. (Paris, 1965–68); E. Balmas, *Un Poeta del Rinascimento francese, Étienne Jodelle: la sua vita, il suo tempo* (Florence, 1962).

Lochianus, Michel: A professor at the College of Auch where Muret taught. (See note on Rudolphe Condom above.) In the same poem mentioned there, see also ll.99–100: *Me duce, perficiet patriae Lochianus honorem, / Cuius tu cinges, Calliopeu, caput.* On p. 128, Bénétrix indicates that, like Vermelianus (below), Lochianus was from Ussel, and that he left behind a short poem (accompanying the longer poem of Du Poey) where Du Poey is said to be to the College of Auch as Homer was to Achilles.

Lomenius, F. Verus: François de Loménie, canon of Limoges (See Dejob, 4, n.1). The "Verus" appears to be a reference to his integrity. Leroux notes that he was, as Pierre Crouzeil, a friend of Simeon DuBois and calls attention to a note in Baluze's copy of the 1552 *Iuvenilia* (now in the BNF), p. 54: *Fuit hic Lomenius / canonicus Ecclesia[e] / Lomovicensis, / amicus etiam / Simeonis Bosii / Praetoris Limo- / vicensis.* One assumes he is related to the F. Gratus Lomenius addressed in epigram 28.

Lomenius, F. Gratus: probably the same person as the previous entry. Leroux believes "Gratus" is a nickname.

Macrin, Salmon: or Jean Salmon (1490–1557), often called the French Horace, because of his success in writing Latin odes. See *Épithalames et Odes*, a critical edition with introduction, notes, and translation by Georges Soubeille (Paris, 1998); I. D. McFarlane, "Jean Salmon Macrin (1490–1557)," *BHR* 21–22 (1959–60): 55–84, 311–49, 73–89.

Molza, Francesco Maria: Poet from Modena (1489–1544) of Italian and Latin verses. He gained fame for his pastoral *La ninfa tiberina* (1538). For his Latin works see especially *Elegiae et alia*, ed. M. Scorsone and Rossana Sodano (Torino, 1999).

Moncaudus, François: of Bordeaux. Little is known of him except that Joseph Scaliger attacked him in a scathing satire and that he wrote scabrous poetry that wasn't published. See also *Scaligerana* (2nd ed., Cologne, 1667), 158. Leroux notes a liminary poem of his among the *Poésies* of Pierre de Brach, also a poet of Bordeaux. Martial Monier also addressed an epigram to him urging him to publish his poetry (*Epigrammata, Elegiae et Odae* [Bordeaux, 1573], epig. 209).

Montausier, Charles de: Leroux identifies him as belonging to the house of Sainte-Maure, but his precise identity is unknown.

Montbasius, Guillelmus: or Guillaume de Montbas. DeJob reports this note in the exemplar of the *Iuvenilia* in the Bib. Nat., in the hand of Baluze: "Gul. Montbazius, Lectoriensis episcopus vivebat anno 1567. Fuit autem patria Picto, Ortus e Barthonibus (?) qui alio nomine Mombasii dicuntur." In epigram 29 he is addressed as a "Lectorian Bishop." This would make him the son of Pierre Bart(h)on (d. 1556), who had served in battles against the Venetians (1509) and Picardie (1513), and whose chateau was burned and pillaged in 1547. Guillaume was bishop of Lectoure and Deputy of State of France at the Council of Trent.

Nicolas de Vienne: Leroux believes he could be the son of Claude de Vienne, Lord of Clervaux, chamberlain of the Emperor Charles V.

Noallius: from the de Noailles family? Otherwise unknown.

Pontanus, Joannes Jovianus: or Giovanni Pontano, Italian humanist and poet (1426–1503), an important figure in the Academy of Naples. In 1505 the Aldine

IDENTIFIABLE NAMES　　　　xliii

Press published a posthumous edition of his major poetic works, and then his philosophical works, dialogues, and orations in 1518. His lyric poems influenced the Pléiade. He wrote numerous didactic poems, elegies, hendecasyllabics, and the like, many of them taking as their subject his deep affection for his wife and family. For his biography, see Carol Kidwell, *Pontano: Poet and Prime Minister* (London, 1991).

Querculus, Ludovicus: Louis Chesneau, a barrister and former teacher of Brinon (see above). In 1548 Brinon established for him a life annuity, and then four years later bestowed on him a piece of property at Villiers-Adam.

Quintius, Pierre: a colleague of Muret at Auch. Du Poey (see Condom entry above for reference) refers to him in his poem (ll.103–4) in the following way: *Quintius huc veniet, Latiae facundia linguae; / Proderit his aliqua Barrerianus ope.*

Ronsard, Pierre de: the well-known French poet (1524–1585) of the Pléiade. Of that group he was by far the most creative and energetic. He befriended Muret in Paris and attended the latter's lectures on Catullus. Although he considered writing in Latin at the beginning of his career, his entire corpus is in the French language. For the best overview of his life and contributions, see I. D. McFarlane, *A Literary History of France: Renaissance France, 1470–1589* (London, 1974), 297–326, with bibliography there. Muret's contemporary commentary on his *Amours* is unique for the time.

Rufus, Petrus: Pierre le Roux or Roussanes. See H. Busson, *Le Rationalisme dans la littérature française de la Renaissance* (2nd Ed., Vrin, 1957, 11). Leroux highlights his appearance in a letter of Joseph Scaliger addressed to Jean Dousa (*I. Scaligeri epistolae* [Anvers, 1600] I, 1, 45–46], where he is treated as a notorious atheist. According to Adolphe Magen, *Documents sur Jules-César Scaliger et sa famille* (Agen, 1873), 35–36, he belonged to an old family at Agen.

Sannazaro, Jacopo: Italian poet and humanist (1455–1530) from Naples. He published his influential pastoral romance *Arcadia* in Italian in 1501 (French version by Jean Martin in 1544/6) and *De partu Virginis* in Latin in 1513, which earned him the title of the Christian Vergil. He spent some time in France with Frederick III of Naples during the latter's exile. *The Major Latin Poems of Sannazaro*, ed. R. Nash (Detroit, 1996); and, Carol Kidwell, *Sannazaro and Arcadia* (London, 1993).

Scaliger, Julius Caesar: also, Jules Cesar de l'Escale de Bordonis, classical scholar (1484–1558), father of the more famous Joseph Scaliger. In 1519 he received his doctorate from the University of Padua. He served as physician to the Bishop Antonio de la Rovera of Agen after moving there at age forty-two. Both Nostradamus and Rabelais studied with him for a time at Agen, and it was there that Muret visited him. In the period from 1531 to 1544 he wrote several treatises defending Ciceronianism against the attacks of Erasmus. In 1561 at Lyons he published his *Poëtice,* a systematic treatment of poetry that ran through many editions. His *Poemata* were published at Geneva in 1574. See V. Hall, Jr., "The life of Julius Caesar Scaliger (1484–1558)," *Transactions of the American Philosophical Society,* n.s. 40 (1950): 85–170.

Schleicher, Daniel: probably a student of Muret (DeJob, 53), though otherwise unknown. See the note on *Sat.* 2.

Tilius, Janus: Leroux thinks that this could be Jean du Tillet from Angoulême, who became clerk of the Parlement of Paris and died in 1570. He was possibly a student of Muret.

Valesius, Louis: Moret translates the last name as "Valèse," but with no explanation. Leroux mentions a "Loys de Vallois" as a possibility, a zealous Protestant whom Théodore de Bèze alludes to in a letter, but he does not seem a likely candidate for the circle of Muret.

Vermelianus, Janus: Jan Vermélian d'Ussel, whom Muret knew at the College of Auch. He addressed a short poem to Muret about his tragedy *Julius Caesar.* A translation is given at Bénétrix, 128.

IDENTIFIABLE NAMES

No definitive information could be found on the following individuals:	The following names should be considered fictitious:	
Burge, Claude	Avitus	Pamphagus
Caliantheus, Charles	Collina	Paula
Callée, Antoine	Crassus	Paulus
Corellius	Galla	Phyllis
Crucius, Marius	Gallonius	Pompilius
Crucius, Sanso	Gaurus	Ponticus
Delian, Jean	Gellia	Pontilianus
Nicolaus of Vienna	Grannius	Porna
Ogerie, Anne	Lais	Romanus
Voesie, Claude	Lucius	Rufinus
	Lygdus	Sestius
	Marguerite	Virro
	Otho	

METERS

For the odes Muret employs only two different metrical schemes. All poems save one are written in Alcaic strophes, a favorite meter of Horace (cf. Hor. *Carm.* 1.9, etc.). The Alcaic strophe consists of two Alcaic hendecasyllabics followed by one Alcaic enneasyllabic and one Alcaic decasyllabic. The scheme for this meter is as follows:

1–2. ⏑ / –⏑ / –⏑ / –⏑⏑ / –⏑⏑
3 ⏑ / –⏑ / –⏑ / –⏑ / –⏑
4 –⏑⏑ / –⏑⏑ / –⏑ / –⏑

For example, the first ode begins in this way:

Au/ratĕ / gentis / grandĕ dĕ/cus mĕae
Qui / tensa /docta /fila legens manu
Saeclis inexpertum vetustis
Ambrosi/o iacis / ore /nectar.

In the poem to Ronsard, Muret uses the second Asclepiadean strophe scheme, consisting of three minor Asclepiadeans followed by one glyconic (cf. Hor. *Carm.* 1.6, 15, 24, 33; 2.12; 3.10, 16; 4.5, 12). These measures are sometimes considered choriambic. The scheme for this meter runs as follows:

1–3 –⏑ / –⏑⏑ / – / / –⏑⏑ / –⏑ / –
4 –⏑ / –⏑⏑ / –⏑ / ⏑

For example, the fourth ode begins in this way:
Ronsardĕ Aoni/i // pectinis / arbiter
Qui prin/ceps reso/num // solici/tas ebur
Vento/rumque mi/nas // et cele/res po/tens
Lapsus / sistere / fluminum.

METERS　　　　　　　　　　xlvii

All the epistles and satires are written in hexameters. The elegies are all elegiac couplets, as one would expect. Throughout the book I have not identified hexameters or elegiac couplets, since they are easily recognized.

Most of the epigrams are elegiac couplets as well, but Muret also uses Phalaecian hendecasyllables, one iambic trimeter, and two choliambics (limping iambs or scazons). Respectively, the schemes run as follows:

Phalaecian hendecasyllables
— — / — ⏑ ⏑ — / ⏑ — ⏑ — —
For example, *epig.* 8.3:

— — — ⏑ ⏑ — / ⏑ — ⏑ — —
Aspectuque tui / carere nolunt.

Iambic trimeter (pure)
⏑ — ⏑ — / ⏑ — ⏑ — / ⏑ — ⏑ —
For example, *epig.* 49.6:

⏑ — ⏑ — — — ⏑ ⏑ ⏑ ⏑ — ⏑ ⏑
Ut fraudet ex/spectatio/ne alios facit.

As is obvious from this example, Muret follows the lead of many Latin writers in allowing for the substitution of a long anceps and the resolution of any long (including the substituted long anceps).

Choliambic
⏓ — ⏑ — / ⏓ — ⏑ — / ⏑ — **x**

Many resolutions are allowed here as well, except for the closing metron, which gives the 'limping' effect. An example of the choliambic meter is *epig.* 38.1:

— — ⏑ — — — ⏑ — ⏑ — — **x**
Inter Lati/nos forte sic/ubi assedit.

In the latter two, Muret follows the resolution and substitution conventions of Martial rather than Catullus.

LIMINARY POEMS:
THE POEMS OF INTRODUCTION[1]

---

1. I have omitted three poems—one each of Buchanan, Jodelle, and Jan Vermélian d'Ussel—that only refer to Muret's tragedy *Julius Caesar*.

Comes Alsinous Lectori

Vis, Lector, Tragici sonum cothurni,
Vis, Lector, numeros Catullianos,
Vis, Lector, numeros Tibullianos,
Vis, Lector, numeros Horatianos?
En, libro tibi dat Muretus uno.

Ioannis Aurati in M. Antonii Mureti Iuvenilia

Tam bona posse putas cuiquam iuvenilia credi
   Carmina, digna viro, digna, Murete, sene?
Quae tibi tam tenuis limae solertia rasit,
   Quam quod Praxiteles ungue polivit ebur.
Ipse suum titulum nimia liber arte refutat,
   Auctorisque annos inficiatur opus.
Tu licet affirmes, licet omnia numina iures,
   Contra te facit ars ingeniumque tuum.
Deme igitur titulum libro, vel deme nitorem:
   Aetatem nitidus debet habere liber.

Εἰς τὴν βίβλον Μάκρου Ἀντωνίου τοῦ Μουρήτου

Τίς, πόθεν, ὦ Μουρητ', ἔρχῃ νέος Ἰταλίδαισι
   Κόσμος ἀοιδοπόλοις, σῆς ἕνεκ' εὐεπίης
Ἠνίδ' ὅσον μολπαί σου ἀποστίλβουσιν ἔρωτα,
   Πάντοθι παντοίων βριθόμεναι χαρίτων.
Ἠνίδ' ὅσην Κυθέρειαν ἀποπνείουσιν ἀοιδαὶ
   Αἱ σέο, κληθμῶν πληρέες ἁβρομελῶν.
Ἢ φλογὶ σῶν μελέων φλογερὰν χάριν ἵμερος ἧψεν,
   Ἡ δὲ Κύπρις μελίθρουν ὤπασεν ἁβροσύνην.

Liminary Poems

Nicolas Denisot to the Reader

Do you want, reader, the sound of the tragic cothurnus,
Do you want, reader, Catullan measures,
Do you want, reader, Tibullan measures,
Do you want, reader, Horatian measures?
Behold, Muret gives them all to you in one book.

A Poem of John Dorat about the Iuvenilia *of M.-A. Muret*

Do you think, Muret, that anyone can believe that
such good poems, such mature poems, are "juvenile"?
Your perfecting of these has been as subtle and fine
as the ivory Praxiteles polished with his fingernail.
The book itself with its extraordinary art refutes its own title,
and the work belies the years of the author.
Although you insist, although you swear by all the gods,
the art contradicts you, as does your talent.
So remove the title from your book, or remove the gleam:
A book that glistens requires age.

On the Book of Marc-Antoine Muret [a poem of Jean Antoine Baïf]

What sort of glory, Muret, may come to the Italian bards,
and from where, thanks to your sweet-sounding words?
See with how much love your songs do shine,
laden everywhere with all kinds of charms!
See how much Aphrodite your tunes exhale,
overflowing with enchantment and graceful melodies!
Truly by her flame desire has touched the fiery grace of your songs,
and Cypris has made sweet-voiced charm your companion.

'Ια. Ἀντωνίου Βαιφίου τοῦ αὐτοῦ εἰς τὴν αὐτήν

Σῶν, Μούρητ', ἐπέων ποστὸν τόδε· φράζε λέοντα,
Οἷος ἔφυ, μεγάλων τὸν μέγαν ἐξ ὀνύχων.[2]

In M. Antonium Muretum Iani Antonii Baifii

Seu visum est tibi diis laudes aequasse virorum,
  Haud pudeat Flacci sic cecinisse lyram:
Iulia seu Tragico defleris funera versu,
  Marce, Sophocleo tu pede digna tonas:
Seu fers Margaridem lepido super aethera cantu,
  Cantas, quo invideat Lesbia Margaridi.
Quis tibi cedet honos pro tali carmine? cingat
  Lauro, hedera, myrto texta corona caput.

Comes Alsinous

Musae, noster amor, meum Muretum,
Vestrum et candidum et optimum Muretum,
Qui vos usque adeo canit canendas,
Qui vos usque adeo colit colendas,
Quo nil cultius elegantiusve,
Quo nil candidius venustiusve,
Seu regum Tragico neces cothurno,
Seu scribat, posita severitate,
Venustas Veneres, iocos, lepores,
Et molles elegos decente versu,
Facundo, lepido, aureoque versu:
Musae, inquam, Aonides, meum Muretum,
Vestrum et candidum et optimum Muretum,
Vatem dicite, et approbate vatem.

---

2. A proverb taken from Erasmus' *Adagia* 1.9.34 (*leonem ex unguibus aestimare*), where it is attributed variously to Pheidias (Lucian, *Herm.* 55) or Alcaeus (Plut. *Mor.* 410c). The sense is that, just as the greatness of a lion can be extrapolated from the claw alone, Muret's immense talents can be discerned on the basis of this first publication.

Liminary Poems

Another Poem of Jean Antoine de Baïf, to the Same

This maxim is indicative of what you've written, Muret: "You can tell how great the lion's stature is from the size of his great claws."

A Poem of Jean Antoine de Baïf about M.-A. Muret

You desired to compare the praises of men to the gods—
Horace's lyre would not be ashamed to have sung like this.
You lamented the murder of Caesar in tragic verse—
Marcus, you thunder forth measures worthy of Sophocles.
You lift Marguerite to the heavens with charming song,
and sing so that Lesbia would envy her.
What honor should be given you for such poetry? Let a
crown woven with laurel, ivy, and myrtle gird your head.

Nicolas Denisot

Heed me, Muses, whom I love—my Muret,
your bright and best Muret,
who continuously sings of you who are worthy to be sung,
who continuously honors you who are worthy of honor,
than whom nothing is more cultivated, or more elegant,
than whom nothing is more bright or charming.
whether he writes about the deaths of kings in tragedy,
or, with the seriousness set aside,
writes of Venus' charms, merriment, wit,
and soft elegies in fitting verse,
in clever, urbane, and golden verse—
Aonian Muses, please, proclaim
my Muret, your bright and best Muret,
a poet, and grant the poet your approval.

6   Liminary Poems

In otio negotium.[3]

Stephani Iodelli Parisini

Caesar, Amor, testudo; movet, delenit, inescat;
   Fletum, elegos, aures; sanguine, melle, sonis.

---

3. According to Leroux, this line is taken from the device of Denisot and appears also among the liminaries of the *Amours* of Magny (ed. Courbet, *Les Amours d'Olivier de Magny: texte original* [Paris, 1878], 14) and at the beginning of the *Monophile* of Étienne Pasquier (ed. Balmas [Milan, 1957], 58).

In leisure, work

A Poem of Étienne Jodelle of Paris

Caesar, Cupid, the lyre; causes, sweetens, entices;
weeping, elegies, ears; with blood, with honey, with sounds.

Marci Antonii Mureti in librum Iuvenilium ad clarissimum virum Ianum Brinonem in senatu Parisiensi consiliarium Regium.

About the book *Iuvenilia* of Marc-Antoine Muret, to the very distinguished gentleman, Jean de Brinon, royal counselor in the Parisian Parliament

Praefatio

Saepenumero sum admiratus, Iane Brino, vir illustrissime, quo tandem fato contigerit, ut cum e Gallia nostra paene innumerabiles extiterint in omni genere scientiae praestantes viri, poetarum tamen magna semper a nobis fuerit inopia laboratum: idque eo admirabilius videri potest, quod quae ad poetas efficiendos plurimum valere dicuntur, ingenii bonitas, linguarum peritia, et multarum magnarumque rerum comprehensa cognitio, ea in perplurimis nostrorum hominum, nihilo caeteris nationibus, ne quid arrogantius dicam, inferiora reperiri queunt. Neque vero illud dicere possumus, graviorum artium scientiae addictos homines Gallos operam ponere in his levioris operae studiis noluisse: eorum enim qui ad versus faciendos animum adiecerunt, quaedam prope infinita vis facile non tam voluntatem eis, quam eventum defuisse declarat. Quod si id nobis Graeco tantum, aut Latino sermone contigisset, forte causam illius paucitatis in earum linguarum peregrinitatem reiicere liceret: nunc vero cum idem in eo contigerit, quem a nutricibus, una cum ipso, ut dicitur, lacte combibimus, aliam omnino causam necessario cogimur suspicari. Scio, hoc quod dicturus sum, quantopere nonnullorum animos mordeat; sed tamen et verissimum est, et mehercule iam notius, quam ut negari amplius possit. Qui se vernaculo nostro sermone poetas perhiberi volebant, perdiu ea scripsere, quae delectare modo otiosas mulierculas, non etiam eruditorum hominum studia tenere possent. Primus, ut arbitror, Petrus Ronsardus, cum se eruditissimo viro Ioanni Aurato in disciplinam dedisset, eoque duce, veterum utriusque linguae poetarum scripta, multa et diligenti lectione trivisset, transmarinis illis opibus sua scripta exornare aggressus est: cuius postea exemplum insecuti I. Antonius Baifius, I. Bellaius, aliique permulti, brevi tempore tantos fecere progressus, ut res vel ad summum pervenisse iam, vel certe haud ita multo post perventura esse videatur. Idem in lingua Latina multum abest, ut dicere liceat: in qua cum ex veteribus ab Ausonio, ex recentioribus a Salmonio, et aliis duobus forte, aut summum tribus discesseris, ut Graeci proverbio dicunt esse multos quidem qui boves stimulent, sed raros aratores,[1] ita dicas, licebit, multos quidem esse qui versus faciant, sed raros, planeque εὐαριθμήτους poetas. De iis loquor, qui scripta sua in publicum edidere: scio enim et alios esse sat

---

1. Diogenianus, *Paroemiographi* 7.86 (Leutsch and Schneidewin): "Πολλοὶ βουκένται, παῦροι δέ τε γῆς ἀροτῆρες" Cf. the similar "πολλοί τοι ναρθηκοφόροι, παῦροι δέ τε βάκχοι" of Plato's *Phaedo* 69C (also attributed to Diogenianus at 7.86) and *Anthology* 10.106, the Latin of which is given by Erasmus, *Adagia* 1.7.6. Erasmus explains proverbs of this type (cf. Matt. 20.16, 22.14) as meaning that many exhibit the outward signs and even enjoy the reputation of a particular talent or virtue, but few possess the talent or virtue in reality.

Preface

Oftentimes I have wondered, Jean de Brinon, very honorable sir, why it has happened that, though a virtual untold number of men excelling in every kind of knowledge have emerged from our France, nevertheless we have always suffered from a short supply of poets. And that seems all the more remarkable because those things which are said to be especially beneficial for producing poets, namely, goodness of temperament, skill in language, and the comprehensive knowledge of many great things, can be found in numerous of our people to no lesser degree—lest I sound too arrogant—than in other nations.

Nor can we say that, since French people are devoted to the more serious arts, they have been unwilling to give attention to these less demanding pursuits. For the nearly infinite number of them who have cast their mind to making verses certainly indicates that not so much did they lack will as success. But if that paucity of success happened to us only in Greek or Latin, perhaps we could ascribe the cause to the foreignness of those tongues. But now since the same thing happens in that tongue which we drank down from our wet-nurses, together with the milk itself, as they say, we are compelled by necessity to seek a totally different cause.

I know how much what I am about to say will gnaw at the egos of several, but still it is both true and, by Hercules, is now too widely known to be denied any more. Those who were wishing to be called poets in our vernacular speech, for a great while wrote those things that were able to delight only leisured women, but not also to hold the interest of erudite men. As I see it, Pierre de Ronsard, when he had studied under a very learned man, Jean Dorat, under whose guidance he spent time in the writings of the ancient poets of both tongues, with much diligent reading, was the first to try to begin adorning his own writings with those imported riches. Later, having followed his example, Jean Antoine de Baïf, Joachim du Bellay, and a great many others, made such great progress in a short time that it seemed perfection had been achieved, or certainly was about to be achieved very soon.

The same is far from being true in the Latin language. As you could say, as the

multos, et imprimis eum quem supra nominavi, Ioannem Auratum, qui vel solus, vel praecipue, si quando sua emiserit, effecturus est, ne ulterius suos Iovianos, Actios, Molsas, Flaminios Italiae invideat Gallia. Cum igitur, ut ad institutum redeam, in tanta ingeniorum bonitate, in tanto doctissimorum virorum proventu, in tanta adolescentum poetices studiosorum aemulatione, quasique rivalitate, tantam poetarum raritatem animadverto, nihil fere aliud comminisci possum, nisi esse quandam, ut caeterarum rerum, ita studiorum quoque tempestivitatem, statisque quodammodo coeli conversionibus fieri, ut modo in hac, modo in illa facultate certi homines praestantes et egregii existant. Quod si est, bona spes me tenet fore, ut sub Henrico rege Christianissimo, tamquam olim sub Augusto, poetarum ingenia excitentur. At de his quidem satis: nunc tempus est, ut de meipso tibi dicere aliquid incipiam qui cum etiam puerulus, et a teneris, ut Graeci dicunt, unguiculis[2] admirabili quodam poetices amore flagrassem, multa etiam paene* in omni genere carminis, veteres, quoad per vires licuerat, imitatus conscripseram; quorum, paulo grandior factus, nonnulla tardipedi, ut ait Catullus,[3] deo dicaram, nonnulla proieceram, nonnulla etiam, ut fit, penes me retinueram. Ea igitur cum haud ita pridem amicis quibusdam meis,[4] quibus ego plurimum in hoc genere tribuo, communicassem, non eis solum illi calculum suum adiecere, verum etiam auctores mihi fuerunt, ut edenda eorum saltem aliqua parte iudicia hominum experirer. Assensus sum, ut quod verum est ingenue fatear, non admodum gravate: tum quod res non magni periculi videretur; tum quod facile confiderem fore me, si non, ut ait Horatius, extremum primorum,[5] at certe extremis usque priorem. Subsecivis igitur horis, aliquod mihi tempusculum a philosophiae, et iuris civilis praelectionibus, quibus assidue occupatus distineor, ad haec exscribenda, et in ordinem utcunque redigenda sumpsi; nam perpolire et limare accuratius neque magnopere libebat, neque per eas, quas modo dixi, occupationes licebat. Feci autem, quod locupletes interdum oenopolae solent, qui multa hospi-

*paene *om. 1789, 1834*

---

2. That is, "a prima infantia," meaning, "from a very young age." Cf. Cic. *Epist. ad Fam.* 1.6.2 (*qui mihi a teneris, ut Graeci dicunt, unguiculis es cognitus*) and Hor. *Od.* 3.6.24 (*de tenero meditatur ungui*).

3. Cat. 36.7. The idea is that the poems are low quality and fit for the fire, Hephaestus being the "slow-footed" god.

4. It is noted in Ruhnken's edition (1789, followed by Frotscher in 1834) that Muret should have written, "amicis *cum* quibusdam meis . . . ," but was misled by a corruption of the text of Caes. *De bello civili* 3.18: *quibus communicare*. Modern editors have restored the missing "cum" (in the OCT ed., R. L. A. du Pontet notes that the reading was first suggested by Gronov, who lived after Muret). The construction, "communicare aliquid cum aliquo" is common in Cicero (e.g., *De amicitia* 70: *impertiant ea suis communicentque cum proximis*) and other ancient authors.

5. Hor. *Epist.* 2.2.204, a figure from the racecourse.

Greeks say in a proverb, that, aside from Ausonius of the ancients, from Salmon Macrin of the moderns, and two or three others at the most, there are many who drive oxen, but ploughmen are rare, so you could say that there are many who compose verses, but poets are scarce enough to count on one hand. I am talking about those who have published their writings. For I know that there are plenty, especially the one I named above, John Dorat, who either alone, or even chiefly, should he publish his own, would make it so that France would not begrudge Italy her Pontanos, Sannazaros, Molzas, and Flaminios.

So, to return to my plan, when, amid such excellence of natural talent, such a great supply of learned men, such a great emulation and, as it were, rivalry of eager young people in the discipline of poetry, I notice the great rarity of poets, I can only believe that there is a certain season for disciplines, just as for everything else, and that it happens somehow by the regular revolutions of heaven that now in this ability, now in that, certain men who are excellent and above the rest emerge. But if so, I have great hope that under the most Christian King Henri II, as once under Augustus, the talents of poets might be sparked.

But, about these things, enough for now. It is time that I begin to say something to you about myself, who, while still a little boy, and, as the Greeks say, from tender fingernails, burned with a certain wondrous love of poetry. I had even written many things in almost every poetic genre, imitating the ancients as best I could. After growing up a bit, I dedicated some to the slow-footed god Vulcan, as Catullus says, I discarded others, and, as happens, I retained some. When recently I had shared these with my friends, whose opinions about such things I respect very much, they not only approved of them, but also encouraged me to test the judgments of people by publishing at least some part of them. I agreed, and to tell the truth, not at all reluctantly, both because there didn't seem any harm in it, and because I certainly believed that I would be, if not, as Horace says, behind the foremost, then certainly always ahead of the last.

In my spare hours, whatever small amount of time there was for me after my lectures of philosophy and civil law, with which I was detained constantly, I took to writing these things out and in one way or the other putting them into some kind of order. For I didn't really care to polish it up and edit it in detail, nor did my work, which I just mentioned, allow for that. I did do, however, what the wine sellers do from time to time, who set out many kinds of wine for their guests so they can choose what most pleases their palate. For likewise I have set forth

tibus vini genera gustanda proponunt, electuris quod ad palatum maxime fecerit: nam ita et nos multa poemation genera proposuimus, ut si forte in aliquo lectoribus fecissemus satis, in eo plura porro emittere pergeremus. Hoc autem quicquid erat libelli, *Iuvenilia* inscribere placuit, ut si quid forte interdum lascivius dictum esset, ipsa nos apud severiores excusaret inscriptio. Ac initio quidem decreveram eum nemini cuiquam dicare, ut qui tanti esse non ducerem: quod consilium cur postea mutaverim, intelliges. Cum iam in eo excudendo librarii essent, forte die quodam accidit, ut ex studiorum laboribus peiuscule me haberem. Venere ad me, pro nostra familiaritate, Comes Alsinous, I. Antonius Baifius, Stephanus Iodellus, ut alloquio suo et partem meae molestiae allevarent, et paulatim eximerent diem. Ibi multis ultro citroque habitis verbis, tandem de his etiam nugis iniectus est sermo; primusque Baifius rogavit ex me, eccuinam librum meum dicare meditarer; tum ego, id quod res erat, nemini. Ibi tum Comes valde hortari me coepit, tibi ut eum inscriberem; pergratum id tibi, perque acceptum fore: simulque nactus dicendi campum, cum alia multa de te honorificentissime commemorare coepit, tum ea quae tu in Ludovicum Querculum, hominem optimum et doctissimum, institutorem olim tuum, benignissime et fecisti et quotidie facis: quae etsi omnes optime noveramus, nemo tamen erat, qui non in Comitis de tua laude dicentis oratione libenter acquiesceret. Quid quaeris? Cum aliquandiu reluctatus fuissem, veritus ne parum decorum videretur ista tam pusilla in tuo tanti viri nomine apparere, ad extremum tamen me[6] persuaderi passus sum: quod eo dico, ut si forte mea tibi parum probabitur audacia, Comes ipse mecum culpae sustineat partem. Valde autem te oro, vir illustrissime, ut dum tibi alia graviora molimur, hoc, qualecunque tandem est, aequi bonique consulas. Tibi quidem integrum est, huius veluti glebae apprehensione totum agrum, uti optimus, maximusque est, si collibuerit, vindicare.*[7] Quod ut facias, vehementer te etiam atque etiam rogo. Vale. Lutetiae, 8. Calend. Decemb. 1552.

*vendicare *1553*   vindicare *om. al*

---

6. It is noted in the 1789 and 1834 edd. that this should properly be *mihi*.
7. Poetry can be described as a field for ploughing (cf. Ovid *Trist.* 2.327: *tenuis mihi campus aratur*) or, particularly in the case of epic, a field for doing battle (cf. Muret's own first elegy, line 5). Propertius (3.3.17–18) says that the elegist's fields are "soft" ones: *non hic ulla tibi speranda est fama, Properti: / mollia sunt parvis prata terenda rotis,* i.e., "No hope of fame for you here, Propertius. Soft are the meadows to be worn down by your wheels." On the sense of *mollia* here, see note on *epig.* 32.11. Leroux: "En prenant cette motte de terre, vous être libre de réclamer la propriété de tout ce que le champ contient de meilleur, si vous avez apprécié. Et je vous engage le plus vivement du monde à le faire."

many kinds of poems, so that if in any particular genre I have performed well enough, in that one I will continue to publish more things in the future. Whatever of a little book this was, I decided to entitle it *Iuvenilia,* so that if by chance anything is spoken too playfully from time to time, the title itself would excuse me with the harsher critics. And in fact at the outset I had decided that I would not dedicate the book to anyone; you'll understand why I changed my mind.

When the typesetters were already in the process of setting the type, by chance on a certain day I happened to be feeling a little ill from the labors of my studies. Nicolas Denisot, Jean Antoine de Baïf, Étienne Jodelle came to me out of friendship to ease part of my discomfort by their consolation, and little by little they caused the day to pass. We had many conversations on various topics, and finally the talk fell on these *nugae.* Baïf first asked me to whom I was planning to dedicate my book. I said, "To no one," which was the truth. Then at that point Nicolas began to urge me to dedicate it to you, saying that it would be very pleasing to you and welcome. And as soon as he had obtained the lead in the conversation, he began to relate things about you that do you great honor, and also those things that you did and do daily for Louis Chesneau, the best and most learned man, once your teacher.

Although we knew these things very well, there was no one who was not gladly keeping quiet during the oration of Nicolas as he spoke your praise. In short, although for awhile I was reluctant, fearing that it would seem inappropriate that those petty things would appear with the name of such a great man—your name—still at last I allowed myself to be persuaded. To that I say, if you don't appreciate my audacity by chance, let Nicolas himself take part of the blame with me. I plead with you, most illustrious man, that, until I construct other more serious things for you, you might receive this favorably and be satisfied with it. In fact, it is in your power, if you want, to vindicate the entire field by the acceptance of this clod, so to speak, for it is the very best field of all. I plead with you that you do so, again and again in the strongest terms. Farewell. Paris, November 24, 1552.

Elegies

1.

Non ego Cadmaeos meditor committere fratres,
 Quorum inimicitias ipsa locuta pyra est,
Non veteris Troiae lacrymosa reponere bella:
 Bella canenda aliis, bella cavenda mihi.
Hoc aliis per me liceat decurrere campo, 5
 Illa meis non est versibus apta seges.
Me Venus et Veneris certo puer improbus arcu
 Enervant numeros attenuantque meos,
Nec, praeter dominae blandum ridentis ocellos,
 Carmine me quicquam concelebrare sinunt. 10
Forsitan ista senes culpabunt scripta severi:
 Quid faciam? res est imperiosa decor.
Quem non ille hominum, quem non movet ille deorum?
 Saepe etiam caelo diripit ille Iovem.
Me quoque Margaridos decor admirabilis urit, 15
 Et sibi devinctum magna sonare vetat.
Nec vero Aonides vestro me excludite coetu,
 Si qua ego virginibus non satis apta canam;
Nempe etiam e vobis iuvenili capta decore
 Oeagro tenerum subdidit una latus. 20
Si nulla e vobis ullum sensisset amorem,
 Unde foret, quaeso, dicite, natus Hymen?
Sanctus Hymen, qui seductas a matre puellas
 Abripit, inque viri collocat ipse sinu?
At tu, quae in me oculis nimium violentibus usa, 25
 Nunc spolia e nostro sanguine opima refers,
Hos numeros hilari (quid enim vetat?) accipe vultu,
 Et vide, ut in speculo, quid tua forma queat.

2.

Prima meae quisquis deliramenta iuventae,
 Et specimen tenuis respicis ingenii,
Sic tibi, si quid amas, semper contingat amari,
 Invidia vacuus, si legis ista, legas.
Nec tibi sit duros acuisse in carmina dentes, 5

1.

I am not planning to pit the Cadmean brothers against each other;
the pyre itself has spoken of their enmity.
And I have no intention of rehashing the tear-filled war of old Troy:
It is for others to sing of wars, for me to avoid them.
They would have my consent if they wish to run over this plain,
but that's no field for my verses.
Venus and her naughty boy with his unerring bow
weaken me and make my measures thin,
nor do they permit me to celebrate anything in my verse
besides the eyes of my mistress seductively laughing.
Perhaps harsh old men will find fault with the lowbrow stuff I've written here:
What should I do? Beauty is a powerful thing.
What man or god does it not affect?
Often it even wrenches Jupiter down from heaven.
The wondrous beauty of Marguerite burns me as well,
and puts me in chains and prevents me from singing of great things.
But don't exclude me from your company, Muses,
if I sing of some things unsuitable for virgins,
for even one of you was taken by youthful beauty
and submitted your tender thigh to Oeagrus.
If none of you had ever felt love,
from where would the child Hymen have come, I ask you?
—holy Hymen, who takes girls and leads them away from their mother,
placing them in the loving embrace of a husband.
But you, who have attacked me with your slashing eyes
and now bring back the finest spoils from my blood,
receive these measures with joyous countenance (for what prevents it?),
and see, as in a mirror, what power your loveliness has.

2.

You who take note of these first ravings of my youth
and this token of my slight talent,
I hope you always find the love you are looking for,
and that you hold no grudge when you read these things, if you read them.
But don't whet your hard teeth on these poems;

Carmina quae propriis scripsit Amor manibus.
Seu sunt grata tibi, qua fronte placentia culpes?
    Seu minus, ecquis te cogit ut illa legas?
Seria si quaeris, non sunt hic seria, lector:
    Scribere amatorem seria posse putas?   10
Nos ignes canimus, pueri nos tela volantis,
    Omine non fausto cognita tela mihi,
Et dominam, cuius sub amoena fronte relucent
    Lumina, sidereis aemula luminibus,
Lumina materies ardoris maxima nostri,   15
    Lumina, quae mentem surripuere mihi.
Haec ego sola canam, dum florida ver aget aetas.
    Sit procul hinc tragico syrmate Musa tumens.
Post, mea cum multi distinguent tempora cani,
    Venerit et tremulo curva senecta gradu,   20
Tunc mihi sit curae Solis perdiscere cursum,
    Anne, et quae noceant sidera, quaeque iuvent,
Quot caelum teneant zonae, quot partibus orbis
    Constet, et unde cadant fulmina, curve cadant.
Utamur, dum fata sinunt, melioribus annis,   25
    Et tota nobis mente colatur Amor,
Dum decet et postes nocturna frangere rixa,
    Nec pudor est vernis frons redimita rosis;
Dum decet et mentem leni vincire Lyaeo,
    Et dominae clausas ante iacere fores.   30
Auferet haec secum, velut aufert omnia, tempus.
    Cernis, ut hora, dies, mensis, et annus eunt?
Qui modo vagibat, nunc est puer, inde repente
    De puero iuvenis, mox vir, et inde senex.
Quare florentes aptosque caloribus annos   35
    Quisquis agis, Veneris vive sub imperio,
Ne frustra, aetatis meliori parte peracta,
    Vivere tunc cupias, vivere cum nequeas.

3.

Scire cupis quae sit votorum summa meorum,
    Et qua praecipue vivere sorte velim?
Non ego tecta mihi Phrygiis innixa columnis,

these are poems that Love wrote with his own hands.
Or if these poems are pleasing to you, will you crinkle your brow and disapprove?
Or if they are not, who in the world is forcing you to read them?
If you are looking for serious things, reader, they aren't here.
Do you think a lover can write serious things?
We sing about fires, the darts of that winged boy,
the familiar, unlucky darts,
and the lady, whose eyes gleam under a charming brow,
a rival to the starry lights,
eyes that are the greatest cause of my passion,
eyes which have stolen my mind.
I will sing of these things only, so long as my flourishing age enjoys its springtime.
Far away be that Muse who swells with the tragic robe.
Afterwards, when grey hairs cover my temples,
and old age sets in, bent over and with shaking gait,
then I'll care to learn the course of the sun,
or maybe which stars do good, and which ones harm,
how many zones the sky has, of how many parts the world's orb consists,
and whence the thunderbolts fall, or why.
Let me enjoy my better years, while the Fates permit,
and let me honor Love with all my mind,
while it is seemly to break down the door posts in a nighttime quarrel,
and it is no shame to deck the brow with blooming roses,
and while it is seemly to bind my mind with smooth wine,
and to lie before the shut doors of my mistress.
Time will take away these things, as he takes away everything.
Do you see how the hour, the day, the month and the year flee?
The one who was just now wailing, now is a boy, then suddenly
from boyhood to young man, then soon a man, and then an old man.
So to those who are still young enough to feel the heat of passion,
I say this: While you are in your prime, let Venus reign,
lest in vain, with the better part of your life past,
you then desire to live, when you cannot.

3.

Do you want to know what is the sum of my vows,
and in what lot I would most wish to live?
I'm not looking for roofs resting on Phrygian columns

Divitis aut auri pondera mille petam;
Non ab Erythraeo repetendas litore conchas, 5
Aut quae centenus iugera taurus aret,
Sed tecum longae traducere tempora vitae,
Securumque tuo semper amore frui.
Tunc ego purpureos possim contemnere reges,
"Praeque mea sors est," dicere, "vestra nihil," 10
Si me candidulis incinctum, vita, lacertis
In tepido teneas confoveasque sinu,
Me nunc mellitis mulcens sermonibus, et nunc
Continuo fixis impete basiolis,
Semotum strepitu dominaeque tumultibus urbis, 15
Versantem valido pinguia rura bove.
Sic tecum, mea lux, vitae traductus inerti
Vivere si possim, nil prius esse putem.
Tecum ego per montes, tecum per devia tesqua,
Et curram nullo per loca tacta pede. 20
Post, ubi currendo fuerit lassatus uterque,
Fessa in graminea membra reponet humo,
Et rursum certamen erit linguisque labrisque,
Quod vel Chaonias vincere possit aves.
Forsitan et quiddam post basia multa sequetur 25
Multo illis quod sit dulcius et melius.
Non ego tunc loculi metuam gravioris amantes.
Servandae bona sunt rura pudicitiae:
Balnea non illic, non sunt populosa theatra,
Non quidquid mentes sollicitare potest, 30
Sed nemora et placido currentes murmure rivi
Demulcensque rudi carmine pastor oves.
Porro deterior nobis cum venerit aetas,
Sparserit et cana tempora nostra nive,
Tunc curare cutem genioque litare decebit, 35
Dum fuerint vitae stamina rupta meae.
Nam mea tu, sed non longum mansura superstes,
In tumulo condes ossa minuta brevi:
Deinde ubi te pariter saeva mors impia falce
Laeserit, et iuris iusserit esse sui, 40
Quo nos, te poni tumulo mandabis eodem:
Inscriptum lapidi carmen et istud erit:
Cor fuerat binis unum, mens una, viator,
Quorum nunc unus contegit ossa lapis.

for myself, or piles of gold and riches;
not conch shells that must be retrieved from Erythraean shores,
or fields that a hundred bulls would plough;
but to draw out the seasons of a long life with you,
to be carefree and always enjoying your love.
Then I would be able to hold in contempt richly clad kings,
and to say, "Your lot is nothing compared with mine"
—assuming, my life, you hold me disrobed in your tender white arms,
if you fondle me in your bosom,
now soothing me with your honeyed words,
now with little kisses planted with unrelenting passion,
while I plough the fertile fields with a strong ox,
far from the noise, from the bustle of the capital.
So, my life, if I can live with you,
withdrawn to a quiet existence, I would think nothing could be finer.
I would run with you through mountains, through the remote wilds
and places never tread before.
Then, when we are both tired from running,
we will place our wearied limbs down on the grassy ground,
and again there will be a struggle of tongues and lips,
which even Chaonian birds could not surpass.
Perhaps also something will follow after the many kisses
that is much sweeter and better than those.
Then I will not fear well-heeled suitors.
Country places are good for preserving modesty.
There are no baths here, no crowded theaters,
nothing that can trouble our minds;
but here are groves, streams running with a peaceful murmur,
a shepherd calming his sheep with a simple song.
And when a decrepit age has come upon us,
and has sprinkled our temples with white snow,
then we should pamper our bodies and refresh our souls with wine,
until the threads of my life have been broken.
For you—but you are not going to survive for long after—
will bury my crumpled bones in a small grave.
Finally, when impious Death with his dire scythe
has cut you down as well and has laid his claim on you,
you will ask to be placed in the same tomb with me,
and this poem will be inscribed on the headstone:
"These two shared one heart, one mind, traveler,
and now a single tombstone covers their bones."

4.

Virgo oculis ipsis merito mihi carior, ac non
　　Solum oculis ipsis, quin etiam ipsa anima,
Quam niveus morum candor, mens nescia fraudis,
　　Plus quam maiorum stemmata nobilitant,
Nobilitent licet ipsa licetque a sanguine claro, 5
　　Et non obscura sit tibi stirpe genus,
Quanta, putas, nostram vexarunt taedia mentem,
　　Ex quo diversis coepimus esse locis?
Mitius hostili ruerent cum Pergama dextra,
　　Laomedontiadas indoluisse puto; 10
Mitius Electran, falsas cum tristis ad aures
　　Venit Orestaeae nuntia fama necis;
Scilicet haud alius campis errabat Aleis
　　Excussus patrio munere Bellerophon.
O! quoties aegro suspiria pectore duxi, 15
　　Atque ignis, dixi, quam procul hinc meus est!
O! quoties quavis libuit mihi morte pacisci,
　　Possemus paucos ut simul esse dies!
Occurrunt animo ridentia lumina nostro,
　　Occurrit fusco blandus in ore lepos; 20
Nunc molles subeunt risus, nunc gratia fandi,
　　Nunc subeunt sciti, sed sine dente, sales,
Verbaque, amarescunt mihi prae quibus omnia mella:
　　Ah! me his tam longum posse carere bonis?
Improba, Persephones educta ex carcere Pestis, 25
　　Vix tua plus ulli, quam mihi, tela nocent:
Falx tua non paucos leto multavit amaro,
　　Falx tua corde meo me iubet esse procul.
Illis finis adest vitae, finisque dolorum,
　　At mea perpetuus pectora languor habet. 30
Hem! nunquamne ego te posthac, mea cura, revisam?
　　Nunquamne os istud suaviloquum aspiciam?
Nunquam erit ut veteri Sol nos de more iocantes
　　Conspiciat surgens conspiciatque cadens?
Certe equidem eveniet. Viden' ut iam fulgure laevo 35
　　Firmarit nostras Iuppiter ipse preces?
Spes fovet in medio iactatos aequore nautas,

26 ulli *1553* illi *1757, 1779*

4.

You are a maiden dearer to me than my very eyes—rightfully so—and not
only my very eyes, but also the breath of life itself.
The splendor of your character, as dazzling as snow, a mind that knows no deceit
ennoble you more than your pedigree
(even though that does ennoble you, and though your family
comes from famous blood and illustrious stock)—
do you realize how tormented my mind is
since we began to live apart?
Milder grief the Trojan women suffered, I think,
when Troy fell by hostile hand.
Milder grief Electra felt when she heard the sad (but false) report
Announcing Orestes' murder.
This is how Bellerophon must have felt when he wandered
the fields of Ale after being knocked from his father's gift.
O how many times did I sigh from my aching chest,
and say, "How far from here is my flame!"
O how many times I would have gladly agreed to any death,
so we could be together for a few days!
Your laughing eyes come to mind,
the coaxing charm in your swarthy face.
Now comes soft laughter, now charming conversation,
now comes clever wit, but without the bite,
and words, compared with which all honey is bitter to me.
Ah! Can I stand to be without these things so long?
Wicked Death, plague drawn from the dungeon of Persephone,
your weapons scarcely harm anyone more than me.
Your scythe slaughters multitudes with bitter death,
your scythe bids me be far from mybeloved.
The end of life is at hand for them, the end of grief,
but constant weariness possesses my heart.
Shall I never see you again after this, my dear?
Hah! Shall I never gaze upon that sweetly speaking mouth of yours?
Will it never be that the rising sun sees us
playing the way we used to, nor the setting?
Yes, it will come to pass. Do you see how now Jupiter himself
has affirmed our prayers with a flash of lightning from the left?
Hope sustains sailors buffeted about in the middle of the sea,

Spes fovet armatos, spes fovet agricolas.
Spes fovet inclusos tenebroso carcere sontes,
    Et nos in vita spes quoque sola tenet.   40
Haec modo ne quando temere concepta putetur,
    Fac, fiat scriptis certior usque tuis.

5.

Non ego Cumaei peragam si pulveris annos
    Vivere Margaridos liber amore queam;
Nec si se lecto Venus offerat aurea nostro,
    Margaridem Veneri postposuisse velim.
Tam mihi confixit iaculo praecordia certo   5
    Idalius cornu notus et igne puer.
Haec quoque nascenti cecinerunt fata sorores,
    Quas Nox antiquo sustulit ex Erebo.
At Paris Oenonen quamvis ardenter amarat,
    Sustinuit visa linquere Tyndaride.   10
Dixerat et Theseus, ego te Minoi relinquam?
    O! ea sit leto tardior hora meo.
Vix bene vectus erat spumosa ad litora Diae,
    In viduo coniux sola relicta toro est.
Submergi, dum per Neptunia prata vagatur,   15
    Dignus et iste fuit, dignus et ille fuit,
Qui potuere suos alio transferre calores,
    Et vitas vita deseruere prius.
Tale ego si faciam facinus, mihi terra dehiscat
    Et rapiar Siculae vivus in antra Deae;   20
Illic me Tragicae vexetis Erinnyes, illic
    Omnia cunctorum solus acerba feram.
Sed neque tam dubius neque sum tam fictus amator;
    Una dies vitam finiet, una fidem.
Quandocunque igitur fatalia tempora mensus   25
    Ad vacuas lucis cogar adire domos,
Margaris ipsa mihi natitantes claudat ocellos
    Vitamque ore suo carpat ab ore meo.
Post, effusa comas, nostrum fleat ante sepulcrum,
    Serta ferens lacrymis humida facta suis,   30

9 amaret *1757, 1779*

hope sustains soldiers and farmers.
Hope sustains the guilty locked in their dark cell,
and hope alone keeps us in life as well.
Only lest this hope ever be thought rashly conceived,
bolster it by writing to me constantly.

5.

If I should exhaust the years of Cumaean sand,
I would not be able to live free from the love of Marguerite;
and if golden Venus should offer herself to my bed,
I would still prefer Marguerite over her.
The Cyprian boy, known by his bow and his fire,
has pierced my heart with so sure an arrow.
The sisters whom Night bore from Erebus
also sang of these fates at my birth.
"But," you might object, "Paris could bear to leave Oenone,
however passionately he had loved her, once he saw Helen;
there was a time when Theseus proclaimed, 'Shall I leave you in Crete?
Oh! I would sooner die!'
Scarcely had he sailed his ships to the foaming shores of Naxos,
and she his wife was left alone on her widowed bed."
They deserved to be sunk as they wandered Neptune's meadows,
those who could transfer their passions to another,
and desert the loves of their life sooner than life.
If I could commit such a crime, may the earth swallow me up,
and may I be snatched away living into the caves of the Sicilian goddess.
There may you, tragic Furies, torture me,
there may I alone bear the bitter blows of all.
But I am not so fickle, I am not a lover who deceives you.
The same day will end my life as ends my fidelity.
Therefore, when my time has come
and I am compelled to approach the homes devoid of light,
let Marguerite herself close my failing eyes,
and may she pluck the life from my mouth with her own lips.
Afterwards, let her weep before my tomb with streaming hair,
bearing garlands made wet with her tears.

Et dicat: Vates nuper, Murete, fuisti
  Non bonus, at certe fidus amator eras.

6.

Margari, quis mihi te reddat deus, aut tibi quis nos,
  Aspectu ut grato possit uterque frui?
Nec solum aspectu, sed et oscula ferre citato
  Impete, quae nullus dinumerare queat;
Ut colludentes iucundo murmure linguae 5
  Committant avidas per patula ora animas.
Non ita laeta fuit quondam Icariotis, Ulyssem
  Cum vidit salvum post duo lustra suum,
Nec tam iterum accepta Lyrnesside laetus Achilles,
  Qua quondam abducta fleverat ipse diu, 10
Quam te conspecta scis me, mea vita, futurum,
  Quam me conspecto te scio, vita, fore.
O quam avide, o quoties, o quot, formosa, figuris
  Isti ori roseo basia pressa darem!
Non hedera annosas complectitur arctius alnos, 15
  Non ulmum vitis pressius ulla tenet.
Tunc mea turgidulas tractaret dextra papillas,
  Tractarent avidae lactea colla manus.
Longa vetant, eheu, spatia interiecta viarum,
  Quanta Hypanin vix sunt inter et Eridanum: 20
Nam te Pictonicae retinent felicia terrae
  Oppida, qua Clanus pinguia culta secat,
Me vero invidiae procul a te dentibus actum
  Fortia lunatae moenia Burdigalae,
Pocula quae veteri non inferiora Falerno 25
  Ducit ab innumeris glarea trita rotis.
Et tamen, heu, sine te mihi iam nec dulcia vina,
  Tristia nec quidquid corda levare solet.
Ipsa mihi est invisa dies, Sol ipse videtur
  Opposita vultus abdere nube suos. 30
Et merito, quid enim sine te non triste putandum est,

And let her say: "Lately you haven't been a good poet,
Muret, but you were indeed a faithful lover."

6.

Marguerite, what sort of god will give you back to me, or me to you,
so that we both can enjoy each other's pleasing sight?
Not only sight, but also to kiss with wild
abandonment, kisses which no one could tally;
so that tongues playing together with sweet groaning
might join our eager breaths through open mouths.
Not so happy once was Penelope, when she saw
her Ulysses safe after ten years,
and not so happy was Achilles when he got back Briseis,
whom he had wept for so long when she was taken away,
as you know I would be, my life, once I see you,
as I know you would be, life, when you see me.
How eagerly, how many times, in how many ways, beautiful woman,
I would kiss that rosy mouth of yours.
Not more tightly does the ivy embrace the aged alder,
nor any vine more closely hugs an elm.
Then my right hand would caress your swollen breasts,
my greedy hands your milky neck.
Long stretches of roads lying in between forbid, alas!—
those between Boug and the river Po barely rival them.
For the prosperous towns of Picton hold you
where Clain cuts through fertile fields.
The strong walls of moon-shaped Bordeaux
hold me, driven far from you, by their teeth of envy,
where the gravel roads worn by countless wheels
transport drinks not inferior to old Falernian wine.
And yet, without you—alas!—to me now no wine is sweet,
and nothing can lighten my sad heart.
I hate the very day, the sun itself
seems to hide its face behind the cloud.
And rightfully so: What can cheer me when you are absent?

Qua sine vel vita est ipsa molesta mihi?
O di, si miseros vestrum fovet ullus amantes,
    Vos tandem faciles in mea vota date:
Reddite me dominae, vel si id per fata negatur,   35
    Finiat angores nex inopina meos.

7. Ad P. Cruselium Medicum

Dum tu conaris Parcarum extendere fila,
    Semineces luci restituisque viros,
Conclamata novam mittens in corpora vitam,
    Atque Charonta levi currere nave iubens,
Interea quo me, Cruseli docte, putares   5
    Ducendos sine te fallere more dies?
Scilicet, ut semper, nostros agitamus amores,
    Quae vitae nobis sola terenda via est.
Et modo damnamus, toties quem sensimus, arcum,
    Nunc de crudeli conquerimur domina,   10
Nunc, qua placari possit ratione, rogamus,
    Omnia quae quivis tactus amore solet.
Haec mea laus, haec sint famae praeconia nostrae:
    Non alio ad manes nomine notus eam,
Ut quondam iuvenis telo percussus eodem,   15
    Quo nos, assidue carmina nostra legat
Agnoscatque suos nostris in versibus ignes
    Reddaturque meis cautior ipse malis.
Tu, cui fatipotens artem concessit Apollo,
    Morborum pelli qua genus omne queat,   20
Perge salutifera miseris succurrere dextra
    Regnaque Persephones fac populosa minus,
Ut tibi laeta viro gratetur sospite coniux,
    Et paene amisso turba minuta patre,
Ut te fama ferat candentibus aurea pennis   25
    Hippocrati Coo, Phillyridaeque parem.
At sine me, qui sum sectando natus Amori,
    Inter inexhaustas vivere nequitias.
Me disperdat Amor, semper me torqueat, inque
    Corde meo accensas ventilet usque faces,   30

6 Ducentos *1834, seq. a Leroux*
8 qua *1834*

Even life itself is burdensome without you.
O gods! If any of you pities poor lovers,
at long last be favorable to our vows.
Return me to my lady, or if the Fates do not permit,
let an unexpected death put an end to my anguish.

7. To the Physician Pierre Crouzeil

While you're busy trying to extend the threads of the Parcae,
and restoring half-dead men to the light,
and sending new life into bodies already long lamented,
and while you force Charon to proceed with ship light in weight,
how do you think, learned Crouzeil, that in the meantime
I while away the days that I must spend without you?
Of course, as always, I am playing the lover,
a way of life I have to tread.
And just now I am complaining about the bow that I have felt so many times,
now I am complaining about my cruel mistress,
now I am asking how she can be placated.
I'm doing all the things someone touched by love usually does.
This is my source of praise, these are the heralds of my fame:
Known by no other name shall I go to the ghosts below,
so that anyone struck sometime by the same arrow of the boy
as I might read my poems through
and recognize his own fire in my verses,
and be rendered more cautious by my misfortunes.
You to whom life-giver Apollo has granted the skill
by which every kind of disease can be driven away,
continue to aid the suffering with your healing right hand,
and make the kingdoms of Persephone less populated:
so that the happy wife with her husband safe might give thanks to you;
and so too the little troopers who almost lost their father;
so that golden fame might bear you on gleaming wings
as an equal to Hippocrates of Cos, an equal to Chiron.
But permit me, who was born for pursuing love,
to live in inexhaustible futility and worthlessness.
Let Love ruin me, always let him torture me,
and let him fan the flames in my heart:

Qui si te pariter certo concusserit arcu,
   Hei mihi! quot curas perpetiere miser?
Tunc tandem disces quid sit servire puellis,
   Tunc tandem excludi quid sit, amice, scies.
Nil tibi multiplices cognoscere proderit herbas, 35
   Hunc etenim morbum pharmaca nulla iuvant.
Quippe etiam Phoebum virgo Peneia torsit,
   Profuit auctori nec medicina suo.
O quam saepe mihi, mallem carissime, dices,
   In gelidis Scythiae montibus esse lapis. 40
Haec te, et plura manent; sed quae tua cunque futura est,
   Ingenio saltem digna sit illa tuo.

8.

Basiolum blando tetulit mihi Margaris ore,
   Ambrosia et dulci nectare dulce magis,
Quale thymo aut casiae, verni sub primula Solis
   Lumina, cum blando murmure libat apis.
Inde fugit propere pedibus lasciva protervis, 5
   Dum sese in tenebris posse latere putat.
Sed nihil est, non sivit eam latuisse Cupido:
   Erranti faculas praetulit ille mihi.
Iam te igitur rursus teneo formosula, iam te
   (Quid trepidas?) teneo, iam, rosa, te teneo. 10
Da mihi pro grata sumpti mercede laboris
   Ter tria terque tribus basia ducta modis.
Dic age num sentis animos concurrere nostros,
   Dum sibi dimidium quaerit uterque sui?
Sic age, sic mea vita, animos iungamus utrinque, 15
   Nulla ut eos possit dissociare dies,
Quin tandem ambiguae post iura precaria lucis
   Unicus e gemino spiritus ore fluat.

If he ever strikes you with his sure bow like this,
oh, poor man! how many cares will you endure?
At long last you will learn what it is to sit in servitude to girls,
then at last you will know, my friend, what it is to be an excluded lover.
Your sundry medicines will in no way avail you,
for this disease no drugs can cure.
In fact, even the Peneian maiden tortured Phoebus,
nor did it help him that he was lord of medicine.
How often you will say to me, "I would prefer, dearest friend,
to be a rock in the chilly mountains of Scythia."
These things, and even more, await you: But whatever girl is in your future,
may she at least be worthy of your heart and spirit.

8.

Marguerite gave a kiss to me with her seductive mouth,
a kiss sweeter than ambrosia and sweet nectar;
like that the bee sips with soothing murmur from thyme and mezereon
in the morning light of the vernal sun.
Then the playful girl fled hastily with running feet,
until she thought she could hide herself in the shadows.
But it is no use, Cupid did not allow her to lie hidden:
He lit the way for me as I wandered.
So now I hold you again, lovely little girl, now I hold you
(why do you tremble?); now I hold you, my rose.
Give to me countless kisses, and kisses kissed
in countless ways, a reward for my effort.
Come, tell me, do you feel our souls meeting,
as each is seeking its other half?
Come, my life, let us join our souls with one another
in such a way that no day can separate them.
Instead, at long last, after the prayed-for right of waning light,
let one single breath flow from our twin mouths.

9.

Margari, flammeolis quae me comburis ocellis,
    Per quos in cineres, hei mihi, vivus eo,
Dic mihi, qui facias tam multa incendia, cum sis
    Candidior prima frigidiorque nive?
Namque ea quae molles exest mihi flamma medullas,   5
    A te, si qua fides, non aliunde venit.
Tu tamen, heu, tanquam glacie circumdata pectus,
    Edure nostras respuis usque preces.
Esse quid hoc dicam? neque enim potis est in eodem
    Cum summo summus frigore inesse calor.   10
Scilicet et quae nos fieri non posse putamus,
    Cum libet, et quoties, perficit unus Amor.
Is tibi cor mixto circumdedit igne geluque,
    Quae possent ferri singula, iuncta necant.
O igitur glacies quovis ardentior igni,   15
    O ignis quavis frigidior glacie,
Aut ne me perdant tua frigora, mitius ure,
    Aut ne flamma, gelu proice, Diva, tuum!

10. *Ad F. Verum Lomenium*

Hei mihi, cur genio vis me pugnare, Lomeni,
    Naturaeque iubes vertere iura meae?
Curve parum gratas impellis durus ad artes,
    Musica cui solum sacra placere vides?
Nam nec acris miles fieri nec idoneus armis,   5
    Cui semel arrisit rustica vita, potest;
Nec si quem placido nascentem lumine Clio
    Viderit admota contigeritque manu,
Aut bonus hostiles unquam foedare catervas,
    Aut ad saeva fori iurgia promptus erit.   10
Omnia sed fugiens tranquillae inimica quieti,
    Exiget aetatis mollia fila suae,
Magnarum securus opum, securus honorum,
    Omnia despiciens, quae leve vulgus amat.
Ille etiam summos audax contemnere reges,   15

9.

Marguerite, you who consume me with your blazing eyes,
eyes that turn me from the living—alas!—into ashes:
Tell me, how do you cause so many fires, when you are
whiter and colder than freshly fallen snow?
For that flame which eats away at my soft marrow comes,
believe me, from nowhere else but you.
Yet you—alas!—have encircled your heart as with ice,
and you harshly spit out my entreaties.
What will I call this? For it is not possible that in the same thing
the utmost heat exists along with the utmost cold.
Of course, even what we think is not possible,
whenever and as often as it pleases, Love alone accomplishes.
He has encircled your heart with fire and chill mixed,
which individually can be borne, together kill.
So ice, hotter than any fire,
and fire, colder than any ice,
either burn more mildly, lest your cold destroy me;
or lest your fire destroy me, cast off your frost, goddess!

10. *To F. Verus de Lomenie*

I can't stand this! Why do you want me to contend with the inclinations of my spirit,
Loménie, why do you bid me to change my natural bent?
Or why are you so intent on pushing me into the unpleasant arts,
when you see that I like only the sacred rites of the Muses?
For the one on whom the rustic life has smiled
cannot become a spirited soldier or suited for arms.
And if Clio gazes favorably upon someone and, drawing near, touches him with her hand,
he, assuming he is good, will never be inclined to mutilate hostile troops with wounds
or be drawn to the wrangling of the law courts.
But fleeing all enmity, he will draw out the delicate threads of his life in tranquil peace.
Unconcerned with great riches, with office,
he despises everything the fickle mob loves;

Praeque sua miseros conditione putans.
Castra iuvent alios bellique inamabile murmur
    Missaque non siccae corpora multa neci,
Queis rapiat primae teneros lanuginis annos
    Acceleretque suum Parca severa diem.   20
Gaudeat hic miseros inter clamare clientes
    Et pavidos duro terreat ore reos.
Hic adeat terras alio sub sole calentes
    Litoraque instructa plurima classe legat,
Seu ferat Herculeas animus spectare columnas,   25
    Seu ferat annosos ire ad Hyperboreos.
Durus, qui fragili vitam committere ligno
    Audet et ignotas aequoris ire vias,
Nec timet inverso decumanos marmore fluctus
    Securusque animi squamea monstra videt.   30
Non sic divini, mitissima pectora, vates,
    Aethereo quorum flamine corda calent.
Otia sectantur sed enim tacitosque recessus,
    Et sua neglectis urbibus arva colunt
Splendidaque et multo spectanda palatia luxu   35
    Contemnunt humiles anteferuntque casas.
Illic et siccant generoso plena Lyaeo
    Pocula, Bistonia frigidiora nive,
Et si nescio quid seu vultu ancilla sereno,
    Seu non informis villica pollicita est,   40
Protinus ut capta reduces ex urbe triumphant.
    O hominum felix terque quaterque genus!
Sic ego sim liceatque mihi, mea Margari, tecum
    Non alia vitam ducere sorte meam.
At tu, quantum in te est, alio nos ducere tentas   45
    Astraeaeque sequi numina, Vere, iubes.
Et quid, ais, quaeso, molli tibi carmine quondam
    Proderit aut homines aut cecinisse deos?
Scilicet ut toti fueris cum fabula vulgo,
    Cumque erit in vultu plurima ruga tuo,   50
Fortiter esurias, ut te mala cogat egestas
    Multa pati forti non patienda viro,
Sectari mensas, blande appellare potentes,
    Tollere mentitis laudibus astra super.

he also dares to hold the highest kings in contempt,
thinking that compared with his lot they are miserable.
Let others enjoy camps and the loveless murmur of war,
and many bodies sent to a bloody death.
These are the ones from whom harsh Fate snatches the tender years
of their first beard and hastens their final day.
Let this one rejoice to shout among poor clients,
and with a hardened face to frighten the trembling guilty.
Let that one approach lands blazing under a foreign sun,
and let him skirt countless shores with his well-stocked fleet,
perhaps to see the Pillars of Hercules or to visit the aged Hyperboreans.
Hard is he who dares to entrust his life to fragile wood,
to travel uncharted waters,
and does not fear the immense waves when the sea is in turmoil,
and gazes on scaly sea monsters unconcerned.
Not so the divine poets, whose hearts burn
in their gentle breasts with the ethereal fire.
No, they hunt for leisure and quiet retreats,
they dwell in fields and neglect the cities.
They scorn palaces splendid and wondrous in their extravagance,
they prefer humble cottages.
There also they drain their cups, full of fine
wine, colder than the Thracian snow. And if a smiling servant girl
or a decent-looking overseer's wife has promised them something or other,
straightaway they exult like those returning from a captured city.
O! three and four times blessed breed of men!
Thus may I be, my Marguerite, and may I be allowed
to spend my life with you and not in any other way.
But you try with all your might to divert me;
you bid me, Verus, to pursue the will of Astraea.
And you say, "Please tell me what good will it ever do
for you to sing of men or gods with elegiac song?
I'll tell you: When everyone in the world is gossiping about you,
when your face is full of wrinkles,
you will be very hungry, and evil need
will compel you to suffer many things,
things a brave man ought not to suffer;
to hunt for meals, to sweet-talk the powerful,
to raise them to the stars with your sycophantic lies.

Quod nisi desiperes, poteras in luce forensi 55
    Versari et laudem quaerere opesque tibi.
Excute decepta blandum de mente furorem,
    Qui tibi, ni caveas, perniciosus erit.
Advertit tardas qui recta monentibus aures,
    Exitium demens fabricat ipse sibi. 60
Ergo ego ut hirsuti verbosa volumina Baldi,
    Ut discam leges, Iustiniane, tuas;
Dediscam teneri modulamina blanda Properti,
    Dediscam numeros, culte Tibulle, tuos?
Ah peream prius et saevo me fulmine tactum 65
    Trudat in obscuras Iuppiter ipse domos.
Quam melius dulces dominae in complexibus annos
    Ponere et in caro saepe iacere sinu!
Dispeream, si quicquid opum, si quicquid honorum est,
    A genere hoc vitae me revocare potest. 70

But if you were not foolish, you could be employed in the legal profession,
and seek praise and wealth for yourself.
Shake this seductive madness from your deceived mind,
which, if you are not careful, will be your undoing.
The one who turns slow ears to those warning the truth,
himself goes mad and devises his own ruin."
Then you are asking me to learn the wordy volumes of unpolished Baldus,
to learn your laws, Justinian;
to forget the charming songs of tender Propertius,
your measures, refined Tibullus?
Ah! I would sooner perish, and sooner Jupiter himself strike me
with his thunderbolt and shove me down into the dark abodes.
How much better to spend sweet years in the embraces of my lady,
and often to lie in her dear bosom!
May I be damned if any riches or honors
could recall me from this kind of life!

COMMENTARY ON THE ELEGIES

ELEGY 1

A *recusatio* following the pattern of Ovid's *Am.* 1.1, where the poet begins, *Arma gravi numero violentaque bella parabam,* and goes on to complain that Cupid stole a foot from every other verse, leaving him nothing to write about but the lighter subjects. Similarly, under the influence of Cupid, Muret has surrendered to the power of beauty. Note the initial refusal to write about military exploits, and then the concluding military terminology (*violentibus* and *spolia*) applied to love (a metaphor best known from Ovid's *Am.* 1.9, where it is said that every lover is a soldier; cf. also Prop. 1.1.35–38; 1.7.13–14).

1. Cadmaeos ... fratres: Polyneices and Eteocles, sons of Oedipus, who killed one another as they vied for the throne of Thebes; cf., with similar purpose, Prop. 1.7.1–2: *Dum tibi Cadmeae dicuntur, Pontice, Thebae / armaque fraternae tristia militiae ...* **committere:** The writer claims to be doing what he is only describing; cf. Juv. 1.162–63: *licet Aenean Rutulumque ferocem / committas.* Also, Hor. *Carm.* 2.1.17–20. **2. pyra:** According to Stat. *Theb.* 12.429–446, the flames of the brother's funeral pyres were said to have leapt apart (Leroux). **4. canenda ... cavenda:** note the word play. He avoids writing about wars because he cannot sustain the grandeur of the dactylic hexameter line after line. **5. decurrere campo:** Muret continues the military theme, here with a phrase normally applied to equestrian exercises (see Stat. *Theb.* 7.415; Aug. *contr. Ac.* 3.5: *ne in quaestionis campis tua equitaret oratio*). For similar metaphorical uses, see Juv. 1.19 (of *satire*) and Colum. 10.226 (Calliope wants Columella to run in narrow confines and help her weave poems of a "slender thread"). Muret might have in mind Prop. 2.10.1ff., where the poet describes the writing of epic poetry as "giving rein to the Haemonian steed upon the open plain (*campum*)." Cf. also Ovid's description of his poetic task in terms of an arena for chariot racing, *AA* 1.39–40. **6. seges:** Leroux translates with "moisson" (= "harvest"), a translation which produces a sharp break from the military language at play here. It is true, however, that *seges* does not work well as a synonym of *campus.* Perhaps Muret is thinking of Tibullus' *seges*

41

(1.1.43, *parva seges satis est*), a modest rustic field that signals the poet's rejection of martial violence in favor of a peaceful, "elegiac" existence. Thus, by unexpectedly applying *seges* to the military sphere, a *seges* in which he does not want to work, he conjures up the positive image of the landscape of Tib. 1.1, the kind of *seges* to which he does aspire. **8. attenuantque:** Poets often speak of the thinning of their verses or the song sung on slender reed (e.g., Verg. *Ecl.* 6.8 [of pastoral]; Prop. 3.1.5, 8), especially when evoking Callimachus' Alexandrian style as their model. **9. blandum:** for the adverbial use, cf. Petr. 127: *delectata illa risit tam blandum.* **11. ista:** in a self-deprecating, pejorative sense. So Mart. 11.16.1–2: *Qui gravis es nimium, potes hinc iam, lector, abire / quo libet: urbanae scripsimus ista.* Also Bèze, *Epig.* 1.3: *Iste tamen poterat, lector, liber esse, libellus.* **senes . . . severi:** Cf. Catullus 5.2 and the apotropaic sense there. **18. non satis apta:** phrasing and line position borrowed from Ov. *Ars Am.* 3.706. **20. Oeagro:** Thracian king who produced Orpheus with the Muse Calliope (Apollod. 1.3.2). **latus:** a euphemism for sexual intercourse, found frequently in ancient literature (sometimes with *femur* instead of *latus*). Cf. Ov. *Her.* 2.58, *lateri conseruisse latus; id.* 19.138, *molle latus lateri composuisse tuo.* **23–24. seductas . . . abripit:** reminiscent of Catullus' description of Hymen at 62.21–23: *Qui natam possis complexu avellere matris,* etc. According to Cat. 61.2, Hymen was the child of the Muse Urania. Other writers make him the son of Calliope or Terpsichore, or, according to Servius (*Aen.* 4.127), of Bacchus and Venus. **24. collocat ipse sinu:** cf. *Eleg. in Maec.* 2.34 (*te Venus in patrio collocet ipsa sinu,* which perhaps itself is drawn from Cat. 66.56: *et Veneris casto collocat in gremio*). *Collocare* is often used idiomatically of marriage (e.g., Cic. *Div.* 1.104: *filiam in matrimonium collocare;* Tac. *Ann.* 4.39: *in collocanda filia*). **25. tu:** Marguerite. **oculis . . . violentibus:** Similarly, Ovid says that Corinna is *violenta* because of her lovely face (*Am.* 2.17.7); here the loveliness of the eyes cuts through Muret like a sword. **26. spolia . . . opima:** specifically, spoils stripped off a general by another general after one-on-one combat. The picture here is of one general pitted against another in single combat. **28. in speculo:** Leroux refers to a long tradition of comparing literary works to mirrors. She calls the reader's attention to two works on the topic (I give a different edition and pagination for the first): E. R. Curtius, *European Literature and the Latin Middle Ages,* vol. 2 (Princeton, 1967), 336, esp. n56; and Einar Màr Johnson, *Le Miroir, naissance d'un genre littéraire* (Paris, 1995). The idea is that by reading (or watching a play about) the lives of others, one is really looking into a mirror at one's own reflection (on this see esp. Ter. *Adelph.* 415–16). **quid:** cognate accusative; Moret: "Quel est de ta beauté le souverain pouvoir."

ELEGY 2

Muret encourages his readers to "seize the day" before old age saps them of their vitality and passion (Hor. *Carm.* 1.11; *Ep.* 1.4.13, etc.). Many elements here are picked up from the end of Tib. 1.1: "Let others occupy themselves with serious or dangerous matters, I prefer my girl; now is the time to break down doors and start a lively brawl; old age is setting in and the passion of love will soon fade." Muret warns his readers that his own poetry reflects this exuberant philosophy. For this reason he bids the pedantic and the stuffy to stay away, nor does he have patience for doddering old men or moralizing critics who disapprove of his carefree attitude.

1-2. deliramenta . . . respicis: echoing Catullus' appreciation of Nepos in *c.* 1.4: *aliquid putare nugas.* **3. si quid . . . amari:** literally, "so may it happen to you to always be loved, if you love at all." Cf. Ov. *Ibis* 561: *Nec tibi, si quid amas, felicius Haemone cedat.* The *sic* at the beginning of the lne recalls the structure of Hor.*Carm.* 1.3, also signaled by a penultimate *sic*-clause: *sic te diva.* Moret: "Je voudrois, si ton coeur est pris de quelque amour, / Que l'objet des tes voeux pût t'aymer à son tour." **5. acuisse . . . dentes:** closely paralleling Tib. 3.9 (= 4.3), *nec tibi sit duros acuisse in proelia dentes.* Lions and boars are said to whet their teeth against their prey; cf. also Hor.*Carm.* 3.20.10 (*haec dentes acuit timendos*). **7. fronte:** as at Mart. 1.7, concerning Domitian's disapproval of his poetry. **17. florida ver aget aetas:** from Cat. 68.16: *Iucundum cum aetas florida ver ageret.* Leroux points to the following comment of Muret *ad loc.* in his commentary on Catullus (1554 = Ruhnken, 2.841): "Elegans iuventutis descriptio. Eratosthenem autem dixisse tradunt, primam illam viriditatem aetatis, ver vitae esse; corroboratam aetatem, constitutamque, aetatem, et autumnum; quibus senectutem, quasi hiemem quandam succedere." **18. Sit procul hinc:** On the importance and prevalence of this and similar phrases in Latin poetry see K. Summers, "Catullus' Program in the Imagination of Later Epigrammatists," *CB* 77 (2001): 147–60. **20. tremulo curva senecta gradu:** a phrase taken from Erasmus (*Carm.* 95.56), who perhaps drew it from his friend Fausto Andrelini, *Livia* 1.3.20. Cf. Ov. *AA* 2.670, with the same *carpe diem* advice: *Iam veniet tacito curva senecta pede;* also, id. *Met.* 7.601. **23. Quot caelum teneant zonae:** from Verg. *Georg.* 1.233: *quinque tenent caelum zonae.* Cf. Cic. *ND* 1.24 and Ov. *Met.* 1.45–51. The ancients divided both the heavens and the earth (Muret's *orbis* later in the line) into five zones or belts. Muret prefers to reserve use of his youthful mind for love (l. 26) and wine (l. 29) rather than theoretical science. **25. melioribus annis:** Ovid (*Trist.* 4.93–94) complains that white hairs had already driven away his "better years" before he was sent off into exile: *iam mihi canities pulsis melioribus* *annis / venerat.* **27. postes nocturna frangere rixa:** Ovid (*AA* 3.71) warns noncompliant women to beware the old age creeping upon them, a time when no longer their doors will be broken by the nightly brawl: *Nec tua frangetur nocturna ianua rixa.* **30. clausas . . . fores:** an allusion to the well-known "excluded lover" motif (paraclausithyron), in which the poet-lover is barred from his sweetheart by an unyielding gate or doorkeeper (on this see Frank O. Copley, *Exclusus Amator* [Madison, WI, 1956; repr. Chico, CA, 1981]). For examples see esp. Lucr. 4.177–82; Hor. *Carm.* 1.25, 3.10; Prop. 1.16.17–44; Tib. 1.2; Ov. *Am.* 1.6. **32. Cernis . . . eunt:** echoing Cic. *De senect.* 69: *horae quidem cedunt et dies et menses et anni, nec praeteritum tempus umquam revertitur, nec, quid sequatur, sciri potest.* For the idea of fleeing time, cf. Verg. *Georg.* 3.284: *Sed fugit interea, fugit irreparabile tempus;* Hor. *Carm.* 2.13–14: *currit enim ferox / aetas;* Pers. 5.153: *Vive memor leti, fugit hora.* **36. Veneris vive sub imperio:** a play on various exhortations of ancient writers to live the day to the fullest (Hor. *Sat.* 2.6.96–97; Pers.5.153; Sen. *Ep.* 45.12–13, 101.10; Mart. 1.15.11–12, 8.44.1).

Elegy 3

Muret takes as his theme the praise of country life modeled on Horace's description of his Sabine farm (Sat. 2.6) and its contrast with a busy day in Rome. The beginning echoes Horace's first line and its contempt for riches: *Hoc erat in votis: modus agri non ita magnus.* For Muret, the countryside provides an ideal locale for lovers to conduct their romantic affairs in private, without concern for extraneous factors that could stifle their passion and vitality (Catullus' *vivamus atque amemus*). This poem takes us away from the pressures of the bustling city, the business, the noise, the crowded streets and disapproving gossips, to an unfettered place of simplicity and happiness, where life is lived to the fullest. Likewise, Tibullus found success in love only when he was in a rural setting.
2. qua praecipue vivere sorte velim?: Leroux points to a poem of Ronsard that translates a similar expression in Posidippus (*AP* 3.59: Ποίην τις βιότοιο τάμη τρίβον;). In Ronsard's poem, Muret's name is expressly mentioned, an indication that Ronsard is thinking of this elegy: "Quel train de vie est-il bon que je suive, / Affin Muret, qu'heureusement je vive . . ." (Pierre Ronsard, *Oeuvres complètes*, critical edition by Paul Laumonier, completed and revised by Raymond Lebèque, Isidore Silver et al. [Paris, 1914–1990], 20 vols., V: 77). Antoine de Baïf responds to this with an epigram in his *Passetems:* "A M. A. de Muret, contre *Quel train de vie est-il bon que je suive, etc."* (ed. Marty-Laveaux [Geneva, 1965], IV: 414). **6. centenus . . . taurus:** The singular is poetic; cf. Verg. *Aen.* 10.207: *centenaque*

arbore fluctum verberat; Stat. *Theb.* 6.213–214: *centenus . . . eques.* **16. Versantem:** a double-entendre, given the erotic context. For "ploughing" as a sexual metaphor, see Adams, 154. **17. vitae . . . inerti:** "the quiet life"; cf. Tib. 1.1.5. **18. Chaonias . . . aves:** Ov. *AA* 2.150; Verg. *Ecl.* 9.13. The reference is to the doves that predicted the future at Dodona. Doves were considered especially affectionate creatures. **27. loculi . . . gravioris:** i.e., a purse more weighed down with money, the sort one would expect rivals to carry in the big city whereby they can corrupt the modesty of young girls (line 28). For *loculus* = purse or money casket, cf. Juv. 1.89 (see Courtney's note *ad loc.*); Mart. 5.39.7; Suet. *Galb.* 12. Moret: "Là je ne craindray point de voir d'autres galans." Leroux: "Alors je ne craindrai pas les amants de ce lieu plus sévère . . ." **29. Balnea . . . theatra:** In line 31 these find their natural counterparts in the rivers and the groves. Ovid (*AA* 1.89–100 and 253–58) recommends the baths and theaters as good places to meet the opposite sex. **30. mentes sollicitare:** In line 32, in contrast, the shepherd is able to calm his sheep with song (*demulcens . . . oves*). **35. curare cutem:** proverbial (also used in the title of *Epig.* 106, below); cf. Hor. *Ep.* 1.2.29, 1.4.15; Erasmus, *Adag.* 2.4.75, who applies it pejoratively to people who care more about bodily pleasures than reputation. **genioque litare:** The phrase could mean any number of things. Leroux makes the following observation: "Le mot *Genius* désigne le génie tutélaire d'un homme, qui lui permettait d'engendrer des enfants. Il était honoré par des offrandes. Voir Hor. epist. 2, 1, 143–144 et carm. 3, 17, 14–16." Here, though, the focus seems to be on indulging one's senses (cf. Plaut. *Pers.* 5.151: *indulge genio: carpamus dulcia*) as a sign of enjoying oneself. Both Horace passages mentioned by Leroux, in fact, speak of offering wine to the *Genius,* and so, given the context, appears to be what Muret has in mind: Drinking wine is an appropriate way to make a sacrifice to one's genius. **36. vitae stamina rupta:** a reference to the activity of the Parcae. **44. unus . . . lapis:** Muret has in mind Ov. *Her.* 11.124, with Canace, daughter of Aeolus, speaking about herself and her dead son: *urnaque nos habeat quamlibet arta duos.*

Elegy 4

The poem begins with an emotional declaration of love, which leads in turn to the deep pains caused by separation comparable to death, and finally builds to its main theme, the paradoxical nature of hope. Hope steadies the wavering heart and offers strength in times of trouble; but for all its fortifying power, hope itself can barely be sustained sometimes, and itself relies on something concrete and certain to steady it. At times Muret echoes Catullus' lament for his brother in c. 65.

11. Electran: This is the version found at Soph. *Elect.* 788–90. **14. Excussus patrio munere Bellerophon:** After he was thrown from Pegasus and blinded by a blast from Jupiter, Bellerophon wandered the fields of Ale around Lycia (the region where he had killed the Chimaera). See Hom. *Il.* 6.201 (trans. Cic. *TD* 3.26.63); Hyg. *Fab.* 57; Ov. *Ibis* 259 (*qui miser in campis maerens errabat Aleis*). The horse is a "father's gift" because Poseidon, Bellerophon's father by some accounts, sired the horse. **35. fulgure laevo:** a propitious omen in terms of Roman augury; cf. Verg. *Aen.* 2.693 (*intonuit laevum*) and Ov. *Fast.* 4.833–34 (*tonitru dedit omina laevo / Iuppiter*). **41–42:** Moret: "Mais l'espoir de vous voir, sera bien plus certain, / Si vou le confirmez d'un mot de vostre main." Leroux: "Mais pour qu'on ne croie pas que cet espoir est vain, / Confirme-le en écrivant sans trêve."

Elegy 5

Muret is drawing from a topos about the instability of lovers' vows, which, the poets say, never reach the ears of the immortals and ought to be written on water (Soph. fr. 811; Callimachus *Epig.* 29 [Pfeiffer]; Philodemus *Epig.* 36 [Sider]; Cat. 70; Ov. *Am.* 1.8.85–87 and *AA* 1.631–668). Here the poet makes exaggerated claims about his fidelity and constancy while promising to avoid the mistakes of infamous lovers of myth. Despite the insistence on long-term commitment, the poem in fact dwells on infidelity and death. Paris and Theseus abandoned their lovers and so deserve to die. The poet, too, deserves torture and death if he fails to be faithful to Marguerite. It is death in the end, however, that separates the lovers and makes the past tense conclusion appropriate: "You were a faithful lover, Muret." The unexpected mention of poetic quality at the end of the poem subtly invokes two favorite topoi of classical poets: 1) the immortality of poetry (even the stories of infidelity that he rehearses live on in poetry) as opposed to the mortality of love (it dies along with the person); and 2) the difference between the poet's life and his poetry (cf. Cat. 16 and Mart. 1.3).

1. Cumaei ... pulveris: a reference to the story of the Sibyl's request of Apollo to live as many years as there are grains of sand in her hand. According to tradition, she lived for a thousand years. **8. Nox ... ex Erebo:** the Parcae; cf. Cic. *ND* 3.17.44: *quos omnes Erebo et Nocte natos ferunt.* **9. At:** The contrastive signals an objection that could be raised by Marguerite (see TLL s.v. *at,* col. 996, lines 48ff.) and is answered in line 15 by the emphatically positioned *submergi.* Moret understands it differently: "Je ne sçaurois brûler du feu d'un autre objet, / non, je ne feray pas ce que Pâris a fait . . ." **Oenonen:** told in Parthenius, *Erotica pathemata* 4 and Ov. *Her.* 5. Paris loved Oenone while still a shepherd on Mt. Ida, before he met Helen, and swore to her that he would never leave her. In the end, Oenone committed suicide over Paris' infidelity. **13. vectus erat spumosa ad litora Diae:** an echo of Cat. 64.121ff. **20. Siculae . . . Deae:** Cf. Juv. 13.50. Persephone was gathering flowers in Sicily when Hades snatched her away. **15. Submergi:** emphatic by position indicating the poet's forceful and indignant response to the objection. **18. vitas:** "loved ones." Muret has used *vita* throughout as a term of endearment, and so here. **28. vitam . . . ab ore meo:** Leroux refers to the Roman tradition whereby a kinsman would catch the last breath (i.e., soul) from the mouth of a dying person (Cic. *Verr.* 5.45; Verg. *Aen.* 4.684–85). **31. nuper:** "as of late," presumably because erotic poets are at their best when desperate and separated from their lover. Cf. Bèze, *Epig.* 83, which begins, *Esse quid hoc dicam, quoties sum, Candida, tecum, / Cur faveat pigro nullus Apollo mihi?* And see *Eleg.* 6 below. **31–32:** Moret: "Qu'enfin son amitié parfaite / Luy fasse dire hautement, / S'il n'estoit pas un bon Poëte; / Il estoit un fidelle Amant." Leroux: "et qu'elle dise: 'tu n'etais naguère bon poète, Muret, / mais san conteste amant fidèle.'"

Elegy 6

The elegy has its roots in the lament for lost loved ones (see Hor. *AP* 75: *Versibus inpariter iunctis querimonia primum*), as is reflected in Ovid's mournful strains for the death of Tibullus (*Am.* 3.9). And although by Augustan times poets used the elegy primarily to describe a love affair with a mistress, it is particularly the separation from a lover or elusive girl that inspires the poet to write. The love elegy, in fact, often takes on a tone of desperation, marked by the pathetic self-pitying, complaining, and longing for death typical of any lament. See M. E. Clark, "Horace, *Ars Poetica* 75–78: The Origin and Worth of Elegy," *CW* 77 (1983): 1–5.

4. dinumerare: an allusion to Cat. 5 and 7, where the counting of kisses is an issue. In each case, the number of kisses kissed is so large that the envious are not able to tally them. **6. Committant . . . animas:** Leroux notes the parallel in Secundus, *Basia* 10.12: *Et miscere duas iuncta per ora animas.* **15. hedera . . . arctius:** cf. Cat. 61.34–35 and 106, in comparison with the amorous embrace of the bride and groom. **20. Hypanin:** Boug, a river of the Ukraine (ancient Scythia, Herod. 4.52). **Eridanum:** the Po of northern Italy. Both this river and the previous receive mention together at Verg. *Georg.* 4.370–73. **21. Pictonicae . . . terrae:** an indication that Marguerite is living in and around Poitiers in the region of Poitou in central France. **24. lunatae:** The Garonne river makes a crescent shape within the city of Bordeaux, a fact reflected in the city's coat of arms (a small moon in the water) and its motto (*Lilia sola regunt lunam, undas, castra, leonem*). **25. Falerno:** a white wine from northern Campania (from grapes grown on the hillsides just south of Naples) highly prized by the Romans; so, e.g., Varro 1.2.6, *Quod vinum [conferam] Falerno?* **26. glarea trita:** cf. Aus. *Epist.* 4.15–16: *aut iteratarum qua glarea trita viarum / fert militarem ad Blaviam.* **27. sine te . . . vina:** With this sentiment cf. Calp. Sic. *Ecl.* 3.51–52: *Te sine, vae misero, mihi lilia nigra videntur, / nec sapiunt fontes et acescunt vina bibenti.* **29. invisa . . . videtur:** note the play on words and the double-entendre for *invisa.* **34. vota:** Horace lists the votive epigram as the secondary use of the elegy (*AP* 76, *post etiam inclusa est voti sententia compos*).

ELEGY 7

Muret makes subtle contrasts between his own calling and that of the physician Crouzeil, between his *otium* and Crouzeil's *negotium.* Crouzeil treats physical diseases so effectively that he is able to thwart the plans of the Fates (Parcae) by extending life. Fewer people than before step upon Charon's boat for transport into the Underworld. For this skill Crouzeil receives accolades from many quarters and enjoys the greatest fame. Muret, on the other hand, wins immortal praise for grappling with another kind of malady, the disease of love. Love is a disease that no traditional medicine can cure, a sentiment the poet has drawn from Prop. 2.1.57–58: *Omnis humanos sanat medicina dolores: / solus amor morbi non amat artificem* ("Medicine cures all what ails a human being: Love alone hates the art that cures its ill"), which itself may look to Theocritus, *Idylls* 11.1–2 and Callimachus *Epig.* 46 [Pfeiffer]). Even Apollo the Healer could not find a remedy for his love of Daphne, nor will Crouzeil, if Cupid ever strikes him and forces him to exchange his *negotium* for *otium.* But the elegists who suffer the pangs of love can write about the emotionally tortuous vicissitudes of their affair as a caveat and guide to readers caught in the same snare (cf. Prop. 1.1.35ff.; Bèze, *Eleg.* 1.41–42). Treatises from the Middle Ages synthesizing the writings of the ancients show that physicians at least were taking "love sickness" as a serious medical problem. On this see esp. Massimo Ciavolella, *La "malattia d'amore" dall'Antichità al Medioevo* (Rome, 1976); and Mary Wack, *Lovesickness in the Middle Ages* (Philadelphia, 1990). For a discussion of poetry/song in some poets as a remedy for love (a solution invented, supposedly, by Polyphemus in his episode with Galatea), or as a means to win over the girl, see J. K. Newman, *Augustan Propertius: The Recapitulation of a Genre* (Hildesheim, 1997), 464–65.

3. conclamata: a reference to the ritual calling of the dead person's name in

Roman funerary rites; the lament was carried on for several days before burial, perhaps to give the deceased one last chance to revive. Cf. Lucan 2.23: *cum corpora nondum conclamata iacent.* **6. Ducendos ... dies:** Leroux, reading *ducentos,* translates, "deux cents jours." **fallere ... dies:** for the sense, cf. Ov. *Met.* 8.652: *medias fallunt sermonibus horas / sentirique moram prohibent.* **24. turba minuta:** a periphrasis for children drawn from Prop. 2.29.3–4: *obvia nescio quot pueri mihi turba minuta / venerat.* Propertius, however, is not using the phrase to indicate family members; on this see W. J. Slater, "Pueri, turba minuta," *BICS* 21 (1974): 133ff. **26. Phillyridaeque:** Crouzeil outdoes both real doctors and mythological doctors. Chiron, the son of Cronus and Philyra, a daughter of Ocean, was a kindly Centaur who trained many of the heroes and gods in the medical arts. He himself was an accomplished physician and surgeon. His students included Apollo, Asclepius, Jason, and Achilles. **28. nequitias:** used of the life of the poet devoted to love; cf. Prop. 6.26: *huic animam extremam reddere nequitiae.* **37. virgo Peneia:** Daphne.

ELEGY 8

Muret picks up Aristophanes' story about the nature of love from Plato's *Symposium* to create a vivid, almost comic image of a couple merging body and soul in the embraces of love. The poem is a variation on Cat. 99, where Juventius spurns the poet's kisses. The ending, however, echoes Salmacis' prayer for union with Hermaphroditus (Ov. *Met.* 4.371–72: *non tamen effugies, ita di iubeatis, et istum nulla dies a me nec me deducat ab isto!*).
  2. Ambrosia: cf. du Bellay's equation of kisses with "ambrosial flowers" (*Amoenitates poeticae,* 369): *et ambrosios anhelo ab ore / Flores carpere mi licet beato.* **17. ambiguae ... lucis:** The passage is somewhat cryptic. Leroux understands *lucis* here to mean "life" or "existence": "ni empêcher qu'après les lois précaires d'une vie dédoublée." She also argues that *ambiguae* "doit être pris selon son acception étymologique (*ambo:* deux)," as if the poet is contrasting the previously "split" couple with the newly "twinned" couple. She adduces the somewhat convincing parallel from John Secundus, *Basia* 13, 21–22: *Donec, inexpleti post taedia sera furoris, / Unica de gemino corpore vita fluet.* But *precaria* makes better sense here if understood in its basic meaning of "prayed for" or "petitioned" (cf. Tac. *Germ.* 44: *non precario iure parendi*): Muret is praying for the right to kiss his girl to his heart's content. This relates as well to the sense of *preces* at *Eleg.* 9.8 below. *Lucis,* on the other hand, should be interpreted in view of the other references to light in this elegy. In lines 3–4 the image of the bees sipping honey gives the first

hint that this episode takes place early in the morning. Then in line 6 the girl hides in the shadows, while the poet searches for her by the light of Cupid's torch (line 8). Even the girl's shuddering (line 10) makes us think of the flickering of the fire in the early morning hours. Thus we are to understand that in the subtle and ambiguous glow of twilight the poet and his girl are lost in a passionate embrace, with souls joining as one. Moreover the ambiguous light, or, if you will, the interplay of sun and moon, hints at the union of male and female that is taking place here. Salmacis' passionate embrace of Hermaphroditus led to a *forma duplex*, an ambiguous merging of genders (Ov. *Met.* 4.378–79). Likewise, at *Ep.* 3.16 Muret gives Dionysus the epithet *ambiguus*, i.e., "androgynous." Such seems to be the focus of the passage. Moret, in contrast, sees a reference to death in these lines. His translation of the last four lines runs as follows: "Ma Belle il faut ainsi les assembler si bien, / Que personne jamais n'en couppe le lien. / Et que quand de nos jours la mort rompra la trame, / De nos deux corps unis, il n'en sorte qu'une ame."

Elegy 9

The oxymoronic "icy fire" topos is often traced to Petrarch, but of course has its roots in ancient literature, going back to Sappho 31 [LP]. Cf. also Verg. *Aen.* 8.386–90, where Venus' embrace with her "snowy-white arms" [*niveis . . . lacertis*] ignites a flame in Vulcan's marrow; and *Anthol. Lat.* 706:

> Me nive candenti petiit modo Iulia. rebar
>   Igne carere nivem: nix tamen ignis erat.
> Quid nive frigidius? nostrum tamen urere pectus
>   Nix potuit manibus, Iulia, missa tuis.
> Quis locus insidiis dabitur mihi tutus amoris,
>   Frigore concreta si latet ignis aqua?
> Iulia sola potes nostras extinguere flammas:
>   Non nive, non glacie, sed potes igne pari.

The topos refers to the contradictory mingling of joy and despair in the experience of the lover. **8. edure:** the adverb, built from *e(c)durus*, is unattested in classical Latin. **18. Diva:** Marguerite herself, godlike for her ability to deal simultaneously with ice and fire.

Elegy 10

Loménie urges Muret to abandon the "elegiac" life he has chosen for himself in favor of the practice of law. In the city's law courts, Loménie advises, he can earn fame and store up riches for his retirement. But Muret rejects conflict of any kind and scorns riches. As a poet and a lover he prefers the embraces of his lady.
  4. Musica . . . sacra: i.e., poetry. **5. acris miles:** cf. Cic. *Cat.* 2.21: *Hosce ego non tam milites acris quam infitiatores lentos esse arbitror.* Cicero draws a distinction between the active, eager soldier and lazy insolvents. For the form of the adjective (*acris* as masc. sing.), see Neue-Wagener II, 16. Dictionaries point to Ennius, *Ann.* 368–69 (Vahlen²), *somnus . . . acris*, but O. Skutsch (*The Annals of Q. Ennius*, 1985, 12: 367–68) argues that Priscianus was wrong to cite this as an example of *acris* as a masc. nom. sing, since here it should be read as acc. pl. Neue-Wagener has other examples, though, most notably Cels. 8.4 (*vomitus*) and Colum. 12.17.2 (*sapor*). **6. Astraeae sequi numina:** i.e., the study of law. Astraea is the goddess of justice. **7. placido nascentem lumine Clio:** echoing Hor. *Carm.* 4.3.2, where Melpomene is said to gaze favorably on a chosen few when they are being born. Strictly speaking, Clio inspires the writing of history, but here she is to be taken as the Muse of poetry generally. **15. Ille . . . contemnere reges:** cf. *Eleg.* 3.9–10. **18. non siccae . . . neci:** cf. Juv. 10.113: *sicca morte tyranni.* **61. hirsuti . . . Baldi:** Baldus de Ubaldis (1327–1406), born in Perugia, famed Italian jurist. He is *hirsutus* because he wrote in medieval Latin. **62. Iustiniane:** The second syllable is normally long. Justinian, shortly after becoming emperor in 527, commissioned a digest (*Pandectae* or *Institutiones*) of all Roman law into three volumes. A second edition, completed in 534, survives. As Leroux states, G. Budé had greatly improved the text with his *Annotationes in XXIV libros Pandectarum* of 1508. On readings of the text in the Renaissance, see M. Reulos, "L'interprétation des compilations de Justinien dans la tradition antique reprise par l'humanisme," *L'Humanisme français au début de la Renaissance* (Paris, 1973), 273–86.

M. Antonii Muretii ad Petrum Rufum
Druydam, Consiliarium Regium,
Satyrarum Libellus

Book of Satires of Marc-Antoine
Muret to Pierre Roussanes of the
King's Council

Satyra Prima

Iam dudum tumido mihi bilis in hepate fervet,
Et rumpi metuo, nisi te, Auruncane, secutus,
Inficiam tenues mordaci carmine chartas.
Tune ausis satyram conscribere, tot tibi rerum
Conscius, ut satyrae possis satis esse vel unus? 5
Quidni autem? nunquid par est audacia Balbo,
Balbo, Stentorea Christum qui voce professus,
Deinde domi cevet, tremulum crissante Lycinna?
Et tamen hunc torvis oculis, et fronte severa,
Flammatisque genis atque horrifico ululatu, 10
Dum docet et iactat fatuae sua dogmata turbae,
In mores clamare malos si videris olim,
Esse putes supero demissum ex limine Paulum.
O mihi si effossa liceat scrobe dicere, quod mox
Efferat in vulgum foliis vocalibus arbor, 15
Quaenam ego, vel potius quae non ego crimina dicam,
Concitus? optari sed enim quia talia possunt,
Non etiam fieri, dicam tibi, Rufe, sed uni,
(Σοὶ γὰρ ῥητὰ λέγειν καὶ ὅμως ἄρρητα licebit)
Quae mihi sive furor sive haec suggesserit ira. 20
Nam quis enim est adeo patiens (nisi forte Torannus
Deprensis solitus blandiri in coniuge moechis
Et piperis multo saturas offerre placentas,
Dum refugit rixas vitandaque iurgia censet),
Quisnam inquam est usquam, qui, si saecli semel huius 25
Vividius paulo faciem consideret, ira
Abstineat? cum iam oppresso virtutis honore,
Regnet in humanis vitiorum infamia rebus.
Improba quos ludi fecit fortuna choragos
Visceribus reliquorum et sanguine plebis aluntur. 30
Praeficiuntque suis saevi rationibus, haud quos
Longa fides vitae vel constans fama probarit,
Verum aquilas et vulturios, qui rodere norint
Ad vivum atque unum ex membris augere lienem.
Ringitur interea populus miser et prece multa 35
Nequicquam surdas divorum verberat aures.
Audisne haec inquam, magni pater Herculis? audis?

Satire One

For a long time now the bile has been seething in my swollen liver,
and I fear that it will burst, unless I follow you, native of Aurunca,
and imbue my tender pages with a biting song.
"Have you dared to write satire," you might say, "aware of so many
of your own faults, so many, in fact, that you could be the sole subject of a satire?"
Yet why not? Am I as bold as Balbus,
that Balbus who, after having preached Christ with the voice of Stentor,
then at home plays the pathic while Lycinna gets it on?
And yet, if ever you see him preaching against evil ways,
with his eyes wild and brow stern,
cheeks aglow, howling terrifically
as he pontificates and tosses out his dogmas to the foolish crowd,
you would think that he is Paul sent down from the threshold of heaven.
If I could dig a hole in the ground and speak what soon
a tree would divulge to the crowd on vocal leaves,
tell me what would I speak, or rather which faults would I *not* speak about,
once I'm roused? But because such desirables are
but vain fantasy, I will speak to you alone, Roussanes
(for to you I can speak both the speakable and the unspeakable),
things that either my rage or this anger will suggest to me.
For who is so patient (except perhaps Torannus,
who often acts courteously when he catches adulterers on his wife
and offers them peppery cheese cakes,
because he hates quarreling and thinks that conflict should be avoided),
who, I say, is there who observes carefully the conduct of this age
and abstains from anger? when now, with the honor of virtue crushed,
the infamy of vice rules in human affairs?
Those whom coy fortune has made life's stage managers
are fed by the blood and guts of the rest of the people.
These cruel fellows give charge of their business accounts,
not to those who have earned trust in life and who have built up a good reputation,
but to eagles and vultures, types who know how
to gnaw the spleen to the quick and at the same time to fatten it from the limbs.
Meanwhile the poor people are angry, and
nothing from their constant entreaties strikes the deaf ears of the rich.
Do you hear these things, father of great Hercules, do you hear them?
Are you listening, or are you asleep, or drunk from a draft of nectar,

Audisne, an dormis, an nectaris ebrius haustu,
Exerces positis genialia tempora curis?
Non aliter nostri. Similes fortasse tueris. 40
Haec aliquis, sacro cernens qui sulphure quercus
Nil meritas, non monstra illa exitiosa, feriri,
In rabiem versus furiisque agitatus amaris,
Insequitur veteris non sanum dogma Lucreti.
Sic alia ex aliis incommoda. Quomodo enim plebs 45
Ipsa colat divos, cum vos, qui fulmine bruto
Stringitis in vestras ausos mutire tiaras,
Conspiciat divis ipsique oppedere Christo?
Anne libet mecum rationum evolvere libros?
Centum lenoni sestertia, mille Corinnae. 50
Hui! mille infami scortillo? Desine, pulchra est,
Et bene sub domino lumbos vibrare perita.
Quin etiam fessus si quando elanguit, ipsa
Insilit et blande super illum palpitat. Id tu
Quanti esse aut potius quanti non esse putabis? 55
Perge age. In accipitres triginta expensa canesque
(Hos domini potius pasci decuisset omaso);
Eripuit fallax plus millibus alea binis;
Unguenta exoticique tulerunt caetera odores,
Fartoresque coquique et rari opsonia luxus. 60
Interea quantum in viduas, quantum in peregrinos?
Quotnam inopes pavit domini quadra? quot studiosos?
Inscius est morum, quisquis nunc talia quaerit.
Haec fuerant sub rege Numa, sub consule Bruto.
Nunc alia est aetas. Nugalibus hisce relictis, 65
Curant magnanimi ventrem caudamque nepotes.
Nec gratus quisquam est, nisi cui perfricta pudorem
Frons omnem abstulerit, sic ut probet omnia sitque
Et bene ructanti post coenam applaudere porco
Et bene pedenti blandum arridere paratus. 70
Sed satis est. Si forte furor Phoebeius olim
Mentem, Rufe, meam simili concusserit oestro,
Bilem aliis, uni risum tibi, Rufe, movebo.

and having set aside your cares spend your time in ease?
That's how our leaders are. Perhaps you are watching out for those who are like you.
Anyone who sees these oaks undeservedly struck by the holy brimstone,
and those ruinous monsters who get off unstruck,
is turned mad and driven into a bitter rage,
and follows the crazy dogma advocated by old Lucretius.
Thus from worse to worse it goes. For how can the people
themselves worship the gods, when they see that you, who with your brutish thunderbolt
strike down those who mutter against your tiaras,
mock the gods and Christ himself?
Care to unroll their accounts with me?
A hundred bucks to the pimp, a thousand to Corinna.
Whoa! A thousand for an infamous prostitute? "Wait a minute: She's good-looking,
and an expert at moving her hips underneath her customer.
But even if he's weary and can't perform, she herself
climbs on top of him and seductively throbs and humps him. Given that,
will you reckon she's expensive or a bargain?"
Let's look further. You paid thirty bucks for food for your hawks and dogs
(they should have eaten their master's tripe instead).
Some fraudulent game of dice snatched away more than two thousand.
Ointments and exotic perfumes carried off the rest,
as well as poulterers and cooks and fancy side-dishes.
Meanwhile, how much did you spend on widows, how much on strangers?
How many poor people did the master's table feed? How many students?
Whoever now seeks such things, is unaware of the current morality.
These things existed under king Numa, under the consul Brutus.
Now it's a different time. Brushing aside these minor details,
their great-souled descendants care for their belly and their prick.
They don't like anyone, except the one who has lost all sense of shame,
to the point that he approves of everything and is prepared to applaud
the pig who belches well after dinner and to laugh at the one who farts charmingly.
But it's enough. If by chance Apollo's madness
ever strikes my mind, Roussanes, with a similar inspiration,
I will anger others while provoking you alone to laughter.

M. Antonii Mureti ad Danielem Sleicherum, Ulmensem, adolescentem omnibus et fortunae, et corporis, et animi bonis cumulatissimum Satyra Secunda

Rumpe Lycambea numeros de caede madentes,
Musa ferox, rabieque nova flammata malignos
Fige hominum mores damnataque saecula culpae.
At tua quis poterit patienti volvere vultu
Scripta? quotus tandem feret haec convicia lector?   5
Men' curare putas, mea quis laudetve legatve,
Rideat aut damnet? quasi sint haec iusta laboris
Praemia, post centum vigilatas ordine noctes
Et paene erosos repetitis morsibus ungues,
Insani et semper deterrima quaeque probantis   10
Plus aliis populi suffragia caeca tulisse.
Tu modo, quem nondum saecli contagio vertit,
Tu legito haec, Daniel, primaeque a flore iuventae
Disce quot humana lateant sub imagine pestes.
Hunccine tu, cui laena humeros hyacinthina velat,   15
Lucentem hinc illinc auro gemmisque superbum,
Vinosa facie, vasti qui pondere ventris
Sudantis mulae cedentia terga fatigat,
Aspicis? hic primo abiecta de stirpe creatus
Vilisque ignotusque et terrae denique proles,   20
Non aut virtute, ingenuis aut artibus (illas
Ipse sua ex aequo cum mula novit), at astu,
Sensim subducens fatuis fundosque laresque,
Tandem huc pervenit. rabidi nunc more leonis
Ventrem adipe insontum et miserorum sanguine farcit.   25
Aspice et hunc, qui diducto, ceu simia, rictu
Putris gingivae viduata sedilia pandit.
Quottidie hunc videas nitidi sub primula solis
Lumina, cum trepidus postico limine furtim
Emittit tota vexatam nocte sacerdos,   30
Repere paulatim per delubra omnia et illic
Obstipo capite et trepidantibus usque labellis
Nunc has, nunc illas provolvi cernuum ad aras.
Hinc rediens non ille inopes fraudare recuset,
Non delatori periuria vendere Cordo,   35

7 quasi haec sint *1789, 1834*

Satires

The Second Satire of Marc-Antoine Muret to Daniel Schleicher of Ulm, a young man surpassing all good men in in the blessings of mind, body, and fortune

Break out, spirited Muse, into measures soaked with Lycambean blood,
and inflamed with a new madness pierce
the wicked mores of men and this damned age of sin.
"But who will be able to unroll your writings with patience?
How many readers in the end will endure these outcries?"
Do you think that I care who praises or reads,
laughs at or condemns my poems? As if these are just rewards
for my labor, that, after enduring a hundred sleepless nights in a row,
and fingernails eaten away from the constant gnawing,
I also endured the blind applause of a crazed people
who always approve the worst more than anything else.
I ask only you, Daniel, whom the contagion of this age has not yet perverted,
to read these things and learn from a tender young age
how many plagues lie hidden beneath the human form.
Do you see this one, whose shoulders a dainty cloak covers,
glistening here and there with gold, decked out in precious gems,
with an inebriated glow, who under the weight of his huge belly
wears out the creaking back of a sweaty mule?
He was from humble beginnings: born from a downtrodden stock,
vile, ignoble, a son of the earth, he reached this point,
not by virtue or natural talent or skill
(he's about as gifted as his own mule), but by cunning,
imperceptibly drawing away property and homesteads from the foolish.
Like a rabid lion he stuffs his belly
with the fat of the innocent and blood of the weak.
Look also at this one, who, with his jaws gaping open
like an ape, reveals his toothless rotten gums.
You could see him everyday before the first hint of daylight,
when the nervous priest secretly lets a girl out the back door
whom he has worn out the whole night,
creeping ever so slowly amid all the shrines,
and there with bent head, and with constantly quivering lips,
now throwing himself forward at these altars and those.
Returning from here he does not refuse to cheat the poor,
or sell perjurers to the informer Cordus,

Non facere omnia, quae vel dicere vix sit honestum.
Vim putat hanc demens esse in lustralibus undis
Perque globos precibus distracta mente volutis,
Ut si vel cani iugulum patris ense resolvat,
Dummodo mortales oculos effugerit, ipse 40
Conscia securus contemnere numina possit.
O simulatores, tetrum pecus, ut mihi saepe
Bile iecur vitrea diffinditur ista tuenti!
Creditis esse deum caelo, qui talia curet?
Exprimite hoc factis. non creditis? abicite ergo 45
Hunc fucum, et vultu ruite in scelus omne retecto.
Hoc ego larvarum genus exitialiter odi.
Sed quid ego enumerans nequicquam singula conor?
Res caret illa modo; genera ipsa evolvere longum est.
Stupra, doli, fraudes, periuria, furta, rapinae, 50
Crimina erant olim; nostro sunt tempore lusus,
Quos pueri teneris meditantur ab unguibus et quos
Ipse docet natos genitor materque puellas.
Venimus ad summum. ruptis et prorsus habenis
Oppressa rerum potitur virtute libido. 55

to do anything which is hardly right even to mention.
The mad fellow reckons the power in the lustral waters
and in the rote prayers uttered among the crowds
to be such that, even if he slits the throat of his old father with a sword,
so long as he escapes mortal eyes, he can
contemptuously disregard all the watching divinities.
Pretenders! Foul heart! How often my liver
is split by clear bile while watching those deeds of yours.
"Do you think that there is a god in heaven who cares about such things?"
Back up your words with actions. You don't believe? Strip off the make-up,
rush into every misdeed without the mask.
I hate to death this kind of masquerading.
But why in vain am I trying to enumerate each individual crime?
There is no end to that: The list of the types of crimes themselves is long.
Foul behavior, deceits, cheating, perjury, thefts, seizures
—these were once crimes. Nowadays they are games
that kids contemplate from their earliest days,
passed down from dad to boys and mom to girls.
We have come to the end. The reins are snapped
and lust holds sway while virtue lies vanquished.

COMMENTARY ON THE SATIRES

SATIRE ONE

Muret models his first satire closely on the patterns and subject matter set by Juvenal in his introductory poem. The satirist feels compelled by his conscience and anger to attack the evil in the world (Juvenal's *facit indignatio versum*), not because he himself is free from fault (he could be the sole subject of a satire, an unidentified respondent suggests), but because the very ones who should be fighting corruption and immorality are in fact wallowing in it. Debauchery reigns in high places. Balbus, the priest, breaks his vows and indulges in sexual pleasure with a girl after preaching against such sins. Civic leaders enrich themselves on the backs of the honest working class. The nobility is marked by decadence and excess à la Marc Antony. This disregard and contempt for Christian values among the leadership disheartens the masses and causes them to doubt the sovereignty of God. The satirist, with his slashing sword of wit, endangers himself by provoking the high and mighty, but it is his heroic duty not to lay them low, but to cause those who are noble at heart to deride them.

    2. Auruncane: The satirist Lucilius was from Suessa Aurunca (Juv. 1.20). **6. Balbo**: with the meaning, "the stammerer." The pun is that he speaks loudly and confidently even though he has this defect. **7. Stentorea**: cf. Hom. *Il.* 5.785–86 and 859–61; Juv. 13.112. Stentor was a Greek warrior at Troy known for his strong voice. **8. cevet**: used by Juvenal (2.19–21) in a similar context about those who preach virtue yet practice vice: *. . . qui talia verbis / Herculis invadunt et de virtute locuti / clunem agitant. Ego te ceventem, Sexte, verebor?* See also Mart. 3.95.13 (coupled with *pedicaris*) and Pers. 1.87. On the history and connotations of the word, see Joachim Mussehl, "Bedeutung und Geschichte des Verbums *cevere* (Mit zwei Exkursen über Verwandtes)," *Hermes* 54 (1919): 387–408. E. Fraenkel, *Kleine Beiträge zur klassischen Philologie* (1964), vol. 2, 45ff.; Adams, 136–37. **tremulum**: adverbial; cf. Mart. 14.203.1: *tam tremulum crissat.* **Lycinna**: a name borrowed from Propertius. According to Prop. 3.15.3–10, she was his first love interest and a source of jealousy for Cynthia. She was a courtesan, perhaps, given that the poet did not bother to engage her in conversation (*vix memini nobis verba coisse decem*), and thus particularly apropos for the passage at hand. **10. horrifico ululatu:** Note the hiatus on the model of *femineo ululatu* (Verg., *Aen*.4.667; 9.477) and *Bacchei ululatus* (Ov., *Met.* 11.17). **14. effossa . . . scroba:** an allusion to the story of Midas. According to the myth, Midas had run afoul of Apollo and been punished with the ears of an ass. Midas kept his ears covered with a headdress all the time so that only his barber knew the secret. The king threatened to execute him if he told anyone, but the barber could not bear to keep such a secret. Finally, when he could contain it no longer, he dug a pit where he could whisper to the deep earth that Midas had the ears of an ass, whereupon the reeds that grew in the area of the pit began to repeat the news to the wind. **19. Σοὶ ἄρρητα:** Soph. *OC* 1001. **23. piperis:** Pepper has long had the reputation of being an aphrodisiac. The idea is that Torannus is so intent on winning over his wife's lovers that he actually encourages them by fueling their lusts. **29. choragos:** generally speaking, the manager of a play (particularly among the Romans; the role of the choregus was more limited among the Greeks); used here of those in charge. **31. suis . . . rationibus:** echoed in l. 49 below. **34. lienem:** an allusion to Alciato's emblem (Lyons, 1550, no.147), that "the wealth of the tyrant is the poverty of his subjects." Alciato writes, "What the spleen is to the human body, Caesar said his treasury was to the common weal. If the spleen swells, the other powers of the body dwindle; if the treasury swells, this shows civic poverty." This refers to Ps.-Aur. Vict., *Epit. de Caes.* 42.21: *ut. . . . fiscum lienem vocaret, quod eo crescente artus reliqui tabescunt.* Here, the agents of the wealthy stuff the purse of their masters by robbing the common people and then rob their masters by helping themselves to the purse. **41. Haec . . . quercus:** i.e., the *populus miser* of 1. 35, poor but morally strong, the true nobility. **42. monstra illa exitiosa:** i.e., the *divorum* of 1. 36. **44. dogma Lucreti:** i.e., Epicureanism, particularly its insistence that the gods are not involved in human affairs. **50. Corinnae:** the name of Ovid's mistress in the *Amores* (e.g., 1.5). **54. super illum palpitat:** Cf. Juv. 3.134, *ut semel aut iterum super illam palpitet.* The implication is that she is superior to the prostitutes mentioned in the Juvenal passage, since they are only passive. **59. exoticique:** The line cannot scan correctly with this word.

Satire Two

The theme of this satire is the utter decline of morals. From the vast sea of depravity the poet singles out two types of individuals, a lowlife fellow who by his unethical business skills has risen in society and taken on the trappings of high standing, and a hypocritical priest who abuses his position while scoffing at the gods. What these two characters have in common is that they prey on the weak and credulous in society while giving the appearance of holiness and gentility. The respondent believes that neither gods nor men will hear the satirist's complaints, but the satirist himself writes directly to the young man who is searching for the right path of life.

1. **Rumpe Lycambea numeros de caede:** echoing Mart. 7.12.6: *si qua Lycambeo sanguine tela madent.* Martial is comparing his relatively tame and innocuous epigrams with others' verses that are but "darts dipped in Lycambean blood," that is, poetry of a harsher satirical bent. Lycambes was a Theban whom the Greek satirist Archilochus lampooned so viciously that he hanged himself. Ovid (*Ibis* 54) also mentions verses that are "darts tinged with Lycambean blood," as if they are the harshest imaginable. Horace (*Ep.* 1.19.25ff.) claims to have toned down the iambic meter by taking the meter and tone of Archilochus, but not the attack he unleashed on Lycambes. Since Muret is asking the *Musa ferox* for help in writing the most condemning of verses (such is the concern in verses 4–5), *rumpe* here must not mean "interrupt, break off," as often, but "break out into, utter." So too Leroux: "Fais jaillir des vers humides du sang de Lycambe." 2. **Musa ferox:** not a classical collocation. Occasionally, but not always, the ancients designated Polyhymnia as the Muse of satire. 3. **Fige hominum mores:** hendiadys, repeating the idea introduced by *rumpe* in line 1. Iambs are said to "pierce" because they are like spears (see note on line 1). **damnata saecula culpae:** Horace (*Od.* 3.6.17) too refers to the age teeming with sin (*fecunda culpae saecula*) occasioned by the neglect of the gods' cults. 4–5. **At tu quis . . . ?:** so also Pers. *Sat.* 1.2: *Quis leget haec?* 15. **Hunccine tu . . . :** echoing Juv. 1.26–28. 9. **erosos . . . ungues:** said of Lucilius at Hor. *Sat.* 1.10.71. Horace imagines that if Lucilius were alive in his day, he would "scratch his head and bite his nails" as he adds polish to his satires. Cf. Pers. 1.106, where again the biting of nails is proof of pains given to writing: *Nec pluteum caedit nec demorsos sapit ungues.* 17. **vasti qui pondere ventris:** fat from his new-found wealth, as Matho at Juv. 1.32–33: *causidici nova cum veniat lectica Mathonis / plena ipso.* 27. **diducto . . . rictu:** i.e., ready and eager for food (see Juv. 10.230). 28. **Quottidie:** or more properly, *cottidie*. Codex *V* of Catullus has *c*. 68.139 ending with *cotidiana,* but in all other cases the first syllable is short. Lachman emended the line to *concoquit iram.* 30. **vexatam:** Leroux has "malmenée." Adams (p. 200) lists several passages where the word has a sexual connotation, particularly Petron. 139.1; Mart. 8.46.7, 11.81.1. 35. **Cordo:** Juvenal (1.2) makes Cordus a shabby writer of epics (and see other characterizations at Juv. 3.203, 208; Mart. 3.15). 42. **O simulatores, tetrum pecus . . . :** an adaptation of Hor. *Ep.* 1.19.19–20: *O imitatores, servum pecus, ut mihi saepe / bilem saepe iocum vestri movere tumultus!* 54. **ruptis . . . habenis:** i.e., "with all restraints lifted." Cf. Bede (?), *De die iudicii* 73: *Ignis ubique suis ruptis regnabit habenis.*

Epigrams

1. *Divo Julio Caesari Scaligero*

In tenues numeros, primi monumenta furoris,
   Quo mea non simplex corda subegit Amor,
Dirige siderei radiantia lumina vultus,
   Caesar, et haec nati ludicra nosce tui.
Neu pigeat studiis aliquot gravioribus horas   5
   Subtrahere: interdum deserere illa leve est.
Nempe ducum haud quisquam, licet imperterrita gestet
   Corda ferox, gladios semper et arma terit.
Qui populos iussisque regunt nutuque coërcent
   Et retinent forti regia sceptra manu,   10
Non renuunt animos rerum moderamine pressos
   Interdum teneris exhilarare iocis;
Saepe etiam vasti mens unica Iuppiter orbis
   Flectere se a magnis ad leviora solet.
Insequere exemplum regumque, ducumque, Deique,   15
   Dux olim et princeps, nunc mihi paene Deus.

2. *Antonio Goveano*

Summe poetarum, quos saecula nostra tulerunt,
   Cui sacra Castalii fluminis unda subest,
Accipe non tetrica iuvenilia carmina fronte,
   A domino limam iussa subire tuam,
Ut tibi si (quod vix ausim sperare) probentur,   5
   Olim se lucem posse videre putent;
Sin minus, aeterna damnentur ut omnia nocte,
   Aspectu tanti facta beata viri.

3. *Ad Noctem, Sidera et Auroram de Dominae Pulchritudine*

Nox furva atque alis horrenda nigrantibus, et vos
   Fixa meae vultu saepius astra deae,
Audite haec: tu primum Erebi centumplicis uxor,
   Quae veniens uno cuncta colore notas.
Non pudor est ubi flammeolo te Margaris ore   5

Epigrams

1. To Divine Julius Caesar Scaliger

Caesar, direct the radiant eyes of your divine countenance
to my thin measures, the monuments of the youthful madness
with which the band of Erotes conquered my heart,
and recognize these toys of your child.
Don't be upset that you are losing so many hours from your more serious studies;
it makes no difference if you abandon those things occasionally.
You see, no general, though he is warlike and fearless of heart,
always wears out his swords and arms in battle.
And those who rule people with their commands, constraining them with a nod,
and grip royal scepters in a strong hand,
don't refuse to let their minds enjoy trifles and mirth sometimes,
although they are weighed down with governing.
Often even Jupiter, the single intelligence behind the vast world,
turns himself from great concerns to lighter ones.
Follow the example of kings, of generals, and of god,
you who were general once, and a prince, and now almost a god to me.

2. To Antoine de Govéa

Best of poets that our age has produced,
lord of the sacred water of the Castalian spring,
receive my juvenile poems with a brow that is not stern.
Their master bids them to undergo your critique,
so that, if you give your approval (which I scarcely dare to hope),
they might think at some time they can see the light of day;
but if not, may they all be condemned to an eternal night of death,
made blessed by the visage of such a great man.

3. To the Night, the Stars, and Aurora, about My Lady's Beauty

Night, dark and fearful with your black wings, and you,
stars, so often fixated on my goddess' face,
hear these things: you first, wife of hundredfold Erebus,
you who by your coming mark all things with your one color,
aren't you ashamed, when Marguerite strikes you with her glowing

Pellit et invitum cogit adesse diem?
Vos quoque, lucentes Aethrae radiantis ocelli,
   Quorum alta assiduo templa canore sonant,
Non pudor est oculis ubi scintillantibus illa
   Cedere tot vestras lampadas una iubet?   10
Et tu, Dardanii coniux formosa mariti,
   Tangere sol cuius nil nisi terga potest,
Nunquid ubi aspexti, quam te procul illa relinquat,
   Nativus roseo crescit in ore rubor?
Non, puto: quin illi ultro omnes conceditis, in qua   15
   Miratur vires Iuppiter ipse suas.

4. *Ventis furentibus*

Aeolidae celeres, dominae Iunonis alumni,
   Caerula velivoli quos timet unda maris,
Altifremi, alipedes, caeli terraeque tetrarchae,
   Dirigite in pectus flamina vestra meum,
Ut mea vel vestro pereant incendia flatu   5
   Vel me etiam vestris viribus aucta necent.

5. *Ad animum suum*

Quonam abiit mi animus? num quo solet? auguror illuc:
   Pectore se dominae condidit ille meae.
Siccine me tandem miserum, fugitive, relinquis?
   Siccine, desertor, castra inimica petis?
O saltem flammata tuo vel ab igne calescat,   5
   Frigore vel flammas enecet ipsa tuas.

6. *Margaridi*

Dicere dum conor nostros tibi, vita, dolores,
   Ah! misero ex ipsis verba labris abeunt;
Dum tegere et clauso meditor sub corde tenere,
   Ingeminat vires abdita flamma suas.

face, and compels the reluctant day to appear?
You also, gleaming eyes of radiant Aethra,
whose high temples resound with constant song,
aren't you ashamed when by herself with twinkling eyes
she orders your torchlights to withdraw?
And you, lovely wife of Dardanian husband,
of whom the sun can only touch the back,
I wonder, when you see how she leaves you far behind,
does the natural redness increase on your rosy face?
I think it does not: But you all willingly yield to her, in whom
Jupiter himself marvels at his own powers.

4. *To the Raging Winds*

Swift children of Aeolus, foster-children of lady Juno,
whom the azure water of the sail-flying sea fears,
howling on high, swift-footed, tetrarchs of heaven and earth,
direct your gusts into my heart,
so that either my fires might succumb to your blast,
or intensify by your fanning and kill me.

5. *To His Own Soul*

Where is my soul going? to the usual place? I am guessing
it has buried itself in the heart of my lady.
So, you runaway, have you finally abandoned me, wretch that I am?
So, are you going over to the enemies' camp, deserter?
At least let her be inflamed and grow hot from your fire,
or let her snuff out your flames with her coldness.

6. *To Marguerite*

Love of my life, as I'm trying to tell you about my heartaches,
the words disappear right off my lips. Ah, poor me!
As I'm devising ways to conceal them and to shut them in my heart,
the hidden flame doubles its strength.

Quid faciam? ex aequo magnum discrimen utrinque est, 5
   Sive loqui coner sive tacere velim.
O! quae sola meo iam dudum in pectore regnas,
   Tute tibi casus, diva, referto meos.

7. *Somnium*

Euge, an te teneo, mea lux, an somnia demens
   Fingo mihi? certe, lux mea, te teneo.
Somnia non haec sunt. oculis nonne intuor hisce
   Flammeolosque oculos purpureasque genas
Lacteolasque manus et eburnae frontis honorem 5
   Collaque non tacta candidiora nive?
Dulcia collatis ineamus proelia signis,
   Dum tuta alternis lusibus hora datur.
Me miserum! nusquam es. fallax me lusit imago.
   O dolor! o animi gaudia vana mei! 10
Quid queror? exacta si rem ratione putemus,
   Umbra est in misero quidquid amore boni est.

8. *Margaridi*

Dum te, Margari, basiare conor,
Labris protinus invident ocelli
Aspectuque tui carere nolunt.
Quod si contuitu beare ocellos
Tentarim, labra protinus repugnant, 5
Quae ad sese iste tuus vocat trahitque
Candor, purpureo natans in ore,
Ut ferrum Herculeus trahit lapillus.
O vis eximiae superba formae,
Quae me vel mihi dissidere cogit! 10

9. *Eidem*

Sic age, pugnando teneri pascuntur amores,

What should I do? In either case the danger is equally great,
whether I try to speak or I want to keep silent.
Oh! You, goddess, who have long ruled in my heart without challenge,
relate my misfortunes to yourself.

7. *Dream*

Bravo!—wait, am I holding you, my light, or am I losing my mind
and just dreaming? Yes, my light, I hold you;
these are not dreams. I'm sure of it. I really am gazing upon
your blazing eyes with these eyes of mine, your deep red cheeks,
your milky-white hands, the grace of your ivory brow,
your neck whiter than pure snow. Right?
Let us enter sweet battles, our standards engaged,
while a safe hour allows for one game after the other.
How pathetic I am! You are nowhere. A false image has tricked me.
Oh grief! Oh empty joys of the mind!
Why am I complaining? If we really think the matter through,
whatever is good in wretched love is a shadow.

8. *To Marguerite*

When I try to kiss you, Marguerite,
immediately my eyes become envious of my lips,
and do not want to miss out on looking at you.
But if I try to make my eyes happy by staring
at you, immediately my lips object,
and that enticing charmer in your red mouth
calls them to itself and draws them,
like a magnet draws iron.
Oh, haughty power of exquisite beauty,
which compels me even to be at odds with myself!

9. *To the Same*

Go ahead, tender love feeds on fighting,

Invade insanis unguibus ora mihi,
Et turba nostros, audax, laceraque capillos
   Atque interiecta gaudia veste nega.
Illa etenim o quanto magis est perfecta voluptas, 5
   Quae cupiente quidem, sed renuente venit!

10. *Eidem*

Ludamus, mea Margari, et iocemur,
Nos et cum roseum diem reducet,
Et cum se Hesperiis recondet undis,
Deprendat radiatus ora Phoebus
Ludentes simul et simul iocantes. 5
Appellabo ego te meam columbam,
Tu me, blandula, passerem vocabis.
Cum dicam tibi percitus furore,
Da mi basiolum unicum, columba.
Tu collo iniciens meo lacertos, 10
Porges mi oscula delicata mille,
Et mille altera et altera usque mille,
Vibrans improbulam subinde linguam et
   Os morsu tenero meum lacessens.
Dehinc dices mihi, Mi tenelle passer, 15
An non ipsa tibi una sum columba?
Tua una ex animo columbulilla?
Tuum mel, tua suavitas, tuum cor?
En me (nam tua sum) suaviare,
En haec ubera iam retecta cerne, 20
Quae per te mihi primulum tumescunt,
Obiectam et sibi fasciam repellunt.
Quo tu, quo modo, delicate, pergis?
Quo trudis digitos nimis salaces?
Sic nos, sic age, dum viremus ambo, 25
Dum res ad Veneris valemus ambo,
Ne frustra melior teratur aetas,
Ludamus, mea Margari, et iocemur.
Tergo debilis imminet senectus.
Quae cum venerit, ah dolor, columba, 30

so attack my face with your angry nails.
Dare to mess up my hair, tear it,
put on your clothes and deny me happiness.
For how much more fulfilling is the pleasure
that comes when you really want it, but you refuse!

10. *To the Same*

Let us play, my Marguerite, and let us fool around;
and when Phoebus with radiate face draws back the rosy day,
and hides himself in the Hesperian waves,
let him catch us playing and fooling around together.
I will call you "my dove,"
you, sweet-talker, will call me, "my sparrow."
When I am alive with my passion and I say to you,
"Give to me one little kiss, my dove,"
you will throw your arms around my neck
and offer a thousand delicate kisses to me,
and a thousand more, and keep on with another thousand.
And you will move your naughty little tongue back and forth,
biting my mouth with a tender nibbling.
Then you will say to me, "My tender little sparrow,
am I not your only little dove,
the only dovelet of your heart?
your honey, your sugar, your heart?
Come, kiss me, I am yours,
look at these breasts I'm showing you now,
which swell for me for the first time because of you,
and push back my brassiere.
Where, lover boy, are you going, how?
Where are you pushing your fingers burning with lust?"
Like this, come, like this, while we both are young,
while we both have the energy for lovemaking,
lest in vain our better age is worn away,
let us play, my Marguerite, and let us fool around.
Weak old age threatens from the rear,
which, when it comes—ah! grief, my dove,
a terrible cough, and failing health

Nos tussis mala viriumque langor
    Pro ludisque iocisque consequentur.

11. *Ad Paulam*

Basia quod libas cupidis luctantia linguis,
    Res satis ardori non facit ista meo.
Quod mea colla tenens blandis, resupina, lacertis,
    Me dicis vitam, deliciasque tuas,
Hoc nihil est. Dulci Veneris de nectare, Paula,   5
    Aut nulla aut quinta da mihi parte frui.

12. *Ab amica procul positus ob idque noctu quiescere non valens, mortem precatur*

Iam tacitis caelo volvuntur tractibus ignes
    Altaque rorantes Delia flectit equos.
Iam pecudumque atque alituum genus omne ferarumque
    Et quotquot liquido marmore monstra silent
Somnus habet dubioque natans per inane volatu,   5
    Membra papavereis illinit unguinibus.
Te solum, Murete, fugit; tibi cura recursans
    Ire iubet lento tempora moesta gradu.
O caelum! o certis agitati legibus orbes,
    Cuilibet ex ortu qui sua fata datis,   10
Extinctum toties sit fas occumbere! Iam sum
    Non ego sed tantum corporis umbra mei.

13. *In Venerem*

Si Venus, ut mendax docuerunt turba, poetae,
    De mediis vere nata putatur aquis,
Qui fieri potis est, mediis ut fluctibus orta
    Assiduo nostrum torreat igne iecur?
O dolor! o quid iam miseri speretis amantes!   5
    E media vobis nascitur ignis aqua.

will take the place of our games and mischief.

11. *To Paula*

It does not satisfy my burning that
you kiss me with kisses that tangle with lusty tongue.
It is nothing to me that, while you lie on your back and hold my neck
in your gentle arms, you call me your "life," your "sweetheart."
Let me enjoy the quintessence of the sweet
nectar of Venus, Paula, or nothing at all.

12. *Situated Far from His Girlfriend and therefore Unable to Sleep at Night, He Prays for Death*

Already the stars are rolling themselves on their quiet tracks in the heavens,
and the Delian maiden on high guides her dewy horses.
Already every kind of cattle, winged creature, wild beast,
and as many monsters lie still in the marble sea,
sleep holds, and floating through the void with uncertain flight,
anoints their limbs with poppy unguents.
Sleep eludes only you, Muret. The care running through
your mind forces you to pass through the gloomy hours with slow gait.
Oh heavens! Oh heavenly bodies driven by fixed laws,
you who from your rising determine everyone's fate,
may I fall dead as often as you rise! Already I am
nothing but a mere shadow of my body.

13. *About Venus*

If Venus, as the poets, that mendacious band, have taught,
really is supposed to be born from the middle of the sea,
how can it happen that she, who has risen from the midst of the waves,
scorches my guts with a constant fire?
O grief! What hope do you poor lovers have now!
Fire is born to you from the midst of the water.

14. *Ad Margarin*

Quem tu cumque semel blando aspectaris ocello,
  Ni subita exiliat laetitia, lapis est.
Cui vero haec etiam dederis libanda labella,
  Hunc ego felicem terque quaterque voco.
At si quem complexa tuo dignare cubili,   5
  Is non iam felix, Margari, sed deus est.

15. *Lusus cum amica*

Pande oculos, pande stellatae frontis honorem,
  Queis doleat visis invideatque Venus.
Pande, agedum, lasciva. Quid, o, quidnam occulis illud,
  Quo mea versantur corda, supercilium?
Saltem ebur hoc manuum interea spectare licebit;   5
  Ah, etiamne manus? saeva, etiamne manus?
En, iam igitur posthac nihil amplius ipse videbo;
  Claudo etiam ipse meos, en tibi, claudo meos.
Iam, formose dies, iam, lux formosa, valeto:
  Nam vos, nec dominam cernere supplicium est.   10
Audiit inque sinum iecit mea diva meum se
  Reclusitque oculos applicito ore meos.

16. *Eidem*

Cum pluit et radios Phoebus cum subtrahit orbi,
  Tum sane moestus quilibet esse solet.
Ne mirere igitur, si sim, mea Margari, tristis:
  Ecce, pluo lacrimas, tu mihi Phoebus abes.

17. *Ad Gallam*

Novi pro verbis ego sola rependere verba,
  Et pro blanditiis reddere blanditias.
Oscula si qua dabit, sola auferet oscula de me,

14. *To Marguerite*

Whomever you look at once with your seductive eye,
if he doesn't leap up with sudden joy, he is stone.
But the one to whom you have also given these lips for kissing,
I call thrice and four times blessed.
But if you embrace someone and deem him fit for your bed,
he is no longer happy, Marguerite, but a god.

15. *Playing with His Girlfriend*

Open your eyes, open the grace of your starry brow,
on seeing these let Venus grieve and be jealous.
Come, open them, naughty girl. Why are you hiding that
brow, wherein my heart dwells?
At least in the meantime I can see the ivory of your hands.
Ah, even the hands, cruel girl, even the hands?
Look, from now on I myself will see nothing more.
I too close my eyes to you, see, I close mine.
Now, lovely day, now beautiful light, farewell;
for it is torture to see you, while not my lady.
She heard and threw herself into my lap,
and with her mouth pressed against my eyes, she opened them.

16. *To the Same*

When it rains, and Phoebus withdraws the rays of light from the world,
then everyone is usually very gloomy.
So don't be surprised, Marguerite, if I am sad:
Look, I am raining tears, and you, my Phoebus, are absent.

17. *To Galla*

I know how to pay back only words for words,
to return sweet-talk with sweet-talk.
If someone gives me kisses, she will take away only kisses from me,

Pro solis nutus nutibus eripiet.
Haec aliquid praeter tibi me si vis dare, fas est, 5
Haec aliquid praeter, te mihi, Galla, dare.

18. *Julio Caesari Scaligero*

Scaliger Aoniae decus immortale cohortis,
   Qui, quae alios ornant singula, solus habes,
Altera Veronae, maior sed fama priori,
   Cui Clarii munus cessit utrunque dei,
Cui tot se debent animarum millia, per quem 5
   Saepius est Stygii cymba quieta senis,
Quod tantum augusta de maiestate remisti,
   Ut placido versus videris ore meos,
Praemia quae tandem tibi digna reponere possim?
   Devoveam si me, vix satis esse putem. 10
Tune meos versus voce ut laudaveris illa,
   Quam stupet et qua nil grandius orbis habet?
Praemia quaenam igitur reddam tibi digna? sed erro:
   Praemia non debent reddier ulla deis.
Anne tuas igitur describam carmine laudes? 15
   (Laudari humana numina voce volunt)
Deficient humeri tanto sub pondere nec iam
   Tuta erit in tanto nostra carina mari.
Quidnam igitur? taceo. satis hunc dixisse putandum est,
   Se quicunque satis dicere posse negat. 20

19. *In Eundem*

Dic, dea, quod possim scripturus fingere nomen,
   Scaligeri quod par laudibus esse queat?
Cur petis imprudens, quod habes? dic, Scaliger: illud
   Omnia virtutum nomina nomen habet.

she will get nods for only nods.
If you want me to give you anything more,
You have to give to me, Galla, something more.

18. *To Julius Caesar Scaliger*

Scaliger, immortal glory of the Aonian cohort,
you who alone have the things that individually adorn others:
Verona has its own share of fame, but a greater fame goes to you,
to whom both gifts of the Clarian god have submitted.
To you so many thousands of souls are indebted, and under your sway
the skiff of the Stygian old man oftentimes sits still.
Since you relaxed so much from your august majesty
that you looked kindly on my verses,
what suitable rewards can I extend to you?
If I devote myself to you, I think it would scarcely be enough.
Am I to believe that you praised my verses with that voice,
that voice at which the world is amazed and than which it has none finer?
What suitable rewards can I give to you? But I am wrong.
No rewards should be given to gods.
Therefore, I wonder, should I describe your praises in song
(divinities wish to be praised with human voice)?
My shoulders will collapse under such a great weight, nor will
my boat be safe in such a great sea.
What then? I will keep quiet. We have to think he has said enough
who admits that he can never say enough.

19. *To the Same*

Tell me, goddess, as I'm going to write, what name should I create
that will be able to equal the praises of Scaliger?
"Why do you foolishly seek what you possess? Just say, 'Scaliger.' That
name contains all the virtues' names."

20. *In Eundem*

Dicite mi, Musae, cultissima numina nobis,
    Quonam Scaligeri pascitis ora cibo?
Sic ego, sic Musae: quam te sententia fallit!
    Nectare quo potius nos alat ipse roga.

21. *Ad Phyllidem*

Cum ducenda mihi sine te sunt tempora, Phylli,
    Longior est anno mensis et hora die,
At tecum si quando datur mihi vivere, rursus
    Esse diem credo, qui modo mensis erat.
Te sine vel Tauri cum lustrat cornua Titan,   5
    Semper adesse mihi moesta videtur hyems.
At tecum medio gelidae sub tempore brumae,
    Ire tamen veris tempora laeta puto.
Te sine nox mihi fit, medio cum Phoebus in axe est,
    At tecum in media fit mihi nocte dies.   10
Quantum in me miserum iuris tibi fata dedere!
    Quae mihi vel caeli vertere iura potes.

22. *In Carolum Caliantheum*

Philosophum te dicis et hoc te nomine iactas,
    Prae te omnes reliquos ut nihil esse putes;
Nec tamen aut rerum causas et pondera nosti,
    Aut aliud, nomen quo mereare sophi.
Una tuis titulis addenda est littera, Carle: 5
    Nec mihi philosophus, sed *philosomphus* eris.

23. *Rodolpho Condomio, a quo ad cenam invitatus fuerat*

Ad cenam tibi me quoniam condicere cogis
    (Si modo quis cogi, quo cupit ipse, potest),
Accipier qua me cupiam ratione, Rodolphe,

20. *To the Same*

Tell me, Muses, divinities we cultivate the most,
with what food do you feed the mouth of Scaliger?
To that the Muses responded, "How your judgment fails you!
Ask rather with what nectar he sustains us."

21. *To Phyllis*

Since I have to spend my time without you, Phyllis,
a month lasts longer than a year, an hour longer than a day.
But if ever I can live with you,
I believe that what just now was a month will be a day.
Without you, even when Titan surveys the horns of the bull,
it always seems to me that gloomy winter is at hand.
But with you during the midst of chilly winter,
I think the happy springtime is coming.
Without you it becomes night, though Phoebus is in the middle of the sky;
but with you it becomes day in the middle of the night.
How much power the Fates have given to you over me, wretch that I am!
You can overturn for me even the laws of heaven.

22. *About Charles Caliantheus*

You say that you are a philosopher, and you make a show of yourself with this name,
and you think everyone else is worthless compared with you.
But you don't know the causes and consequences of things,
or anything whereby you deserve the name of "sophist."
One letter must be added to your title, Charles:
I'll not consider you a philosopher, but a *philosomphos*.

23. *To Rudolphe Condom, by whom he had been invited to dinner*

Since you urge me to be your dinner guest
(if someone can be *urged* to go where he himself *wants* to go),
hear, Rudolphe, how I desire to be welcomed,

Cognosce et cenae quid caput esse putem.
Non me praecipue vel avis Iunonia ducit, 5
 Vel quae de Scythico flumine nomen habet.
Ista decent reges; nobis cenantibus una,
 Sustineat parcas sobria mensa dapes.
Sit vini tibi cura prior; nisi nobile vinum est,
 Et iocus a mensis et lepor omnis abest. 10
Tunc cibus invito lentescens crescit in ore
 Et levius ferre est, quam recreare sitim.
Sin contra adfuerit generosi copia Bacchi,
 Vix capit undantes vel domus ipsa iocos.
Tunc et convivae per mutua pocula certant: 15
 Hic annos dominae condit at ille suos:
Et veteres memorant flammas et carmina dicunt
 Et laudant cenae concelebrantque patrem.
Quare agedum memori primum hoc sub mente teneto:
 Si tibi cura mei, sit tibi cura meri. 20

24. *In Lygdum*

Ἱππεύειν Lygdus teneris dum discit ab annis,
 Est simul et Chiron factus et Eurytion.

25. *In eundem*

Lygdus blandulus est venustulusque,
Formosusque supra modum et benignus
Non aeris modo, sed sui et suorum;
His multos parat artibus sodales.
Unum est quod nequit approbare multis 5
Nasutis nimium dicacibusque,
Mureto Crucioque Memmioque,
Quod se frugibus unicus repertis,
Multa pascere glande perseverat.

and what I think the main course should be.
Juno's bird does not draw me,
nor that which takes its name from the Scythian river.
Those birds befit kings. For us dining together,
let a modest table sustain a frugal dinner.
Sooner concern yourself with the wine. Unless there is fine wine,
all mirth and charm are absent from the table.
Then the food becomes sticky and accumulates in the grudging mouth,
and it is easier to bear it than to refresh your thirst.
But if, on the other hand, there is a supply of fine wine,
even your home itself will barely hold the overflow of mirth.
And then the dinner guests compete amid the drinking:
this one conceals the years of his lady, that one his own.
And they recall old flames and speak poems;
and they praise and honor the master of the feast.
So come, keep this in mind:
If you care about me, care about the mead.

24.

While from his earliest childhood Lygdus was learning *faire du cheval*,
he became both a Chiron and a Eurytion.

25. *To the Same*

Lygdus is cuddly and charming,
handsome beyond measure, generous,
not only with his money, but with himself and his belongings:
He uses these qualities to acquire many companions.
There is one thing that he is not able to render acceptable
to his many critical and sarcastic friends,
Muret, Crucius, and Memmius:
Although he has tasted of the fruit of the vine,
the odd fellow continues to crack many a nut.

26. De Porna ad L. Memmium

Porna suis tantum, Memmi, substernit amicis.
   Verum: at nulli unquam Porna inimica fuit.

27. In eandem, quae se etiam famulis subigendam praebebat, cum tamen mire arrogans esset

Quam malus est, quisquis dicit te, Porna, superbam!
   Quid? tu te pueris subicis ipsa tuis.

28. F. Gratus Lomenius

Dicere te tactum nullius amore puellae
   Lascivique soles spernere tela dei.
Quid sibi, Grate, volunt igitur, quae saepe notavi,
   Tot data ab arguto signa supercilio?
Quid risus, quid verba manusque oculique loquaces,   5
   Et quae summoto basia teste capis?
Fingo, inquis. Celare tuum cur niteris ignem?
   Quisquis tam belle talia fingit, amat.

29. Gulielmo Mombasio, Episcopo Lectorensi

Quod tam censeris generoso sanguine, Praesul,
   Quodque es tam multis clarus imaginibus,
Illa quidem certe laus est non infima, sed quae
   Tota ad maiores sit referenda tuos.
Quod superas opibus multos, quod honoribus anteis,   5
   Fortunae haec dici munera posse vides.
Quod sis augusto spectandus corpore, forsan
   Natura hanc dotem vendicet ipsa sibi.
At quod tam multis fulges virtutibus atque
   Eximiis rari dotibus ingenii,   10
Quodque tuis lucem praeferre nepotibus illam,
   Quam tibi maiores ante tulere, potes:

Epigrams

26. About Porna, to L. Memmius

Porna only spreads her legs for her friends, Memmius.
True, but Porna is friends with everybody.

*27. About the Same, Who Offers Herself
Even to Servants for Sex, Yet She Is Amazingly Arrogant*

How wrong is he who says that you are high and mighty, Porna!
Why? You place yourself beneath your servant boys.

28. To François the Charming de Loménie

You often say that you are not effected by the love for any girl,
and spurn the arrows of the mischievous god.
What are they after, then, those signals you are giving
with your expressive eyebrow? I've noticed them often.
What about the laughter, the words, the hand and eye communication,
the kisses you steal when no one is watching?
"I'm pretending," you say. Why are you working so hard to conceal your fire?
Whoever pretends such things so well, that one is in love.

29. To Gulielmus de Montbas, Lectorian Bishop

The fact that you are so celebrated for your noble blood, bishop,
and famed for so many family images,
that certainly is not the lowest praise, but it
all has to do with your ancestors.
That you surpass many in riches, that you excel in honors,
you see that these things can be called the gifts of Fortune.
The fact that you must be regarded for your magnificent body, perhaps
nature itself will lay claim to this endowment as its own.
But the fact that you shine forth with so many virtues and
with the outstanding gifts of rare talent,
and that you can pass on that glory to your descendants
that your elders once passed to you,

Haec demum est tua laus; haec, Praesul, laus tua demum est:
   Una haec te superis inserit ordinibus.

30. *In Ponticum*

Saepius hinc illinc video tibi, Pontice, mitti
   Carmina iudicio subicienda tuo,
Idque a divitibus; neque enim tua, Pontice, quisquam
   Emendaturus limina pauper adit.
Quid mirum? neque enim possit dare munera pauper;   5
   Nec te, quae veniunt carmina sola, iuvant.
Mittit at hic gemmas, alius cum versibus aurum,
   Ut constent operae praemia digna tuae.
Tu, quia muneribus caperis, mala carmina laudans,
   Altera mentita retia laude paras.   10
Quid correctoris falso te nomine iactas?
   Id non corrigere est, Pontice, colligere est.

31. *In eundem*

Aurea non vana iactas tua carmina voce;
   Purgari solo nempe quod igne queunt.

32. *Francisco Moncaudo, Burdigalensi*

Moncaude optime, cui novem sorores
Sertis tempora laureis coronant,
Quem vatem geminus suum Cupido,
Quem vatem genitrix suum Dione,
Spretis omnibus, unicum salutat,   5
Illos versiculos perelegantes,
Illos versiculos perimpudicos,
Nec castos nimis et nimis venustos,
Molles, improbulos, libidinosos,
Effrontes, pathicos, Catullianos,   10
Per ludum mihi quos heri dedisti,

this alone is your praise, bishop, this alone your praise;
only this will rank you with the gods above.

30. *Against Ponticus*

Quite often from here and there I see that poems
are sent to you, Ponticus, for you to critique,
and always by rich people; for never does any poor
person come to your house for emendation.
That's not surprising, since a poor person can't pay for your services.
You never like poems that come by themselves.
But this one sends precious stones with his verses, another one gold,
as fitting compensation for your efforts.
Because you are obsessed with payoffs, you praise bad poems
and set other snares with your feigned praise.
Why do you wrongly boast that you are a corrector?
That's not correcting, Ponticus, that's collecting.

31. *Against the Same*

You boast loudly that your poems are "golden";
yes, because only fire can refine them.

32. *To François Moncaudus of Bordeaux*

Best Moncaudus, whose temples
the nine sisters crown with garlands of laurel,
whom twin Cupids, whom mother Dione,
with all spurned, hails as their one and only poet,
those very elegant little verses,
those completely unabashed little verses,
not in the least bit chaste, very charming,
delicate, a tad naughty, erotic,
wanton, pathic, Catullan,
which you gave to me yesterday as a joke,
already, I swear by god, I think I've read a thousand times!

Iam, credo hercule, millies relegi.
Ut sunt molliculi! ut fluunt decenter!
Ut spirant Venerem undiquaque totam!
Ut vincunt Sybariticos poetas! 15
Ut, quod pruriat, incitare possunt,
Non dico senibus modo his pilosis,
Verum decrepitisque mortuisque,
Si quicquam pote mortuos movere est.
   Atqui dicere te tamen solebas 20
Ludorum et Cypriae rudem palaestrae
Meque illa imbueras opinione,
Nil te ut virgineum magis putarem;
Quin et versibus, impudens, in ipsis
Semper dissimulas adhucque sumis 25
Tyronis tibi nomen, Imperator.
   Ohe desine; ten' ego ut pudicum
Posthac arbitrer, ampliusve fallar?
Imo mehercule virginemque Cyprin,
Castratumque putem prius Priapum. 30

33. *Divino ingenio Caes. Scaligeri*

Eminus aetherii collucens luminis aura,
   Quae radios toto disicis orbe tuos,
Certaque cognati retinens commercia caeli,
   Tunc etiam cum te deprimis, astra vides:
Haec tibi pauca tui mirator maximus offert 5
   Carmina, at indocta non bene ducta manu,
Si liceat, tibi templa simul positurus et aras:
   Usque adeo numen suspicit ille tuum.
At tibi pro templo caelum est; humus, ara; nec ipse
   Iam renuit, quin sit victima sacra tibi. 10

34. *Pro Carolo Montauserio ad Margaritam Reginam Navarrae*

Mens regni, sexus lumen, stupor orbis, in uno
   Munera quae divum corpore cuncta tenes,

How smooth they are! How seemly they flow!
How they breathe Venus from every word!
How they beat out the Sybaritic poets!
How they are able to provoke what itches,
I say not only for those hairy old men,
but for the decrepit, the dead, if anything can move the dead.
Yet you *used* to say that you are *ignorant*
of the games of love, of the Cyprian wrestling-mat,
and you had indoctrinated me with that opinion,
so that I was thinking that you were nothing but a virgin.
Yes, but in the verses themselves you
constantly masquerade, dirty boy, and up to this point,
General, you've assumed for yourself the title "raw recruit."
Enough, stop: Do you think I consider you modest
after this, or that I am deceived any longer?
No, I swear, I would sooner think Venus is a virgin,
that Priapus is castrated.

33. To the Divine Genius of Caesar Scaliger

Aura of ethereal light shining from afar,
you who scatter your rays on the whole world,
and even when you bend downward, ever in fellowship
with your brother the sky, you see the stars:
your greatest admirer offers these few poems
to you, but unlearned poems poorly written;
at the same time, if permitted, he wants to set up temples and altars for you,
because he so looks up to your divinity.
But for you the sky serves as a temple, the ground is your altar; nor does
he himself refuse to become a sacrificial victim for you.

34. On Behalf of Charles de Montausier to Marguerite de Navarre

Soul of the kingdom, light of your sex, wonder of the world,
you who hold in one body all the gifts of the gods,

Conspicere in qua una veteres licet heroinas,
  Et quidquid veteri laudis in orbe fuit;
Delicium caeli, terrae decus, accipe, quae se 5
  Advolvunt pedibus carmina pauca tuis.
Nam quamvis tibi nulla dari, nisi magna decebat,
  Parva tamen laeta sumere fronte soles.
Illa tibi cum diis communis, ut omnia, virtus,
  Vili etiam placant quos data thura manu. 10
Fors olim maiora tibi et meliora dicabo,
  Si modo me solita, diva, fovebis ope.
Te sine nil, sed multa tuo cum numine possum;
  Nititur auxilio spes mihi tota tuo.
Ipse quidem prorsus nihil hoc sum tempore, sed tu 15
  Ex nihilo me aliquid reddere, diva, potes.

35. *Caes. Scaligero*

Cum mea tantopere placeant tibi carmina, Caesar,
  Vel si non bona sint, iam bona facta puto.

36. *F. Grato Lomenio*

Quisquis te Gratum primus, Francisce, vocavit,
  Omen, non nomen, tradidit ille tibi.

37. *In quendam*

Mulciber incessu, capite Aeolus, ore Lyaeus,
  Tres uno divos corpore solus habes.

38. *In Rufinum*

Inter Latinos forte sicubi assedit
Pulchellus iste, fusculo ore, Rufinus,
Qui sericatus gaudet ire per vicos,

in whom alone we can see the old heroines,
and what there was of glory in the old world;
delight of heaven, glory of the world, hear these few
poems that fall prostrate at your feet.
For although it was not fitting that you should be given any poems but great ones,
still you often receive small ones kindly.
Your virtue, as everything of yours, is shared with the gods,
whom even incense given with a modest hand appeases.
Perhaps in the future I will dedicate greater and better things to you,
if only you will favor me, goddess, with the usual aid.
Without you I can do nothing, but with your approval I can do many things.
My whole hope relies on your help.
Indeed, I myself am nothing at this point, but you, goddess,
are able to render me something from nothing.

35. *To Caesar Scaliger*

Since you enjoy my poems so much, Caesar,
I think that, even if they are not good, now they have *become* good.

36. *To François the Charming de Lomenie*

Whoever called you "Gratus" first, Francis,
handed to you an *omen,* not a *nomen.*

37. *Against a Certain Person*

You alone possess three gods in one body:
Vulcan in your gait, Aeolus in your head, Lyaeus in your cheeks.

38. *Against Rufinus*

If that cute little Rufinus, with the swarthy face,
who gets his jollies traveling from neighborhood to neighborhood dressed in silk,
by chance has sat anywhere among Latin speakers,

Tria verba molli Graeca voce τραυλίζειν.
　　Graece sed adsit eruditior quisquam, 5
Silentur illa; proferuntur Hebraea,
Quae lividis praemansa dentibus latrans,
Nil prae se Apellas iurat esse Rabbinos,
Suaeque ita obicit imperitiae velum.
　　At scis, apud nos astus iste quid prosit, 10
Doctor trilinguis, architecte verborum?
Scis, inquam, apud nos astus iste quid prosit,
Qui vera fucis iudicamus abstersis?
　　Dum vis videri habere tres simul linguas,
Unaque tentas anteire serpentes, 15
Quod credimus te haud aliud esse, quam linguam.

39. *In Noallium*

Nil immundius est tuis libellis,
Nil obscenius impudiciusque.
Et vis te tamen ut putemus esse
Numa, Fabricioque sanctiorem.
At sententia nostra ea est, Noalli, 5
Quisquis versibus exprimit Catullum,
Raro moribus exprimit Catonem.

40. *In Virgilium. Virgilius ipse loquitur*

Cor Phoebi, Phoebus Latii, vatum pater et rex,
　　Fons ex quo Aoniae prosilit humor aquae,
Par volui primum, maior sed factus Homero,
　　In Graecos Romae iura secunda dedi.
Ad caelos tandem raptus, Iove iudice, dicor 5
　　Nectarea illorum vincere voce sonos.

41. *In Lygdum*

Quod sis tam facilis, quod sis tam, Lygde, benignus,
　　Quam nova nupta suo cum parat ire viro,
Hoc cave te credas nobisve aliisve molestum

he softly lisps three Greek words.
But should anyone a bit educated in Greek come near him,
those words disappear altogether, and Hebrew words are brought to the fore,
which he barks out after chewing on them with his vicious teeth
and swears that Apellas aren't rabbis at all compared with himself.
In this way he casts a veil on his lack of linguistic skill.
But do you know, trilingual doctor, architect of words,
what that craftiness accomplishes around us?
Do you *really* know what that craftiness accomplishes around us,
we who wipe off the make-up and determine the truth?
While you wish to appear to possess three tongues simultaneously,
and likewise are trying to outdo the serpents,
in fact, we believe that you are nothing but a tongue.

39. *Against Noalle*

Nothing is filthier than your books,
nothing more obscene, and more shameful.
Yet you want us to believe that you are
holier than Numa and Fabricius.
But it is our opinion, Noalle, whoever
mirrors Catullus in his verses,
rarely mirrors Cato in his character.

40. *About Vergil. Vergil himself is speaking*

I, the heart of Phoebus, the Phoebus of Latium, father and king of the poets,
fount from which the stream of Aonian water springs forth,
wished at first to equal Homer, but I surpassed him,
and I made Greece second place to Rome.
Finally, after I was taken up to heaven, with Jupiter as my judge, I am said
to surpass the strains of the gods with my nectarous voice.

41. *Against Lygdus*

Don't imagine that you annoy me or others
because you are so agreeable, Lygdus, or because you are so generous
and yielding, as when a new bride is preparing to go to her husband;

Nomine; quin etiam nos magis ista iuvant.
Displicet hoc, quod non tantummodo, Lygde, benignus, 5
Verum etiam, ut fama est, officiosus homo es.

42. *In Apollinem*

Cum timidam cupidus Daphnen sequeretur Apollo,
   Currentem celeri per iuga summa pede,
Improbe, narratur tristis dixisse, Cupido,
   Incaluit pectus cuius ab igne meum,
Aut concede tuas, quibus istam persequar, alas, 5
   Aut tua de nostro pectore tela move.

43. *In Ponticum*

Saepe, velut ridens, Epicuri dogmata laudas,
   Et, quasi per lusum, reicienda negas.
Saepe, velut ridens, dicis tibi vera videri,
   Quin etiam vultus signa probantis habet.
Sic etiam vivis, quasi non alienus ab illo, 5
   Omnia quae iuras te simulare tamen.
Tolle tuas artes: nihil haec mendacia prosunt.
   Qui semper simulat, Pontice, non simulat.

44. *Neque avaros, neque prodigos probandos esse*

Improba quem partis cumulandi plura libido
   Detinet et iuris non sinit esse sui,
Quem vexat damnosa modis insomnia miris,
   Dum sua sub tacita pondera nocte putat,
Qui queritur tardas non saepius ire Calendas, 5
   Quique nihil pensi, dummodo quaerat, habet,
Omnia prae lucro contemnere iura paratus,
   Nec mihi, nec cuiquam, credo, placere potest.
Sed neque qui ternis decies centena diebus
   Fundit et in sumptu nil putat esse nimis; 10

to the contrary, we like that.
This displeases us, that, not only are you an obliging man,
but also, as rumor has it, you are an *accommodating* man.

42. *Against Apollo*

When Apollo was eagerly pursuing the frightened Daphne
as she was running swiftly along the mountain peaks,
he supposedly said gloomily, "Cruel Cupid,
whose flame burns in my breast,
either let me borrow your wings, so I can pursue her,
or remove your arrows from my heart."

43. *Against Ponticus*

Often, sort of laughing, you praise the dogmas of Epicurus,
and as if joking, you say that they should not be rejected.
Often you say sort of laughing that those dogmas seem true to you;
yes, even your face shows the marks of approval.
So you also live that kind of lifestyle,
while swearing that you are just pretending.
Cut out the chicanery; these lies get you nowhere.
The one who is always pretending, Ponticus, is not pretending.

44. *That we should approve of neither greed nor prodigiousness*

The one whom an evil lust for accumulating more and more
possesses, and does not permit him to control himself,
whom accursed insomnia makes anxious in wondrous ways,
while he counts his cash in the quiet night,
who complains that the first of the month doesn't come around often enough,
and who attaches no value to anything but his acquisitions,
ready to hold all laws in contempt in exchange for gain—
this one I don't like, nor do most people, I think.
But neither do we like the one who squanders a cool million
in three days, and thinks that in extravagance nothing is excessive;

Quique etiam noctu, posita cum luserit arca,
   Non alio ritu tempora lucis agit.
Quem Sol si primo locupletem viderit ortu,
   Redditus ex Croeso protinus Irus erit.
Qualis apud Stygiam torquet rimosa paludem   15
   Vano virgineas urna labore manus.
Quisnam igitur? qui se cauta sic temperat arte,
   Ut medium servans, vitet utrunque latus.
Providus, at facilis: parcus sibi, largus amicis,
   Atque etiam largus, cum petit hora, sibi: 20
Qui nec opes terra furtim componere, sed nec
   Perdere discincti more nepotis amat.

45. *In Gelliam*

Quod nimio faciem cultu tibi, Gellia, quaeris,
   Et suffis multo corpus odore tuum,
Hac ratione mihi credis te posse placere,
   Conarisque illa me retinere via.
Quaere alios, isto qui delectentur amore: 5
   Personata mihi nulla puella placet.

46. *Claudio Coleto Campano*

Cum det Rufa rosas, cum det tibi lilia, Claudi,
   Cum det serta tibi crine ligata suo,
Cum te respiciens suspiret pectore ab imo,
   Annuat argutis cum tibi luminibus,
Denique cum quovis solum te sola sequatur,   5
   Conicere hinc quis non ulteriora queat?

47. *In Romanum*

Cum somnus pigris vix dum est excussus ocellis,
   Atque recens orto pluma relicta die,
Inclamas multo puerum, Romane, boatu,
   Ora lavaturas qui tibi portet aquas.

and though he put it all on the line at night,
he keeps right on gambling during the daylight hours;
if the sun sees him rich in the morning,
it won't take long before Croesus is rendered Irus,
as in the Stygian swamp the leaky urn
tortures virgin hands with empty labor.
Who pleases me then? The one who cautiously exercises self-control,
so that he might avoid either side by keeping to the middle road.
He thinks about the future, but is easy-going; he spends little on himself,
but is generous with his friends.
And he even spends money on himself when the time calls for it;
who neither likes to hide his wealth in the earth,
nor to waste it like a reckless prodigal.

45. *About Gellia*

Because you fix yourself up to extremes, Gellia,
and spray perfume all over your body,
you think that you can attract me,
and you try to keep me around that way.
Look for somebody else, who might find pleasure in that love of yours.
I don't like girls who wear masks.

46. *To Claudius Coletus Campanus*

Since Rufa gives roses to you, since she gives lilies to you, Claudius,
since she gives you garlands bound with her hair;
since she looks at you and heaves a deep sigh,
since she nods assent at you with glancing eyes,
and she makes off with you in private,
who can't guess what comes next?

47. *About Romanus*

You've scarcely yet rubbed sleep from your drowsy eyes,
and barely gotten out of bed to start the day,
when you bellow loudly at your boy to bring
water, Romanus, so you can wash your face.

Tunc et gingivas multo sale sesquipedales 5
   Proluis et guttur terque quaterque tuum.
Esse quid hoc dicam, quod cum tam saepe lavetur,
   Nunquam non tamen est sordida lingua tibi?

48. *F. Laccio Cairiechio*

Tune meo elabi possis de pectore, Lacci,
   Aut ego, dum vivam, non meminisse tui?
Ante vel istius mundi compage soluta,
   Tetras in antiquum sit reditura Chaos.
Quin mihi, cum Lachesis summos perneverit annos, 5
   Nostra sonum referent nominis ossa tui.

49. *In Grannium*

Iambicos sine lege Grannius facit:
Miraris? ipse lege Grannius caret.
Fraudem suis idem inserit poematis.
Miraris? ipse fraude sine facit nihil.
Adeoque si quid fraude vacuum unquam facit, 5
Ut fraudet exspectatione alios, facit.

50. *Iohanni Costecaudo*

Ni quantum pote quisquam amare quenquam,
Tantum te ipse amo, Costecaude, ni te
Totum non oculis fero iam in ipsis,
Verum in pectore et intimis medullis;
Contingant mihi cuncta, quae timentur, 5
Et multo graviora, quam timentur,
Tanto ut sim ipse miserrimus malorum,
Quanto tu unus es optimus bonorum.

Then you rinse your sesquipedalian gums with plenty
of salt, and gargle three or four times.
What should I say about this? Even though you wash it so often,
still your tongue is always dirty.

48. *To François Laccius Cairiechius*

Could you slip from my heart, Laccius,
or could I ever forget you so long as I live?
Sooner would the four corners of this old universe come apart
at the seams and be returned to ancient Chaos.
But when Lachesis has spun out my years,
my bones will echo with the sound of your name.

49. *Against Grannius*

Grannius composes iambics without following the rules:
you're surprised? Grannius himself lacks rules.
He also makes mistakes in his poems.
You're surprised? He doesn't do anything without making a mistake;
and, in fact, so much so that if he ever *does* do anything without making a mistake,
he causes a mistake in other people's expectations.

50. *To Jean Costecaudus*

Unless I love you as much
as anyone can love anyone, Costecaudus;
unless I hold you complete not only in my eyes,
but also in my heart and in my very bones;
may I face everything men fear,
and even worse things than those,
so that I might be the worst of the bad,
as much as you alone are the best of the good.

51. Jocosum

Membra sacerdotes si nunc sua caedere moris
    Esset, ut in prisca religione fuit,
Crebra minus ferret spuriorum examina tellus,
    Fraudaret sociam femina rara fidem.
Vera quidem sunt haec, sed si lex illa feratur,   5
    Quaere alium quam me qui tibi sacra canat.

52. In Malos Principes

Iuppiter in faciem, propter sua probra, lupinam
    Mutavit regem, Maenalis ora, tuum.
Ille quidem regum solus, mihi credite, non est,
    De se qui dici promereatur idem.

53. In Corellium

Sutor es et pistor, lanius, lenoque coquusque
    Mercatorque bonus causidicusque bonus:
Te tamen in tota non est mendicior urbe,
    Nec quem paupertas arctius aegra premat.
Dic, agedum, qui fit (nam res est mira, Corelli)   5
    Cum tot res facias, rem facere ut nequeas?

54. In Lygdum

Cur tibi cauta dedit corpus natura pusillum?
    Viderat hoc ipso plus satis esse mali.

55. De monacho quodam

Cordigerum abiecto deprendit forte cucullo
    Hospita non segnem, nec sine mente virum,
Cui tota interior (velut omnia plena dolorum)

51. *A Joke*

If in the present day it were customary for priests to castrate themselves,
as happened in ancient religion,
the earth would hold a smaller crowd of bastard children,
few women would cheat on their husbands.
Yes, these things are true, but if that custom is reinstated,
look for another person than me to sing sacred songs for you.

52. *Against Evil Leaders*

Jupiter turned your king into a
wolf, Arcadia, because of his sins.
Believe me, he's not the only king
who deserves to have this said about him.

53. *Against Corellius*

You are a cobbler and a baker, a butcher, a pimp, and a cook,
a good salesman and a good pleader,
yet nobody in the whole city is worse off than you,
on no one does troublesome poverty press down harder.
So tell us, how does it happen—for it's hard to believe, Corellius—
that, although you make so many things, you don't make anything?

54. *Against Lygdus*

Why did wary Nature give to you a puny body?
She had seen that it is plenty vile the way it is.

55. *About a Certain Friar*

A hostess by chance caught a cordoned friar with his hood cast aside,
a man who was not slow and not without intelligence,
whose whole undergarment beneath his ragged

Serica sub vili tegmine vestis erat.
Hospita quod mirata, quid, o pater optime, nunquid   5
   Vestis, ait, sorti convenit ista tuae?
Ille nihil cunctatus, eho, quidnam vetat? inquit:
   Quippe meo sunt haec parta labore mihi;
Quoque magis credas (grandi mutone retecto),
   Hoc mihi, ait, fusum talia nere solet.   10

56. *In convivatorem nimium prolixum*

Quonam scriblitas, quonam ista sophismata plenis?
   Vis bene convivas pascere? pone famem.

57. *Annae Ogeriae Neapolitanae*

Aurea caesariem, praedulci argentea voce,
   Hei mihi, cur duro ferrea corde manes?

58. *Iohanni Deliano*

Si sacer aetherio furor excitat igne poëtas,
   Eosdemque assidua lampade torret Amor,
Miraris solidos cur nam exhaurire trientes
   Donaque Lenaei sumere patris ament?
Ante diem geminus miseros extingueret ardor,   5
   Ni daret assiduus frigora grata latex.

59. *Stephano Alisio, Burdigalensi*

Si mea se faciles dederint in vota Camenae,
   Ut per plura meum saecula carmen eat,
Tu pariter mecum memori celebraberis aevo

cloak was made of silk. The surprised hostess asked, "How does this garment
fit with your lot in life?" He didn't hesitate—why should he?—and says,
"These were produced for me by my own labor.
So you believe me more" (with that he revealed a huge penis),
"this here spindle," he said, "often spins such things for me."

56. *Against a Long-winded Dinner Host*

Why are you stuffing the pastries and those sophisms of yours?
Do you want your dinner guests to eat well? Assuage their hunger.

57. *For Anne Ogerie from Naples*

Golden haired, and silvery with your pleasant voice,
alas, why are you always iron in your hard heart?

58. *For Jean Délian*

If holy madness goads poets with ethereal fire,
and Love burns them with relentless torch,
do you wonder why they love to drink triple shots,
to take up the gifts of father Lenaeus?
Before their day a double fire would consume the poor fellows,
unless the constant liquid refreshed and cooled them off.

59. *To Étienne Alis of Bordeaux*

If the Muses will be agreeable and heed my vows,
and make my poem endure for many generations,
as with me you will be celebrated by a mindful age,

Et tibi scripta vetus per mea nomen erit.
Sin (sed enim verbis et pondus et omen abesto)   5
　　Non seneant domino longius illa suo,
Non tamen idcirco tibi displicitura putabam
　　Haec magni in te animi pignora parva mei.

60. *Mario Crucio*

Forma aetate perit; vires aetate fatiscunt;
　　Casibus innumeris eripiuntur opes;
Una, Mari, est virtus, quam non vis temporis aufert,
　　Non premit indigno sors inimica pede.
Una suos invicta perennibus inserit astris,   5
　　Fortunae imperio liberat una suos.
Hanc sequere. Insani est postponere firma caducis
　　Veraque quae bona sunt spernere, falsa sequi.

61. *In Ponticum*

Ponticus eximium dum sese ait esse poetam,
　　Hoc solo dici iure poeta potest.

62. *In Laidem*

Non toto est mulier, quam Lais, iustior orbe:
　　Cur ita? nam rectum semper amare solet.

63. *In Avitum*

Cum subigat sterilem, nihil illi donat Avitus:
　　Sic fit, ut ille oleum perdat et illa operam.

64. *In Pontilianum*

Cur tua vix unquam sint salsa epigrammata, quaeris?
　　Diluis haec nimio, Pontiliane, mero.

and through my writings your name will be ancient.
But if (far from my words be omen and ill-consequence)
they only last as long as their master,
even so, I was thinking that these small tokens
of my great affection for you would not displease you.

60. *To Marius Crucius*

Beauty perishes with age; strength fails in time;
riches are stripped away by countless misfortunes;
virtue, Marius, is the only thing that the march of time can't take away,
the only thing hated Chance can't crush under its cruel foot.
Only Virtue unconquered joins its followers with the everlasting stars,
she alone frees them from the tyranny of fortune.
Pursue virtue. It's the mark of a madman to prefer slippery things to firm ones,
and to spurn the true good while pursuing the false.

61. *Against Ponticus*

When Ponticus says that he is an exceptional poet,
that is the only good reason to call him a poet.

62. *Against Lais*

There's not a more upright woman in the whole world than Lais:
Why so? It's her habit always to love the upright.

63. *Against Avitus*

Whenever Avitus screws a sterile woman, he gives her nothing:
So it happens that he wastes his oil and she her toil.

64. *Against Pontilianus*

Why, you ask, are your epigrams scarcely ever witty?
You dilute them with too much wine, Pontilianus.

65. *De virtute et gloria*

Virtus ut solidum quiddam est et corpore constans,
 Aequa sed est umbrae gloria fluxa levi.
Hanc igitur quisquis neglecta amplectitur illa,
 Huic mage quam corpus, corporis umbra placet.

66. *De Lucii cuiusdam memoria*

Esse aliquam si quis memorandi perneget artem,
 Hanc qui confirmet, Lucius unus erit:
Ille etenim nuper curaque adiutus et arte,
 Tres versus totidem noctibus edidicit.

67. *In Paulum*

E lecto surgens ad mensam accedere Paulus,
 E mensa ad lectum rursus abire solet.
Interea attingit libros, ut vina catelli,
 Et queritur sese discere posse nihil.

68. *Fatis Parendum*

Obsequitor fatis: ducent te fata volentem.
 Sin minus, invitum te tamen illa trahent.

69. *De Pompilii Naso*

Pompilio est nasus cubitos tres longus et unum
 Latus, et hunc murus cingit utrinque triplex:
Adsunt et turres, Bacchus quas condidit ipse
 Et minio tinctis usque rubere dedit.
Huic etiam naso vis admiranda tributa est:
 Nam calices siccos illius umbra facit.
Immo etiam longe distans si senserit usquam,
 Ut magnes ferrum, sic trahit iste merum.

65. About Virtue and Glory

Virtue is like something solid and corporeal,
but glory is transient like a faint shadow.
So whoever embraces the latter while neglecting the former,
likes the body's shadow more than the body.

66. On the Memory of a Certain Lucius

If someone insists that there's no such thing as a skill of memory,
Lucius will be one who would confirm this.
For recently, aided by his concentration and skill, he
learned three verses in as many nights.

67. Against Paulus

It's Paulus' habit to rise from the bed and go straight to the table,
and from the table to go straight back to bed.
Meanwhile, he takes to his books, as pups lap wine,
and he complains that he can't learn anything.

68. We Must Obey the Fates

Submit to the Fates: the Fates will guide you when you are willing.
But if you're less than willing, they'll drag you against your will.

69. Concerning the Nose of Pompilius

Pompilius has a nose three cubits long, and one
cubit wide, and a triple wall encircles it on either side.
And towers stand there, which Bacchus himself built,
and painted them with minium and caused them to be red continuously.
And a wondrous power this nose possesses:
Its shadow makes wine goblets dry.
Yes, if ever it smells wine from afar,
as a magnet attracts iron, so that nose attracts the wine.

Nuper eram in mensa, sitiens, potare paratus:
  Pompilius clausas astitit ante fores 10
(Mira canam, sed vera): merum mihi forte paratum
  Attraxit naso protinus ille suo.

70. *In Pauli nasum*

Exiguum si quis nasum vidisse laborat,
  Paulum adeat, Paulo si modo nasus inest:
Non etenim est nasus, sed pars centesima nasi,
  Et quo quis viso dicere possit, ubi est?
Talis inest nasus muscis, sed et his quoque maior, 5
  Et melius nasi nomine dignus inest.
Quam quae per radios volitant corpuscula solis,
  Maiorem nasum vix, puto, Paulus habet.

71. *Sub exortum diei*

Roscida purpureos effert Aurora iugales,
  Et nitidum Soli praevia sternit iter.
Noctis aves dudum rupere silentia cantu
  Nullaque iam caelo rara vel astra micant.
Exit flammivomo Phoebus spectabilis ore 5
  Et tenebras densae noctis abire iubet.
Christe, patris splendor, vero me lumine reple
  Aque meo tenebras pectore pelle procul.

72. *In Gaurum*

Effundas versus una cum luce ducentos,
  Forte poetastris annumerandus eras.
Sed cum te eximium iactas tam saepe poetam,
  Id quoque quod paulum est, incipit esse nihil.

Recently I was at the table, thirsty and ready to drink,
when Pompilius showed up outside my door
(fantastic things I sing about, but true): Immediately
he sucked the wine I was about to drink into his nose.

70. *About the Nose of Paulus*

If anyone is distressed because he has seen a small nose,
let him go to Paulus, assuming Paulus has a nose.
For it's not a nose, but one one-hundreth of a nose,
and looking at it one can say, "Where is it?"
Flies have this kind of nose, I think, except theirs is bigger,
and deserve the name 'nose' more.
Paulus' nose is scarcely bigger than the specks of dust
that swirl about in the rays of the sun.

71. *At Daybreak*

Dewy Aurora brings out her crimson steeds,
and leading the way spreads out the shining journey for the Sun.
The birds have just started to break the silence of the night with singing,
and no stars, or a few only, still twinkle.
Phoebus comes out with his flaming face, a sight to see,
and bids the darkness of the dense night to depart.
Christ, glory of the Father, fill me with true light,
and drive away darkness far from my heart.

72. *Against Gaurus*

When you were pouring forth two hundred verses in one day,
perhaps you were to be counted among the poetasters.
But when you boast so much that you are an exceptional poet,
even that which is small begins to be nothing.

73. In Pamphagum

Pamphagus in patulam tam multa ingesserat alvum,
   Quam poterant denis plus satis esse viris.
Ecce, venit caupo pretiumque expostulat; ille
   Ebria terribili lumina more rotans,
Evomit in patinam vinumque cibosque receptos,   5
   Atque ait, En, merces tu tibi habeto tuas.

74. In Gallonium

Stertit ad octavam Gallonius. inde cubili
   Paulatim assurgens languida membra levat.
Obicitur perdix, quam protinus ille calentem
   Devorat: hac nulli cesserit arte libens.
Spumantis temeti cyathos octove novemve   5
   Adicit, et sacris sic operatus, ait,
Di, date mi constantem animum mentemque quietam;
   Quam multis vita est nostra referta malis!

75. Sestio

Multa quidem, fateor, confers mihi munera, Sesti,
   Devinctum tibi me nec tamen esse reor.
Cur ita? quod quae das, tristi dare mente videris.
   Sic ego quae data sunt vendita dona voco.

76. De voluptate, et ratione

Cum, velut excelsa residens in puppe, Voluptas
   Arbitrio mentem pellit agitque suo,
Horrida bacchantes ineunt certamina venti,
   Navemque in Syrtes et vada caeca trahunt.
Illinc Ambitio, Dolus hinc consurgit et atrox   5
   Ira cruentatas sanguine tincta manus.
At ratio regimen navis si sumpserit, ecce,

73. Against Pamphagus

Pamphagus had stuffed as many things into his fat belly
as would be more than enough for ten men.
Look, the waiter comes and demands he pay the bill; Pamphagus
rolls his drunken eyes in a horrid fashion
and vomits the wine and food that he had consumed into a pan,
and then says: "Here, take your payment!"

74. Against Gallonius

Gallonius snores until two in the afternoon. Then little by little
he rises from the bed and lifts his drowsy limbs.
A partridge is served up, which he gobbles up immediately while it's still hot—
he will yield to no one in this skill.
He adds eight or nine cups of foamy beer,
and after going through this ritual he says:
"Gods, grant me a steady and quiet mind;
my life is beset with so many troubles!"

75. To Sestius

I admit it, Sestius, you bring many presents to me,
and yet I don't think you've won me over.
Why so? Because you seem to be sad when you give them.
I call those gifts you give 'merchandise.'

76. On Pleasure and Reason

When Pleasure, sitting, as it were, on the lofty deck of a ship,
pushes and drives the mind wherever she wishes it to go,
the howling winds engage in a fearsome struggle,
and drag the ship into the reefs and the hidden shallows.
Ambition and Deceit spring up here and there,
and fierce Anger with hands stained red with blood.
But if Reason takes the helm, look!

Compositis undis aequora tuta silent;
Ipsa ratis nullo ventorum exterrita flatu
  In portum certo tramite flectit iter. 10

77. *Sansoni Crucio*

Et bonus et dives, Sanso, simul esse laboras.
  Id fieri nulla sed ratione potest.
Sic utrumque petens, perdes utrunque: necesse est
  Alterutrum tollas alterutrumque petas.

78. *Tumulus Otthonis, hominis voracissimi*

Conditus hac sub humo est gurges vastissimus, Ottho,
  Cui nunc officium iusta rependit humus.
Condidit in ventrem terrae tot iugera vivus:
  Hunc sub ventre suo nunc quoque terra tenet.

79. *In Virronem*

Quod totam Virro furiosi more per urbem
  Discurrit noctu, quod loca sola petit,
Nescio quid secum solus quod mussitat, illo
  Quod nemo est tota sordidus urbe magis,
Hac ratione parat nomen famamque poetae, 5
  Et reperit fatuos sic quibus esse probet.
O valeant, calami, pereat genus omne librorum,
  Reddere si vates mens male sana potest.

80. *In Paulum*

Quae tu condideras, inspexi carmina nuper,
  Lectaque sunt, fateor, terque quaterque mihi;
Nec tamen evalui cognoscere quid sibi vellent.

the waves are calmed and the waters are safe and silent.
No blast of wind menaces the boat;
It makes its way steadily into the harbor.

77. To Sanso Crucius

You're striving to be both rich and good at the same time, Sanso,
but there's no way that's going to happen.
So aiming at both, you will lose both:
You must give up one and go after the other.

78. *The Tomb of Otho, a Very Voracious Man*

Buried beneath this soil is a vast abyss, that is, Otho;
now the ground gives him his just recompense.
While alive he buried in his belly so many acres of earth:
now the earth holds him in her belly too.

79. *Against Virro*

Because at night he scurries furiously
about the whole city, because he prefers solitude;
because, while alone, he mutters something or other to himself;
because no one in the whole city is more vile than he:
for this reason he gets the name and fame of a poet,
and he finds stupid people in whom he finds favor.
O! farewell, quills, may every kind of book perish,
if craziness makes someone a poet!

80. *Against Paulus*

Recently I looked over the poems you had written,
and I swear I read them three and four times.
And yet, I wasn't able to understand what they mean.

Usque adeo obscure scribere, Paule, soles.
Nam tu verba, puto, ex libris accepta Sibyllae, 5
Quaeque Catonis erant tempore prisca nimis,
   Versibus infercis gaudesque obscurus haberi
Et velut inducta singula nube tegis:
   Errasti hoc tantum, quod mittens carmina, Paule,
Debueras una mittere grammaticum. 10

81. *Ad Amores*

Carnifices curae miseraeque incendia mentis
   Et tu cum pharetra, saeve Cupido, tua
Tuque, Erycina ferox, longum aeternumque valete,
   Ferte alio vestras, noxia tela, faces.
Praeteriti vobis nimium concessimus aevi 5
   Iamque dies mores postulat ista novos.
Nunc iuvat et rerum causas tentare latentes
   Inviaque ignavis per loca ferre pedem,
Induere et mores, contracta fronte, severos
   Atque puellares spernere blanditias. 10
Haec loquor, at si me placidis spectarit ocellis,
   Quae fugat aspectu nubila cuncta suo,
Quam vereor ne mox mihi multa et magna locuto
   Omnia cum fastu fortia verba cadant!

82. *In Pontilianum*

Cum rapidus medio desaevit in aequore Titan,
   Fer, puer, huc cyathos, Pontilianus ait;
Cum pluit, en, inquit, deus admonet esse bibendum,
   Qui nunc tam multo proluit imbre solum.
Sic vacua a potu non unquam tempora ducit 5
   Curque bibat semper Pontilianus habet.

You're in the habit of writing so obscurely, Paulus.
For, so far as I can tell, you stuff your verses with words
you've taken from the Sibylline books, words that were
already too old in the days of Cato.
You like being considered obscure,
as if you've shrouded everything in a mist.
This is your only mistake, Paulus, that when you send your poems,
you should also send a philologist.

81. *To Love*

Tormenting cares, flames of an unhappy mind,
and you, cruel Cupid, with your quiver:
and you, wild Erycina, goodbye forever and ever,
take your firebrands and your poisonous darts elsewhere.
We've yielded too much of our life to you until now;
already the day demands we change our behavior.
Now we enjoy investigating the hidden causes of things,
and to tread through places inaccessible to the slothful;
to take on a stern character, with furrowed brow,
and to spurn girlish charms.
I say these things, but, if she looks at me with those serene eyes,
she who scatters all clouds with her face,
how I fear that soon all the great and many brave words
will fail together with my pride.

82. *Against Pontilianus*

When swift Titan blazes at noontime,
Pontilianus says, "Boy, bring here some wine."
When it rains, Pontilianus says, "Look! the gods
who are soaking the soil with so much rain are telling me it's time to drink."
So Pontilianus never spends his spare time without a drink,
and he always has a reason why he should be drinking.

83. *Petro Quintio*

Si dea, quae dubiis huc illuc passibus errat,
    Et regit humanas, lumine capta, vices,
Quem Labyrinthaeis erroribus egit, Ulyssem
    Ad patrios esset passa senere focos,
Membraque lausque viri tumulo caperentur eodem,   5
    Et tegeret nomen, qui tegit ossa, lapis.
At quoniam fatis varie crudelibus actus,
    Dura tulit terra plurima, plura mari,
Vivit et evectus rutilis super aethera pennis,
    Maeonio clarum carmine nomen habet.   10
Macte animo, Quinti: dum te sors invida vexat
    A patriisque procul finibus esse iubet,
Virtutem illa tuam toto disseminat orbe,
    Dumque nocere cupit, sic quoque saeva iuvat.

84. *Claudio Burgo*

Perpetuo moeres nec frontem exporrigis unquam,
    Hoccine tu, quaeso, vivere, Burge, vocas?
Is demum vere vivit, qui mente serena
    Et nitido laetos exigit ore dies.
At qui perpetuis torquet se angoribus, hunc non   5
    Vivere, sed lenta morte perire puto.

85. *In divam Catharinam*

Quo te praecipue commendem nomine, Virgo?
    Laus etenim quae te non minor esse queat?
Magnum erat errores veterum liquisse parentum,
    Maius at imperium deseruisse fuit.
Magnum erat immanis rabiem sprevisse tyranni,   5
    Supplicia at maius sponte subire fuit.
Magnum erat his vitam sponte obiecisse periclis;
    Maius nunquam animo succubuisse fuit.
O decus eximium patriae sexusque polique,
    Dicere te merito nullus honore potest.   10

83. *To Pierre Quintius*

If the goddess who haltingly wanders here and there,
and blindly rules human affairs, had allowed Odysseus,
whom she drove on Labyrinthian wanderings,
to grow old near his paternal hearth,
the limbs and glory of the man would be held prisoner by the same tomb,
and the stone which covers his bones would also cover his name.
But since he was driven about by cruel Fates
and endured many hard things on land and more on sea, he lives on,
and, carried above the ether on golden wings,
he has a name famous from Homer's song.
Press on, Quintius: While jealous Fortune troubles you
and forces you to be far from home,
at the same time she scatters your virtue through the whole world;
and even as she desires to do harm, the cruel lady does good.

84. *To Claude du Bourg*

You are constantly sad, and you do not ever unfurrow your brow—
tell me, du Bourg, do you call this living?
Only he truly lives, who passes pleasant
days with a calm mind and glowing face.
But I think that the one who tortures himself with constant anguish
does not live, but slowly fades away.

85. *To the Divine Catherine*

With what name in particular shall I extol you, Virgin?
For will not any praise fall short of you?
It was a great thing that you abandoned the errors of your old parents,
but it was greater that you gave up power.
It was a great thing that you spurned the madness of a towering tyrant,
but it was greater that you willingly endured punishments.
It was a great thing that you willingly subjected your life to these perils:
It was greater that they never could break your spirit.
O outstanding glory of your country, of your sex, of the heavens,
no one can give you the honor that you deserve.

86. *Eadem de seipsa loquitur*

Illecebras inter medias educta virago,
   Re princeps, mulier corpore, mente dea,
Nixa deo, mundi spernens mala gaudia, vici
   Tum tormenta animo, tum ratione sophos.
Non rota, non gladii, non ipsi horrenda tyranno   5
   Mors potuit mentem sede movere meam.
Scilicet haud quicquam mens Christo afflata veretur.
   Ille meae vires, et mea vita fuit.
Quid, fuit? estque fuitque atque est sine fine futurus.
   Principium vitae mors dedit ipsa mihi.   10
Qui legis haec, sic tu te etiam compone, viator:
   Mors tibi pro Christo vita perennis erit.

87. *In quendam*

Quidam ieiunum me clamitat esse poetam,
   Et mihi, sicca nimis carmina condis, ait:
Ipse nota sed enim carpi ne possit eadem,
   Egregia prudens calliditate cavet,
Nunquam ieiunus, nunquam ut qui scribere siccus,   5
   Sed satur, et vino semisepultus amet.

88. *In Crassum*

Quod ruri maneo studiis addictus honestis,
   Rusticus hoc videor nomine, Crasse, tibi.
Rusticus ille quidem non est, qui rura pererrans,
   Ingenium rerum cognitione colit.
At tu, qui nullam nosti stultissimus artem,   5
   Esse vel in media rusticus urbe potes.

89. *In Gaurum*

Fama est hoc anno morituros esse poetas.
   Quid metuis? nil te, Gaure, timere decet.

86. The Same Speaks Concerning Herself

A heroic maiden reared amid allurements,
a ruler of state, a woman in body, a goddess in mind,
relying on God, spurning the evil joys of the world, I overcame
the torments with my mind, the wise with reason,
neither wheel nor sword, nor death that tyrants fear
was able to make me change my mind.
Indeed, a mind inspired with Christ fears nothing at all.
He was my strength and my life.
What, he *was?* and he is, and was, and will be without end.
Death itself gave to me the beginning of my life.
You who read these things, traveler, pattern your life like this:
Dying for Christ will bring you eternal life.

87. Against a Certain Fellow

A certain fellow shouts that I am a starveling poet,
and says to me, "You compose verses that are too dry."
He himself, so he can't be criticized with the same remark,
is prudently cautious and ever so clever;
since he never likes to write when he's starved or thirsty,
but stuffed and half-buried with wine.

88. Against Crassus

You think I'm a country bumpkin, Crassus, because
I live in the country, devoted to honest pursuits.
Indeed, the fellow who wanders through the countryside
and cultivates his natural talents through learning is not a country bumpkin.
But you no-talent know-nothing can be a country bumpkin
even in the middle of the city.

89. Against Gaurus

There's a rumor that this year poets are going to die:
Why are you afraid? You don't have anything to fear, Gaurus.

90. *In Rufinum*

Cum coenet nemo tota te lautius urbe,
 Ad tua cur rarus prandia, quaeris, eam?
Accubui simulac tecum, Rufine, monetque
 Primus in appositas impetus ire dapes,
Mox onerare meas insulsis versibus aures 5
 Incipis et nugas ingeminare tuas;
Nec retices unquam, sed ab ovo ad mala recenses
 Vix, puto, per centum carmina facta dies.
Quae si quis sanus patienti combibat aure,
 Illum adamantini pectoris esse putem. 10
Miraris cur te non possim ferre canentem?
 Mensa ipsa insipido carmine pressa gemit.

91. *In Fortunam*

Fortuna inconstans et neutro certa paratu:
 Vel fautura premit, vel nocitura favet.

92. *In Commentarios Iuris Civilis Francisci Connani, viri clarissimi. Liber ipse lectorem alloquitur*

Dum tua nil praeter curantis commoda, lector,
 Me patris assiduo cura labore polit,
Dumque diebus amat totas ex ordine noctes,
 Noctibus et totos continuare dies,
Ipse (fatebor enim infelix) dominoque patrique, 5
 Ipse necis properae maxima causa fui.
Verum etiam sine me, fatalia tempora mensus,
 Serius ut paulo, tandem obiturus erat.
Faxo ego ut aeternum per me nunc vivat eroque
 Illi auctor vitae, cui necis ante fui. 10

90. *Against Rufinus*

Since nobody in the whole city dines more fabulously than you,
you're curious, why do I so rarely come to your dinners?
As soon as I recline with you, Rufinus,
and my hunger makes me reach for the food set before me,
immediately you begin to burden my ears with your witless poeticizing,
and to multiply your bantering verse.
And you never shut up, but from appetizer to dessert you recount
poems that I think you could've scarcely written in a hundred days.
If any sane fellow could swallow these things with a patient ear,
I would think he has a heart of adamantine steel.
You wonder why I cannot bear your recitations?
The table itself groans under the weight of your insipid poetry.

91. *Against Fortune*

Fortune is fickle, and she switches her garb back and forth:
Either she hinders a positive development or favors a negative one.

92. *About the Commentaries of Civil Law of François de Connan, a Very Famous Man. The Book Itself Addresses the Reader*

My father always looked out for your well-being, reader,
and his careful attention polished me with constant labor;
and while he loved to work on me day and night,
to work night and day,
I myself (sadly I have to admit it) was the greatest cause
of the hasty death of my master and father.
But even without me, eventually he was going to die,
although a little later, since he had reached the end of his fated thread.
I will see to it that now he lives through me forever;
I will be the source of life for him, whose cause of death I was before.

93. De seipso

Dicebam Euterpae, coeptis in versibus haerens,
    Auxilium fratri porrige, diva, tuo.
Fraterno mota est in risum nomine virgo
    Et nitido sudum reddidit ore diem.
Tunc ego subridens, mirari desine: nam mi
    Si pater est Caesar, tu soror esse potes.

94. In importunos recitatores

Hei mihi, quam res invisa est nimis esse poetam!
    Quantum odii morbus colligit ille suis!
Nil genere hoc hominum est usquam importunius; illos
    Et cane, qui sapiunt, peius et angue cavent.
Nec locus est nec tempus ab his subducere quo te,   5
    Non si mille modis aggrediare queas.
In fora te, in thermas et balnea in ipsa sequentur;
    Quod si in templa gradum ferre parabis, et huc.
Si notos forte aegrotos invisis, et illuc;
    Spectatum ludos forsitan ibis? et huc.   10
Pergis eo, nullum quo ducere quaeris? et illuc;
    Pergis eo, comitem quo tibi poscis? et huc.
Denique, ut exoneres alvum, discedis? et illuc;
    Ut somnum capias, fessus abibis? et huc.
Interea insulsis onerabunt versibus aures,   15
    Auribus ut te tunc ipse carere velis;
Versibus insulsis, queis cantio gratior illa est,
    Quam geminat putri condita rana lacu.
Ex genere hoc, miserum nuper me prenderat unus
    (O lux infelix quam fuit illa mihi!);   20
Fessus ego, insuavis mihi iam ut vita esset, apud me
    Fundebam surdo talia vota Iovi.
Summe deum, te si qua mei miseratio tangit
    (Nam qua sim positus conditione, vides),
Aut abige hunc tandem aut mihi da surdescere, vel iam   25
    Alterutrum nostrum, vel neca utrunque simul.
Venerat ad primae damnata crepuscula lucis;
    Vix abiit vates sole cadente meus.

93. About Himself

I was speaking to Euterpe, while stuck at the beginning of my verses:
"Offer help to your brother, goddess."
Because I said, "brother," the maiden was moved to laughter
and with her shining face she whisked away the clouds.
Then I smiled and said, "Cease to be amazed, for if
Caesar is my father, you can be my sister."

94. Against Troublesome Reciters

Ah me, what a hateful thing indeed it is to be a poet!
How much aversion that disease garners for its practitioners!
Nothing anywhere is more importune than this breed of people: those
who are smart avoid that breed worse than a dog or a snake.
Nor is there a place or time when you can escape them,
not if you try a thousand ways.
They will follow you into the marketplace, into the gym, even into the baths themselves;
but if you are getting ready to walk into a temple, even here they are;
if you go to visit sick friends, by chance, even there.
Maybe you are going to go watch the games? even here.
You are going somewhere by yourself? They are there.
You are taking a friend along? They are here.
At some point you go off to use the toilet? Even there!
You are tired and withdraw to catch a nap? Even here.
Meanwhile, they burden your ears with their witless verses,
to the point that you wish you didn't have any ears:
verses so witless that you'd rather listen
to the incessant croaking of a frog in a swamp.
One of this breed caught poor me recently
(what a rotten day that was!):
I was tired, to the point that I wanted to die, and to myself
I was pouring forth such vows as these to an unresponsive Jupiter:
    Greatest of gods, if you feel any pity for me
    (for you see my current situation),
    either drive this fellow away at last, or let me be deaf, or
    slay one of us, or both of us at the same time.
He had come far too early in the wretched day;
scarcely did my poet leave when the sun was setting.

95. *Paulo*

Das mihi lactucas, centum sed mutua poscis.
  Desine: lactucas, Paule, minoris emo.

96. *In Collinam anum*

Dispeream, nisi te aspicio, Collina, libenter
  Nique etiam tecum saepius esse velim,
Tum quoniam anguicomas sic exprimis ore sorores,
  Terriculi ut facile munus obire queas,
Tum quoniam inprimis potas lepide atque decenter.   5
  Crede mihi, hic demum gratia magna tua est.
Nam tu aliquot, qui sint reliquae praeludia pompae,
  Suaviter immissis ructibus in cyathum,
Sic bibis ut dulcis labiis pendentibus humor
  Assidue alternis influat et refluat.   10
Expers interea ne sit pars ulla decoris,
  Labitur in pinguem spurca saliva sinum.
Crede mihi, id pulchrum est, dentes cum allisus ad atros
  Sic patulo geminus ludit in ore liquor.
Macte age, macte animo, Furiarum sola voluptas,   15
  Delitium Stygii sola futura canis.
Perge citosque bibens Maeandri redde reflexus:
  Id, festiva, simul et bibere et vomere est.

97. *Antonio Collaeo*

Unquamne, Antoni, locupletem te fore credis?
  Et caelo et tota falleris hercle via.
Non es adulator, non fur, non denique leno,
  Non bonus insontes voce onerare reos.
Innocuus vivis fraudisque et criminis expers,   5
  Semper in antiqua simplicitate manes.
Evades nunquam dives rationibus istis:
  Esse bonum nostro tempore stultitia est.

95. *To Paulus*

You give me lettuce for free, but you ask for a hundred presents in return;
Stop: I buy lettuce for less, Paulus.

96. *To the Old Woman Collina*

To hell with me, Collina, if I'm not happy to see you,
if I don't want to spend more time with you;
both because you look so like the snake-haired sisters,
you could easily substitute for a scarecrow,
and especially because you drink with charm and class.
Believe me, here is your great grace.
For with a few belches sweetly emitted into the ladel—
preludes to the remaining parade—you drink in such a way that the sweet liquid
constantly flows in and back out, back and forth, from your drooping lips.
Meanwhile, lest any part miss out on the loveliness,
foul saliva dribbles onto your lap.
Believe me, it's beautiful when the double liquid, hitting itself
against your black teeth, plays this way in your gaping mouth.
Carry on, good work, sole pleasure of the Furies,
dog-to-be, sweetheart of Styx:
Continue, and with your drinking imitate the quick turns of the Meander River:
in other words, cutie, keep drinking and vomiting at the same time.

97. *To Antoine Collaeus*

Do you think you'll ever be rich, Antoine?
I swear, in every way imaginable you are deceived.
You are not a sycophant, not a thief or a pimp,
not a lawyer who overwhelms innocent defendants.
You live without harming anyone, free from deceit and crime,
always upholding traditional values.
You will never come out rich that way:
It's foolishness to be good these days.

98. *Paulo*

Qui capit, inferior; maior, qui donat, habetur.
   Inferior sic te, Paule, libenter ero.

99. *Cuidam*

Hos tibi quid iuras factos ex tempore versus?
   Pagina, si taceas, id satis ipsa probat.

100. *In Phaedram*

Cum Phaedra Hippolyti disiectos cerneret artus,
   Membraque tam multis sanguinolenta locis,
Postquam non potui vivum te inflectere, dixit,
   Persequar ad Stygios te tamen usque lacus.
Dixit et, incumbens gladio, terram ore momordit.   5
   Saepe amor insanus talia monstra parit.

101. *De morte M. Bruti*

Brutus ut Augusto belli succedere palmam,
   Et paulum a victis vidit abesse suos,
Amplexus gladium multa iam caede madentem,
   Ergone te, dixit, sospite, servus ero?
Quin potius fatis id quod praeclusa malignis   5
   Non potuit patriae, dextra datura mihi est.
Haec fatus, rutilum per costas exigit ensem,
   Magnanimoque cadens pectore pulsat humum.
Sic quoque, dum moritur, labris dum spiritus errat,
   Nunc, ait, invito Caesare, liber ero.   10

102. *In quendam*

Quidam Margaridem meam salutat,
Morbosus, capularis, eviratus,

98. To Paulus

He who takes is considered inferior; he is considered greater who gives.
So, Paulus, I'll gladly be your inferior.

99. To a Certain Person

Why do you swear that you composed these verses extemporaneously?
The page itself, if you keep quiet, proves it sufficiently enough.

100. About Phaedra

When Phaedra saw Hippolytus' body torn apart,
and his limbs covered in blood, she said,
"Although I was not able to seduce you while you were alive,
nevertheless I will follow you to the Stygian waters."
She spoke, and falling on her sword, she bit the dust with her mouth.
Often irrational love produces such monstrosities.

101. On the Death of Marcus Brutus

When Brutus saw that he was losing the war to Augustus,
and that his troops were close to being conquered,
he grabbed a sword, already dripping with much slaughter,
and said, "Will I be a slave while you live safe and prosper?
No, that which my right hand was not able to give
to my country, precluded by evil fates, it will give to me."
Having said these things, he drove the blood-red sword through his ribs,
and fell and struck the ground with his stout chest.
And so while he was dying, while his breath was slipping from his lips,
he said, "Now I will be free, despite Caesar."

102. Against a Certain Person

There's a certain fellow who says "Hello" to my Marguerite;
he's diseased, near-death, effeminate,

Ficosus, recutitus, herniosus,
Calvaster, podager, cadaverosus,
Orci victima, pabulum Charontis,   5
Cui iam oris, puto, foetido in recessu
Dentes quinque, nec amplius, supersunt;
Cui centum scabies petita lustris
Artus depopulatur ulcerosos.
   Idem, quod magis ac magis pudendum est,   10
Pauper, dirutus, expeculiatus,
Qui noctu omnia fana pervagatur,
Si quid, perditus, harpagare possit,
A se quo miseram famem repellat.
Atqui surripiat, clepat, quid ad me?   15
   Quidquid fecerit, haud movebor unquam,
Dum ne Margaridem meam salutet.

103. *De morte Ciceronis*

Cum ferus astaret stricto mucrone satelles,
   Sumere supplicium de Cicerone parans,
Immoto vultu atque oculis constantibus, ille,
   Praebens infanda colla secanda manu,
Publica libertas vita mihi carior, inquit.   5
   Me quoque, me fas est, te moriente, mori.

104. *Calendis Ianuariis, iocosum, ad Michaelem Lochianum*

Non tibi pro xeniis fulvi pretiosa metalli
   Pondera, non docta signa polita manu,
Non lana Assyrio tincta et saturata veneno,
   Non gravis argenti lamina munus erit.
Talia non capiunt generosas munera mentes,   5
   Talia magnanimi spernere dona solent.
Cum te igitur, quam sis excelso pectore, norim.
   Non mittam ista tibi dona: quid ergo? nihil.

hemorrhoid-inflicted, circumcised, suffering from hernias,
balding, gout-ridden, cadaverous,
a victim of Orcus, food for Charon;
I think only five teeth remain in the foul recesses of his mouth, no more.
The mange which he has washed a hundred times
makes his ulcerous limbs raw.
Also—and this is the worst part—
he's poor, bankrupt, penniless,
and at night wanders through all the temples,
to see if in his desperation he can pilfer anything
for driving off his miserable hunger.
So he sneaks around, he steals, what difference does it make to me?
He can do what he wants, I don't care,
so long as he doesn't say "Hello" to my Marguerite.

103. *On the Death of Cicero*

When the savage bodyguard stood near, sword drawn,
ready to murder Cicero,
unflinchingly, with steady eyes, he
offered his neck to be cut by the ungodly hand.
"My country's liberty is dearer to me than my life," he said,
"and it is only right that if you die, I die too."

104. *A Joke, on the Calends of January, to Michael Lochianus*

Your gift will not be bars of precious gold,
or statues that a skilled hand polished;
your present will not be wool dipped and soaked
in Assyrian dye, or coins of heavy silver.
Such gifts do not win over noble minds;
the high-minded usually spurn such gifts.
Therefore, since I know you, how you have a lofty heart,
I will not send these gifts to you. What then? Nothing.

105. *Ad Ianum Vermelianum*

Divitias hodie plena depromere ab arca
 Thesaurosque meos iam reserare placet,
Ut te muneribus donem, mi Iane, superbis,
 Iane, inquam, ex animo nunquam abolende meo.
Dona paro tibi ferre, quibus, si dicere fas est, 5
 Attalicae possunt nil dare maius opes,
Munera, Persarum gazas quae vincere possint,
 Munera, Pactoli est prae quibus unda nihil.
Quidnam post tantos feret hic promissor hiatus,
 Qui sua tam elata munera voce canit? 10
Sic tecum: et quae sint ea tandem dona, requiris;
 Atqui iam dudum, quae tibi poscis, habes.
Hui! dices, hoc tu breve chartae et inutile frustum
 Persarum gazis amplius esse putas?
Quid facias? nil possideo, nisi carmina, Iane? 15
 Quare ea thesauros divitiasque voco.
Tu quoque, si natura mihi tua cognita recte est,
 Carmina divitiis pluris habenda probas.

106. *Curandam esse hiemis tempore cuticulam*

Ingere ligna foco, vis frigoris aspera saevit;
 Eia age, quid dubitas? ingere ligna foco.
Non audis quanto Boreas bacchetur hiatu?
 Nonne vides multa ut iam nive canet humus?
Aspicis ut veteres viduentur frondibus orni? 5
 Cernis ut amissas silva queratur opes?
Cernis et ut pigro lentescant marmore rivi?
 Me gelidus totis artubus horror habet.
Ferto, age, ferto huc vina, puer, cyathosque capaces,
 Ante focum mensas explicuisse iuvat. 10
Iam tristi caelum est facie, iam nubilus aer
 Omnia concutiens, nos vetat ire foras.
Ergo domi inclusos genio indulgere necesse est,
 Mos datus a priscis ut teneatur avis.

105. *To Jan Vermélian*

Today I want to draw riches from my full purse
and to unlock my treasure chests,
so I can give you splendid presents, my Jan,
Jan whom I'll always keep in my heart.
I am about to give you gifts greater, dare I say,
than the riches that Attalus could give.
These gifts surpass the treasures of the Persians,
and even the Pactolus river has nothing to compare with them.
"What in the world, after all this blather, will this promise-maker bring,
who sings of his own presents with such an exalted voice?"
So you wonder, and you ask me to finally tell you what these gifts are.
But you already have what you are demanding.
"Really?" you will say, "This short and useless scrap of paper
you think is more bountiful than the treasures of the Persians?"
What do you expect? I possess nothing, Jan, except poems.
For that reason I call these poems my treasures and my riches.
You also, if I understand your character correctly,
agree that poems should be considered more valuable than riches.

106. *That We Should Pamper Ourselves in Winter*

Bring wood for the fireplace, the bitter blast of cold rages.
Quick! Come on! Why are you hesitating? Bring wood for the fireplace.
Do you not hear how loudly the north wind howls?
Surely you see how now the ground is white with deep snow.
Do you notice how the ash trees are stripped of their leaves?
Do you hear how the forest complains that it has lost its treasures?
And do you see how the streams gloss over and grow sluggish?
A chilly shudder runs through my limbs.
Come, bring wine here, boy, bring ample cups:
I prefer to spread my table before the hearth.
The sky is already gloomy. Now storms
shake everything, we can't go outdoors.
Therefore we must stay shut up inside and
enjoy ourselves as our forefathers once did.

107. Lodoico Valesio, adolescenti honestissimo

Miraris, tanto cum te complectar amore,
　Cur tamen extremum hic te, Lodoice, locem?
Pectore nempe mihi penitus defixus in imo es;
　Ultimus, hinc factum est, pectore ut exieris.

ADDITIONAL POEMS BY FREMONT
(INCLUDED IN THE 1552 EDITION AFTER MURET'S EPIGRAMS):

L. Memmii Fremioti in Marcum Antonium Muretum praeceptorem optimum et carissimum

Murete, eximios inter celebrande poetas,
　Cui numerat paucos Gallia tota pares,
Cui pater ipse lyram et plectrum transcribit Apollo,
　Quem sibi Pierides spemque metumque putant:
Hos per te exculti primos cape ruris honores,　　　　　　5
　Quos tibi dat tremula nostra Thalia manu.
Scilicet aurifluae numeroso verbere linguae
　Dum tu corda loquens obstupefacta quatis,
Pectore et a docto gemmarum proicis imbrem,
　Quem rapiat celeri lecta iuventa manu,　　　　　　　　10
Per tua ego ingressus timido vestigia passu,
　Sedulus, haec tandem qualiacunque dedi.
Quae tibi dum placeant, aliorum haud puncta morabor;
　Iudicio tutus despiciam illa tuo.

Eiusdem

Dicebam, mihi Pierides praesto este canenti,
　Et mihi tu vatum ductor Apollo fave.
Aure meas surda Musae sprevere querelas;
　Aure meas surda sprevit Apollo preces.
Verum ubi Mureti me sum de gente professus,　　　　　　5
　Et dixi, Marcus me quoque vester amat.
Mureti audito accurrerunt nomine Musae,
　Sponte et opem Phoebus detulit ipse suam.

107. *To Louis Valesius, an Upstanding Young Man*

You wonder why I've put you here at the end, Louis,
even though I embrace you with such great love.
The reason is, you are planted deeply in the bottom of my heart.
Hence it has come about that you left my heart last.

Additional Poems by Fremont
(included in the 1552 edition after Muret's epigrams):

A Poem of L. Memmius Fremiot about Marc-Antoine Muret, Best and Dearest Teacher

Muret, to be celebrated among the greatest poets,
to whom all of France counts few equals,
to whom father Apollo himself surrenders the lyre and the plectrum,
whom the Pierides reckon for themselves a hope and a fear:
take these rewards of a farm first cultivated by you,
which our Thalia tremblingly gives to you with her hand.
Yes, by the melodious lashing of your golden tongue,
while you have shaken my dumbfounded heart by speaking,
and from your learned heart you have hurled forth a rain of gems,
which a chosen youth snatches up with a swift hand,
I have tread along your footprints with timid step,
diligently, and at long last I have given these, whatever they be.
Should they please you, I will in no wise delay the penning
of others; prudently I will despise them if you so judge.

A Poem of the Same

I was saying: "Be by my side, Pierides, as I sing,
and you, Apollo, guide of poets, favor me."
The Muses spurned my complaints with deaf ear,
With deaf ear Apollo spurned my prayers.
But when I explained to them that I am a
child of Muret, and I said, "Your Marcus loves me
too," at the sound of his name the Muses
ran to me, and immediately Phoebus
himself brought down his aid.

Commentary on the Epigrams

Epigram 1

This epigram recalls Martial's address to Domitian at *Epigrams* 1.4, whereby the emperor is requested to "set aside that brow with which you rule the world" before taking up these poems. But Martial is dealing specifically with censorship, while Muret has broader concerns: a) to underscore the difference between Scaliger's serious endeavors and his own comedic ones (the familiar *negotium-otium* dichotomy found in the elegiac and epigrammatic poets), and b) to advertise the worth of his compositions by suggesting that the famous scholar should take a break from his academic pursuits to read them. Much as the learned Nepos once read the *nugae* of Catullus and deemed them *something*, Scaliger too should recognize that such recreational diversions contribute to a healthy psyche. Epig. 18 below indicates that Scaliger did indeed read Muret's poetry.

2. non simplex: In Greek and Roman literature numerous Erotes attend Aphrodite and their names are variously given (e.g., Himeros, Pothos, Peithos, Anteros). Propertius (2.2) describes a "thousand tender Cupidines [Erotes]" attending the birth of Venus. Catullus (3.1) calls on the Cupidines to mourn his girlfriend's sparrow (*Lugete, o Veneres Cupidinesque*). See also note on *epig.* 32.3. **3. radiantia lumina:** used of the rays of the sun at Ov. *Trist.* 2.325. **4. ludicra:** Horace (*Ep.* 1.1.10) implies that the writing of verse is *ludicrum* (and cf. *Sat.* 1.10.37: *haec ego ludo*) when compared to more serious philosophical pursuits. But "even the Muses enjoy their *ludicra*, and work must be mingled with leisure," according to Ausonius (*Protrep. ad nep.* 1–2). **16. Dux . . . princeps:** Scaliger claimed that he was an offspring of the house of La Scala, which had ruled over Verona until it submitted to the Venetians. In his youth he served as an officer (*dux* seems a stretch, though) in the army of Maximilian and in 1512 distinguished himself in the Battle of Ravenna. It seems better to make those associations here than to follow Leroux's suggestion that Muret plays on the identification with the general Julius Caesar. The unqualified comparison would have been an insult, however, since consistently Muret exhibits a negative attitude toward the partisans of Caesar when talking about Roman history (see epigs. 101 and 103, for example). Leroux points to a parallel in Nicolas Bourbon's *Nugae* 8.24, where Julius Caesar and Julius Caesar Scaliger are explicitly brought together, but, even so, there the poet is drawing a sharp distinction between the two: Julius Caesar is the *monstrum* who conquered the previously unbeaten Gauls, whereas Scaliger conquered them, so to speak, by humane and peaceful means, with his pen and words.

Epigram 2

Renaissance poets often sent out their poetry for criticism (see epig. 30 below), typically to their friends or to another poet with an established reputation. If the readers exhibited sufficient enthusiasm, the author would feel encouraged to publish the work.
   2. Catalii fluminis: the spring of Parnassus sacred to Apollo and the Muses. **3. iuvenilia:** an allusion to the title of the work. **6. lucem posse videre:** i.e., to be published. **8. facta beata:** Even though the poems must be tossed in the garbage, signaling their death, so to speak, at least briefly and to their lasting benefit they were in the hands of a great poet.

Epigram 3

The poet employs the "outbidding" formula so familiar in Roman and neo-Latin authors, whereby mythological or historical figures yield to the superiority of someone in the present. The hyperbole is often signaled by such words as *superare* (e.g., Cat. 51.2) and its synonyms, by *unus* or *solus* (e.g., Ennius *Epigr.* 23–24), by comparatives (e.g., Cat. 35.16, *Sapphica puella Musa doctior;* Verg. 6.164, 9.772, et saep.), or a culminating *cedere* (Prop. 2.2.13, *cedite iam, divae, quas pastor viderat olim;* 3.22.17, *omnia Romanae cedent miracula terrae;* and 2.4.65–66 [about Vergil], *cedite Romani scriptores, cedite Grai! / nescio quid maius nascitur Iliade*). Here, the three ladies of the nighttime sky, Nyx, Aethra, and Aurora, are all mesmerized by his lady's natural glow, her starry eyes, and the redness of her cheeks. She is so serenely and wondrously beautiful, in fact, that they feel no shame in admitting her superiority (line 15, *ultro omnes conceditis*). Propertius (1.4), in a similar vein, believes that his Cynthia outshines the famous women of myth: *Cynthia non illas nomen habere sinat.* Leroux mentions Q. Lutatius Catulus' poem (quoted by Cicero, *ND* 1.79), where the "dawning" (*exoritur*) Roscius is said to "seem more beautiful than the god," presumably the sun. She mentions an imitation by du Bellay (*L'Olive*, 1549–1550, sonnet 83). One could also com-

COMMENTARY ON THE EPIGRAMS   139

pare Meleager, *AP* 12.127 and Theocr. 18.26–28. **3. Erebi centumplicis uxor:** Erebus (Darkness) was both brother and husband to Nyx (Night), with whom he produced Ether and Day. The epithet "hundredfold" suggests a darkness of deep intensity. **4. uno . . . colore:** black. **6. invitum:** reluctant, because the morning hour has not yet come. **7. Aethrae:** daughter of Oceanus and Tethys (Ov. *Fast.* 5.171); here, simply used as a personification of the heavens, with her "gleaming eyes" as stars and with the music of the spheres. **11. Dardanii coniux formosa mariti:** Aurora, wife of Trojan ("Dardanian") Tithonus, and personification of the dawn (= Eos). The sun can only see her leaving and thus "touches the back."

Epigram 4

Here Muret draws heavily from Vergilian language (cf. the striking transferred epithet, *mare velivolum* of *Aen.* 1.224) and imagery (Aeolus and the winds, *Aen.* 1.50ff.), along with coined compounds (e.g., *altifremi*), à la Lucretius, to add an epic gravity to a very non-epic subject matter.

1. Iunonis alumni: an allusion to Verg. *Aen.* 1.78–79: *Tu mihi quodcumque hoc regni, tu sceptra Iovemque / concilias.* **3. tetrarchae:** i.e., the four winds.

Epigram 5

An apostrophe to his own soul, which is compared to a runaway slave and an army deserter. Muret draws on an image already present in Q. Lutatius Catulus fr. 1 (Courtney, *The Fragmentary Latin Poets,* 70–71, 75–76), who himself adapts an epigram of Callimachus (*Epig.* 41 [Pfeiffer]): *aufugit mi animus; credo, ut solet, ad Theotimum / devenit.* . . . Often such addresses to the departing soul are put into the mouth of the dead or the dying (e.g., Hadrian's stanza inscribed in his mausoleum [today the Castel San' Angelo], *"Animula vagula blandula / hospes comesque corporis, / quae nunc abibis in loca, / pallidula rigida nudula, / nec ut soles dabis iocos?*), and may be the dramatic effect Muret wishes here: He is a desperate lover whose soul is leaving him as it would a dying person. Cf. Plaut. *Pseud.* 30ff., particularly 32: *nam istic meus animus nunc est, non in pectore.*

5. ab igne calescat: Muret may mean that the soul burns sexually for his *domina,* or this may be a reference to the fiery nature of the soul, as the ancients saw it (cf. Cic. *Tusc.* 1.18.42, *ardore animi concalescunt*). **6. Frigore . . . flammas:** the icy fire motif, for which see the comments on *eleg.* 9 above.

Epigram 6

The lover is torn between disclosing his longing and suppressing it. Unable to keep quiet or speak, to vent his passions or control them, he conveys his beffudlement with the simple and familiar, *Quid faciam?* He decides, in the end, that his *vita* (line 1) is really his *diva* (line 8). Leroux points to a similar situation described by Valerius Aedituus (fr. 1): *dicere cum conor curam tibi, Pamphila, cordis, / quid mi abs te quaeram, verba labris abeunt.* . . . Valerius goes on to describe physical effects that his emotions have on him reminiscent of those found in Sappho fr. 31 (L-Page) and Cat. 51: sweating, dumbness, dizziness, and so on.

1. dolores: i.e., the torments of love; cf. Hor. *Sat.* 2.3.263: *an potius mediter finire dolores?* and Ov. *AA* 2.519: *tot sunt in amore dolores.* **8. diva:** playing on the *vita* of line 1 by the inversion of some letters. She is fittingly *diva* now because she has a domain that she rules (*regnas* in line 7).

Epigram 7

Muret uses the "lover in a dream" motif (cf. *AP* 5.2, 5.243 [Macedonius the Consul], 12.124, 12.125, and 12.127; Prop. 2.26A; *Corp. Tib.* 3.4; Ov. *Am.* 3.5; Bèze *epig.* 19; Secundus, *Eleg.* 1.10 [=*Amoenitates*, 248–49]; du Bellay, *Amores*, "Somnium," [=*Amoenitates*, 366–67]; and many others) to touch on a well-known Lucretian topos, the vanity of sensual pleasure (desire is not attained in the dream, as *AP* 5.243.8: ἄφθονός ἐστιν Ἔρως κέρδεος ἡδυγάμου. Compare especially *DRN* 4.1106ff.: *iam cum praesagit gaudia corpus* | . . . *nequiquam, nihil inde abradere possunt,* etc.

5. honorem: here "grace," as at 15.1 below. Cf. Verg. 1.591 (*laetos honores* = "joyous grace") and note of Austin *ad loc.*

Epigram 8

Phalaecian hendecasyllables. Body parts vie with one another for Marguerite's affections, reducing the lover to a state of civil war (cf. Secundus, *Basia* 6). Note how the poem begins with an active and aggressive "I" acting on the *te* (line 1) and ends, once the lover has been confronted, with a passive and submissive *me* (line 10).

7. candor . . . natans: i. e., *lingua,* the "tongue" (cf. *epig.* X.13: *vibrans improbulam . . . linguam*). **8. Herculeus trahit lapillus:** The magnet or lodestone was often called *Herculeus/Heracleus lapis* (or ʽΗρακλεία λίθος) and was associated with the attraction of love. Pliny (*NH* 36.16.25) connects the epithet not with the hero Hercules/Herakles, but with Heraclea in Lydia. See also Erasmus, *Adag.* 1.5.87, where there is mention of the "stone of Hercules that attracts iron to itself." For a discussion of the various theories concerning the name, see the commentary of Munro on Lucr. 6.906ff. (vol. 2: 384).

Epigram 9

The strikingly paradoxical contrast between "tender" love and the violent passion that ensues leads the reader to comprehend the perfect pleasure that comes from the unresisting resistance at the end of the poem (cf. Horace's girl with the "teasingly resisting finger" of *Carm.* 9.24) and more broadly, perhaps, to contemplate the contradictory nature of love. Marguerite adds to the pleasure when she hides her real desires (the *cupiente quidem* of 1. 6) by presenting obstacles (the *sed renuente* of 1. 6). Two examples cited by Leroux are particularly relevant: Ov. *Am.* 3.4.17 (*Nitimur in vetitum semper cupimusque negata*) and Claud. 14.11–13 (*Crescunt difficili gaudia iurgio / Accenditque magis, quae refugit, Venus. / Quod flenti tuleris, plus sapit osculum*).
 1. **pugnando teneri pascuntur amores**: Leroux cites Maximianus, *Eleg.* 3.69 (*unguibus et morsu teneri pascuntur amores*) and Secundus, *Epithal.* 85 (*Pugnando teneri volunt Amores!*), among other parallels. **6. cupiente . . . renuente**: both participles refer to Marguerite.

Epigram 10

Phalaecian hendecasyllables. Catullan images and language are brought together to make a variation on the *carpe diem* refrain (Hor. *Carm.* 1.11; Ov. *AA* 2.669–674; Mart. *Epig.* 1.15, Ausonius *De rosis nascentibus*, etc.), particularly in lines 25ff. The abundance of diminutives and "pillow-talk" throughout conjure up an aura of erotic intimacy that touches on the elegiac. There is much influence here from Secundus' *Basium* XVI as well.
 1. **ludamus . . . iocemur**: a play on Cat. 5.1, *Vivamus . . . amemus . . .* Catullus urges his girlfriend to live life to the fullest now since the final setting of the sun, death, approaches, and the chance for love is gone forever. Muret inverts this image in the next line. **2. cum . . . diem reducet**: cf. Cat. 5.5: *cum semel occidit brevis lux . . .* In contrast to the finality of Catullus' setting sun,

Muret's sun brings the chance for play. **6. columbam:** doves, as especially affectionate creatures (Cat. 29.8), were deemed sacred to Venus (see Ov. *Met.* 15.386: *Cythereiadasque columbas*). Ovid (*Am.* 2.6.56) describes a place in Elysium where pure birds flock, including the cooing dove who tenderly "kisses" her mate: *oscula dat cupido blanda columba mari*. *Columba* is also used as a term of endearment at Plaut. *Cas.* 138. On the amorous connotations of doves in the Roman poets, see A. Sauvage, *Étude de thèmes animaliers dans la poésie latine* (Brussels, 1975), 250–55. Du Bellay delineates the erotic associations of the dove in some detail in a poem entitled, "Cognomen Faustinae" (*Amoenitates poeticae*, 362). He praises their snowy-white color, their playfulness and cooing, their gentle nipping and kissing, and their delicateness. **7. passerem:** The sparrow, also a favorite bird of Venus, is the subject of Cat. 2 and 3, often taken as the equivalent of *mentula*. For *passer* as a term of endearment, see again Plaut., *Cas.* 138. **9. Da mi basiolum unicum:** Catullus (5.7) demands *basia mille*, and adds hundreds and thousands from there. Muret asks for but one but receives thousands of erotic ones. **13. vibrans . . . linguam:** conjuring up images of the snake's quivering tongue (cf. Lucr. 3.657 and Verg. *Aen.* 2.111). **29. tergo . . . senectus:** from Sen. *NQ* 3, praef. 2: *premit a tergo senectus*. **31. tussis mala:** The cough is a sure sign of failing health (Hor. *Sat.* 2.5.106–7; Mart. 1.10.4).

Epigram II

The poet prefers that the girl not fan the flames of lust (*ardor*) but quench them with intercourse.

1. basia . . . libas: *libare* in the sense of "to touch"; cf. Verg. *Aen.* 1.256: *oscula libavit natae*. **3. resupina:** Muret creates an image of tender love drawn from Cat. 45 and Lucr. 1.35–36. **6. quinta . . . parte:** from Hor. *Carm.* 1.13.15–16: *quae Venus / quinta parte sui nectaris imbuit*. This is a Pythagorean concept, that in addition to the four elements (earth, wind, fire, water), there is a finer fifth element, far superior to the rest, that animates them. It came to mean, generally speaking, "the best part," and here, more specifically, "intercourse."

Epigram 12

Love torments the lover and causes insomnia. Thus Ovid (*Am.* 1.2.1–4) complains that Love makes his couch seem hard and causes him to toss and turn all night (McKeown, *ad loc.*, collects other relevant passages). For the *solus ego vigilo* topos (the rest of the world sleeps while the lover lies awake), cf. Stat. *Silv.* 5.4.1ff.: *crimine quo merui, iuvenis placidissime divum, / quove errore miser, donis ut solus egerem, / somne, tuis?* Other passages, though typically in the third person (how would the sleepless person know that the rest of the world is at rest?), are discussed by B. J. Gibson, "Statius and Insomnia: Allusion and Meaning in *Silvae* 5.4," *CQ* 46 (1996): 457–68. In particular, he points to love-sick Dido's torment at *Aen.* 4.522–32. For invocations to sleep among the Italian neo-Latin and vernacular poets, see S. Carrai, *Ad somnum: L'invocazione al sonno nella lirica italiana* (Padova, 1990). Du Bellay employs the same topos in a poem entitled, "Somnium" (*Amoenitates poeticae*, 366), where he describes how Cupid troubles him during the night while everything else sleeps: *Nox erat, et placidum carpebant cuncta soporem . . . / . . . Ille meos cernens vigili sub mente dolores / Luminaque e lacrimis turgida facta meis. . . .*

 1. **tacitis caelo volvuntur tractibus ignes:** cf. Verg. *Aen.* 4.524: *cum medio volvuntur sidera lapsu.* 2. **Delia:** Diana from Delos, here as the moon goddess. **rorantes equos:** In Statius' *Achilleis* (1.242–43) it is Titan who drives the "dew-bringing horses" (*humilique ex aequore Titan / rorantes evolvit equos*). 3. **Iam pecudumque . . . ferarumque:** a hypermetric line, with *atque alitum* as an example of diastole or perhaps a mistake of quantity. 5. **Somnus habet:** Sleep is said to "possess" or "not possess" individuals, as at *Il.* 2.2: Δία δ' οὐκ ἔχε νήδυμος ὕπνος. 6. **papavereis:** opium poppy, with soporific qualities (Verg. *Georg.* 1.78: *Lethaeo perfusa papavera somno;* Celsus, *De med.* 2.32: *somno vero aptum est papaver*). 11. **occumbere:** to contrast with *ex ortu* of line 10. 12. **umbra:** i.e., a shade of the underworld.

Epigram 13

Muret complains that the traditional story of the origins of Venus seems to stand at odds with her typical *modus operandi.* He seems to have in mind the lines of Meleager (*AP* 5.176.5–6): θαῦμα δέ μοι, πῶς ἄρα διὰ γλαυκοῖο φανεῖσα / κύματος, ἐξ ὑγροῦ, Κύπρι, σὺ πῦρ τέτοκας ("I am amazed, Cypris, how, though you arose from the blue-green sea, you brought forth fire from the water").

 1. **mendax . . . turba:** It had become proverbial to speak of poets as liars

because of their dependence on a special metaphorical language (see, e.g., Plaut. *Pseud.* 401), but the characterization is not necessarily a negative one. Ovid (*Fast.* 6.253) speaks dismissively of the *mendacia vatum*, while elsewhere excusing them from being chroniclers of history's truth (*Am.* 3.12.42). Likewise, Pliny the Younger (*Ep.* 6.21) concedes that a license to lie is granted to the poets (*poetis mentiri licet*).

Epigram 14

Marguerite raises the status and happiness of a man in proportion to the degree that she surrenders herself.

1. Quem tu cumque: a favorite tmesis of Vergil for a line beginning, with variation on case and pronoun (*Aen.* 1.610, 8.74, 11.762, etc.). **2. lapis:** for the cold and unyielding heart; cf. Tib. 1.1.64, *nec in tenero stat tibi corde silex;* Verg. *Aen.* 6.471, *quam si dura silex aut stet Marpesia cautes.*

Epigram 15

Muret imagines a kind of childish game played between himself and his lover, whereby she hides her face with her hands then hides her hands, and he responds in kind. Here the poet returns to various topics that he has handled before: The torturous nature of love (*supplicium* in line 10), the superiority of his girl to the gods (*invideatque Venus* in line 2), the longing for death when the girl is absent (*dies . . . valeto* in line 9), and the power of the girl over the obsessive lover (*Quo mea versantur corda* in line 4).

1. Pande oculos . . . : *Ad Lydiam,* 9–10: *Pande, puella, stellatos oculos, / Flexaque super nigra cilia.* **honorem:** see note on *epig.* 7.5 above. **3. occulis:** Leroux incorrectly reads *oculis* and thus mistranslates here. **5. manuum:** At first, it seems, his girl covered her eyes and her brow with her hand, then somehow after that hid her hand as well (perhaps she turned her head away). **7. videbo:** A similar line is found in a du Bellay poem about his Faustina (orig. pub. 1558; p. 358 of *Amoenitates poeticae* [1779]): *Ergo te posthac nunquam, mea vita, videbo?* Both authors appear to be adapting lines from Vergil (*Ecl.* 1.75–76) and Silius Italicus (*Pun.* 2.569).

COMMENTARY ON THE EPIGRAMS 145

Epigram 16

Muret rehearses the theme of epig. 12: Marguerite's absence is equated to the setting of the sun and the coming of night.
4. pluo lacrimas: a clever variation on the more common *flere lacrimas*. Here *pluo* keeps to the weather theme, though this verb never appears in the first person in extant classical literature.

Epigram 17

Galla appears to be objecting that the poet is not passionate and loving to the degree she desires, or perhaps she is coyly resisting the "something more." The latter would fit well the character of Martial's Galla at 2.25. The poet responds matter-of-factly by informing her that his is not a selfless conferral of affection, but a transaction in which he expects an equivalent reciprocation. It is noteworthy that Muret turns away from Marguerite to another girl's name when the sentiments described are less than exemplary.
6. Galla: Her name itself is a pun, meaning "French-girl."

Epigram 18

A clever variation on the *recusatio:* Muret cannot sing the praises of Scaliger because he is not up to the task. Even so, his brief verses here do the job for him.
1. Aoniae . . . cohortis: the Muses. **3. Veronae:** Mention is made here of Verona because Scaliger's family (La Scala or Della Scala) was prominent in Verona (on this see epig. 1.16 above). Verona was also famous as the birthplace of Catullus, and later poets often mention the fame that her native son brought to her (see in particular Mart. 10.103). **4. munus . . . utrumque:** i.e., the gifts of medicine (he served as the physician to the Bishop of Agen for a time and wrote works on the medicinal properties of plants) and poetry, which both belong to the domain of the Clarian god Apollo (*Clarii . . . dei*). **6. Saepius . . . cymba quieta:** The idea is that Scaliger heals so many people that Charon, boatman of Styx, has less work with which to occupy himself. **7. remisti:** In other words, only after Scaliger loosened his lofty standards could he have stooped to look kindly upon Muret's poetry. Cf. Cic. *2 Ver.* 1.25; *Phil.* 1.12; *Brut.* 17. **11. Tune . . . ut laudaveris:** For the syntax, cf. Cic. *TD* 2.42: *Egone ut te interpellem?*

Epigram 19

The Muse tells Muret that he need not look afield for a word to describe the virtues of Scaliger, since the scholar's very name, through the reputation won by his accomplishments, implies them all.

1. Dic, dea: The epic beginning invites the reader to think of Scaliger in heroic terms. **3. imprudens:** Muret allows himself to serve as a foil to Scaliger's virtues. **4. Omnia . . . nomen:** The alliteration of *m*'s and *n*'s along with the interlocking word order reinforces the identification of the name of Scaliger with the names of the virtues.

Epigram 20

A variation on the previous poem (note the similar epic beginning). Muret wonders about the source of Scaliger's inspiration and learns that in fact Scaliger serves as an inspiration for the Muses themselves.

3. te sententia fallit: borrowed from.Verg. *Aen.* 10.608: *nec te sententia fallit.*
4. Nectare: normally a gift from the Muses to poets (cf. Pindar, *Olymp.* 7.7).

Epigram 21

Merely through her presence or absence, Phyllis affects Muret's perception of the passing of time, the cycle of the seasons, and the interchange of night and day.

2. Longior . . . die: Leroux compares Macrin. *carm.* 4.5.9–12: *Toto videtur hora brevis die / et mensis anno longior, at dies / (tecum ipse si vivam modo) hora, / mense etiam brevior sit annus.* **5. Tauri . . . Titan:** When the sun (Titan) enters the constellation of the bull beginning in mid-April, spring arrives (Ov. *Fast.* 4.713–20).

Epigram 22

Caliantheus (identity unknown) puts on airs that he possesses scientific and philosophical knowledge, while, in fact, he knows nothing of these fields beyond the external accouterments themselves. Thus Muret feels the need to adjust his name from a "lover of wisdom," to a title that better fits his character, a "lover of void." That Muret is adapting Martial's poem to Pannice (9.47) with its similar subject is evident from the correspondence between line 3 here and Martial's line 7: *Tu qui sectarum causas et pondera nosti . . .*

6. philosomphus: The Greek *somphos* refers to something porous, such as a sponge; thus, he is a "lover of void." Leroux, however, believes that this term signifies that Caliantheus "absorbs" everything without comprehending it.

Epigram 23

A twist on the common dinner-invitation poem (cf. Bacchylides fr. 21, Philodemus 27 [Sider], Cat. 13; Mart. 5.78, 11.52, etc.): Instead of sending the invitation, Muret responds to it. As often in such poems, food is not the main attraction of dinner, rather wine, wit, and song. On the dinner invitation as a sub-genre, see L. Edmunds, "The Latin Invitation Poem: What is it? Where did it come from?" *AJP* 103 (1982): 184–88, and E. Gowers, *The Loaded Table: Representations of Food in Roman Literature,* chapter 4, "Invitation Poems" (Oxford, 1993).

5. avis Iunonia: the peacock, which was for the Romans an expensive delicacy.
6. Scythico flumine nomen habet: The pheasant takes its name from the Scythian (or Colchian) river Phasis. Juvenal (11.139) calls them *Scythicae volucres.*

Epigram 24

Chiron and Eurytion were Centaurs, half-horse, half-man. Eurytion, who had attempted to carry off Hippodamia during her nuptials with Pirithous, was the typical kind of Centaur, with a voracious sexual appetite, but Chiron was the wise tutor of many heroes. Lygdus has taken on the qualities of both. Even so, the bestial desires that Lygdus developed appears to be the real issue here, given the description of his tendencies in the next poem.

Epigram 25

Phalaecian hendecasyllables. Muret make a pun at the expense of Lygdus and his inconsistent behavior: Although he has found success in the high life (*frugibus repertis*), he continues to indulge himself in the low life (*multa pascere glande*).

2–3. benignus . . . suorum: i.e., he gives freely of himself and his possessions. The use of the genitive here is a poetic idiom; cf. Hor. *Sat.* 2.3.3: *quod vini somnique benignus.* Also, ibid. 2.2.62 (for *non parcus*) and id., *Epist.* 1.7.42 (*prodigus*).

7. **Memmius:** Probably Memmius Frémiot of Dijon, whose poems are included at the end of the collection and whose effigy was burned at Toulouse along with that of Muret (see introduction above). **9. pascere glande:** a sexual metaphor; cf. Mart. 12.75.3: *pastas glande natis habet Secundus.* See also Adams, 72. Leroux points to Cic. *Orator* 31, from which Muret borrowed, but the key to the pun lies with Martial. The irony is that Lygdus' generosity and handsomeness translates unexpectedly into passive sexual behavior.

Epigram 26

The poet addresses his friend Memmius (see the previous poem) in the first line, and Memmius gives his objection (note the strong *at* indicating the reply) in the next line. The name of the girl, Porna, suggests her occupation, so we are incredulous concerning the naivete apparent from Muret's initial assertion, but without it we cannot have the pun between *amicis* and *inimica.*

Epigram 27

How can Porna be so proud, the poet asks, when her professions requires her to lie flat on her back in submission?

2. pueris: here, an attendant boy, as often in classical authors (e.g., Hor. *Sat.* 1.6.116). **subicis:** The word stands in stark contrast to the *superbam* of the previous line.

Epigram 28

François claims not to have any interest in love, but exhibits all the signs of someone who is flirting. The poet, however, knowing his Ovid well, recognizes the covert techniques of flirtation that he employs and exposes him for what he really is, a man in love.

2. lascivi ... dei: Cupid (cf. Tib. 1.10.57, *At lascivus Amor rixae mala verba ministrat;* also Ov. *Am.* 3.1.43 and *AA* 2.497). **4. supercilio:** The eyebrow was a favorite means of furtive communication and frequently is mentioned in regard to love trysts (e.g., Ov. *Am.* 2.5.15 and 1.4.19). Ovid (*AA* 1.499) recommends its use in the theater as a part of a broader strategy to seduce a mistress.

Epigram 29

A favorite aphorism of the Stoics and found frequently in Greek and Roman writers: True nobility comes from character rather than privileged birth. Muret explores the theme further in *epist.* 1 below.

2. imaginibus: Given the context, the word must refer not so much to representations of the bishop himself, but to the ancestral images (*maiorum imagines*) so often alluded to in Roman literature. For this, cf. Seneca's assertion (*Ep.* 44.5) that "an atrium full of smoke-begrimed images does not make a nobleman" (*Quis est generosus? Ad virtutem bene a natura compositus . . . Non facit nobilem atrium plenum fumosis imaginibus*). **11. nepotibus:** spiritual descendants. Nothing about the poem suggests that Muret is being ironic when he ascribes children to a bishop. Cf. the sentiment antithetical to the one here, with a similar broad sense to *nepotes*, at Juv. 2.128–29: *haec tetigit, Gradive, tuos urtica nepotes? / traditur ecce viro clarus genere atque opibus vir.*

Epigram 30

This profiteering Ponticus, an imaginary figure appearing in many Roman and Renaissance poems, is the antithesis of the generous Scaliger in epigram 1. It was common practice in the Renaissance to send out poems for critique by other scholars. Ponticus, however, does not render this service for free, but for a fee, thus tainting the process.

10. altera . . . paras: i.e., Ponticus has ulterior motives when he praises bad poems: he hopes to bring in more business.

Epigram 31

Ponticus' poems are only "golden" in the sense that they need to be submitted to the fire to burn off the impurities (cf. Erasmus' *Adag.* 4.1.58, *Aurum igni probatum*).

1. Aurea . . . carmina: Ponticus' opinion of his own poetry harks back to Lucretius' characterization of Epicurus' teachings as *aurea dicta* (Lucr. 3.9).

150   COMMENTARY ON THE EPIGRAMS

EPIGRAM 32

Phalaecian hendecasyllables. The poem contains layer upon layer of dissimulation. Muret plunders the entire arsenal of Catullus and Martial to accuse Moncaudus playfully of the very charge that those two poets had staunchly denied, namely, that their poems reflect their morals.

3. geminus . . . Cupido: i.e., "Love" and "Love Returned (= Anteros)." Pausanias describes altars to these two in Elis and Athens (6.23.3 and 1.30.1, respectively). Cf. Ov. *Fast.* 4.1 (*geminorum mater Amorum*); Sen. *Oed.* 500f. (*geminus Cupido / concutit taedas*, sc. "as Ariadne was escorted to heaven") and *Phaed.* 274ff. (*Diua non miti generata ponto, / quam uocat matrem geminus Cupido: / impotens flammis simul et sagittis / iste lasciuus puer et renidens / tela quam certo moderatur arcu!*). Contrast *non simplex* from line 2 of epigram 1 above. **4. Dione:** Venus (cf. Cat. 56.6; Ov. *Am.* 1.14.33). **11. mollis:** meaning soft, yielding, pliant, sensitive, a word often applied to elegy and epigram. When used as a stylistic term, it often carries a negative connotation, describing a less dignified, unsubstantial and theatrical oratory, or it can refer to a speaker or statesman of questionable character. But Catullus in *c.* 16 openly admits that his poems are *molliculi*, coupling that with *parum pudicum*, both of which are necessary to set the reader (or listener) itching (*pruriat*). Propertius approves of the characterization of his art as well (1.7.19: *Et frustra cupies mollem componere versum;* 2.1.2: *unde meus veniat mollis in ore liber*). Thus *mollities* is not unwelcome in the poet's craft, inasmuch as it speaks to its dramatic and emotive aspects, as when Cicero (*Div.* 1.31.66), citing a particularly moving passage of Ennius, exclaims, *O poema tenerum et moratum atque molle!* Note, too, Muret's use of *dissimulas* in line 25. For a full discussion of the word, see J. K. Newman, *Augustan Propertius: The Recapitulation of a Genre* (Hildesheim, 1997), 195–202. **15. Sybariticos poetas:** The city of Sybaris had become synonymous with luxury, debauchery, and voluptuousness in ancient times. The phrase "Sybaritic poets" refers, not to specific poets, but to a particular brand of poets, namely, lewd ones who reflect the spirit of Sybaris. Cf. Mart. 12.95.1–2: *Musseti pathicissimos libellos / qui certant Sybariticis libellis* . . . **21. Cypriae . . . palaestrae:** Cyprian, because that's where Venus was born. "Wrestling" is often used as a sexual metaphor (on this see Adams, 157–58). For "palaestra" specifically, cf. Mart. 10.55.4. **26. Imperator:** The direct address is part of the military simile that Muret is playing on: Muret sees Moncaudus as "General Pervert" rather than the innocent tyro he claims to be. **30. Castratum . . . Priapum:** an absurd figure taken from Mart. 1.35.

COMMENTARY ON THE EPIGRAMS 151

Epigram 33

Muret equates Scaliger, or at least his *ingenium,* with the gods because of his poetic greatness (from celestial places comes poetic inspiration) and offers himself up as a humble sacrifice in his honor.
3. cognati retinens commercia caeli: Given the many Ovidian echoes here, Muret probably drew the notion of a "kindred" (*cognati*) sky from Ov. *Met.* 1.81 (*cognati retinebat semina caeli*), but the idea is originally Pythagorean (see Diog. L. 1.28: "They say that the soul is a piece of the ether."). For *commercia caeli* he may have been thinking of Ov. *AA* 3.549: *Est deus in nobis [sc. poetis], et sunt commercia caeli*. Cf. also Man. *Astr.* 2.466: *quin etiam propriis inter se legibus astra / conveniunt, ut certa gerant commercia rerum*. Moret: "*Eslevé jusqu'aux Dieux / Tu baisses ta lumière| Jusqu'au dessous des Cieux*. **4. astra vides:** According to Ovid (*Met.* 1.86), the divine seed in human beings causes them to stand erect and raise their eyes to the stars. In contrast, Scaliger can see the stars even when looking downward. **9. templo:** Muret plays on the double sense of *templum* as both a place for worship and a region of the sky.

Epigram 34

Muret writes on behalf of a friend trying to obtain the patronage of Francis I's sister, Marguerite de Navarre (also called Marguerite d'Angoulême, 1492–1549). The king's sister was an accomplished humanist in her own right and supported the arts in many ways.
10. vili . . . manu: as in Cic., *Leg.* 2.24–25, Pers. 2.68–75, Sen. *Ep.* 115.5, and Hebrews 9.12–14, the gods are more concerned with a pure heart than expensive gifts. Human beings are often deluded into believing that the gods have the same nature as themselves and will respond accordingly to gifts, groveling, and bribes.
12. diva: He continues to address Marguerite de Navarre, this time as if she were a patron divinity. He promises her "better things to come" (*maiora et meliora*), that is, more substantial encomia, if she lends him aid.

Epigram 35

Part of the cycle trumpeting the great humanist's approval of Muret's poetry (see epigrams 1 and 18 in particular).

Epigram 36

The pun looks to the name of the addressee himself: L*omen*ius.

Epigram 37

After several epigrams in which individuals receive praise for being like the gods, Muret turns the tables and ridicules "a certain someone" for possessing the more dubious qualities of some gods.
    1. Mulciber . . . Aeolus . . . Lyaeus: Vulcan walked with a limp, perhaps because he was born with a club foot, or because Jupiter cast him from heaven while arguing with Juno. Aeolus was keeper of the winds, and so could be described as an air head or a windbag. Lyaeus (i.e., Bacchus) had rosy cheeks as a result of his drinking. **2. tres uno divos corpore:** Recalling, yet avoiding, the wording of the Trinitarian formula.

Epigram 38

Choliambics. Rufinus claims to know three languages, but in fact knows almost nothing about any of them. He hides his lack of knowledge by switching tongues according to his audience, speaking pseudo-Greek around Latinists, pseudo-Hebrew around Hellenists, and so on. Despite the dissimilation, Muret has discovered that Rufinus is nothing but a tongue, that is, all talk.
    8. Apellas: The name "Apella" had become proverbial for the stereotypically superstitious and credulous Jew; see Hor. *Sat.* 1.5.100: *Credat Iudaeus Apella, non ego.* **15. serpentes:** snakes have forked-tongues, so Rufinus bests them with his three.

Epigram 39

Phalaecian hendecasyllables. An inversion of Cat. 16 and variation on epigram 32: Noalle writes poetry with extremely risqué content, and Muret is not willing to believe that they are not at least somewhat self-revelatory.
    4. Numa, Fabricioque sanctiorem: Numa, the successor of Romulus during the kingly period of Rome, established many of the religious institutions of Rome. Fabricius was a Roman commander and statesman who flourished in the

COMMENTARY ON THE EPIGRAMS 153

3rd century BCE. Later writers admired him as a model of incorruptibility and austerity. **7. Catonem:** Possibly Cato the Elder (Leroux), but just as likely Cato Uticensis, who served as a stock exemplum of strict virtue in the writings of the Latin poets (see Mart. 1, *praef.*).

Epigram 40

This poem is inspired by the iconic tradition that had become popular in the Renaissance (for a discussion, see Summers, 190–96). The icon celebrates the life of some historic person, typically in a few distichs, and can use the first, second, or third person. Muret includes the familiar "outbidding" formula (*vincere*), but also seems to have in mind the plot of Aristophanes' *Frogs*, where Aeschylus and Euripides vie for preeminence in some sort of heavenly ranking system.

6. Nectarea: see note on *Carm.* 1.4. **vincere:** cf. Prop. 2.4.65–66, *cedite Romani scriptores, cedite Grai! / nescio quid maius nascitur Iliade.*

Epigram 41

The compliant Lygdus is always willing to give of himself, but sometimes in ways that Muret does not approve.

1. quod sis: the subjunctive, because the reasons are rejected; the *quod* is introduced by the *hoc nomine* ("for this reason") in the following lines. **3. cave:** sc. *ne*, as often. **6. officiosus:** Adams, 163: "Pathics were modishly called *officiosi* [sc. after a slip of the declaimer Haterius recorded by Seneca Rhetor]." **6.** Moret: "Mais on te tient un homme à rendre un bon office."

Epigram 42

The story is that Cupid, as a mischievous trick, struck Apollo with an arrow that inflamed him with love for the nymph Daphne, but then turned around and struck Daphne with a blunt arrow that caused her to find Apollo repulsive. The imagery is one of hunter pursuing prey. For "lover as hunter" see Callimachus, *Epig.* 33 (=*AP* 12.102); Hor. *Sat.* 1.2.94–134; Ov. *Am.* 2.9.9, 2.19.35, and *AA* 1.253–74.

2. Currentem celeri per iuga summa pede: used often of hunters; cf., for example, Ov. *Her.* 4.42: *Hortari celeris per iuga summa canes.*

Epigram 43

Jokes often conceal truths, and that is the case, so Muret believes, with Ponticus. The theme is similar to that of *epig.* 39 above, where Noalle's rather raunchy poetry is said to mirror his true character, despite his protestations otherwise. "Ponticus" is a stock character in epigram (see *epig.* 30 and 31 above, 61 below), usually described as being selfish, arrogant, and immoral (see, e.g., Mart. 2.32.1, 2.82.1, 3.60.9, etc.), sometimes as a bad poet.

1. Epicuri dogmata: "Epicureanism," while technically not a philosophical school still active during the Renaissance, was a term frequently being applied, at least by Catholic writers, to anyone who led an indulgent lifestyle. **7. Tolle tuas artes:** borrowed from Mart. 9.35.11; cf. also Ov. *AA* 3.594.

Epigram 44

The golden mean. The best known treatment of the theme is at Hor. *Carm.* 2.10.5–8, but see also Theognis 335–36 and Hor. *Sat.* 2.2.65–70. The philosophical basis is Aristotle's discussion of "mean" states at *Ethics* 2.7.

5. tardas . . . Calendas: Payday or rent checks come too slowly, though Leroux translates as follows: "qui se plaint de ce que les Calendes n'arrivent pas plus souvent plus tard." **11. posita cum luserit arca:** Cf. Juv. 1.90, *posita luditur arca*, i.e., "to stake one's life savings on the gambling table." **14. Croeso:** Lydian king of the 6th century BCE famed for his wealth. **Irus:** The beggar whom Odysseus fought to amuse the suitors in his palace (Hom. *Odys.* 18.1ff.). **15–16. rimosa . . . urna:** i.e., the money soon disappears like water in the urn of the Danaid sisters.

Epigram 45

This theme may have been suggested to Muret by Propertius' subtle diatribe against cosmetics at 1.2. Gellia, a stock character of epigram with a notoriously dissembling personality (e.g., Mart. 1.33.1, etc.), uses so many feminine enhancements that Muret sees her as an actor playing a woman rather than a woman herself.

6. personata: a term applied to actors performing in their roles; see Hor. *Sat.* 1.4.56.

Epigram 46

Given what people *can* see happening between Cladius and Rufa, it's fairly certain what goes on when people *can't* see. The anaphora and repetition of *cum* builds to a crescendo that culminates in the final rhetorical question.

Epigram 47

Romanus, given his meticulous oral hygiene, should be the paradigm of cleanliness, but the poet notices that this is not the case (see the note on line 8 below). The emphasis of the final line is likely, not on the inadequacy of the hygiene for removing such a stigma, but on the frequency with which Romanus engages in the activity itself.

5. sesquipedales: an echo of Cat. 97.5, undoubtedly to cast the same unfavorable light on Romanus as Catullus did on Aemilius. **8. sordida:** The implication is sexual (i.e., his tongue is dirty because he engages in oral sex). Cf. Plaut. *Truc.* 380–81: *verum tempestas quondam, dum vixi, fuit / quom inter nos sordebamus alter de altero.*

Epigram 48

The poet pledges his undying devotion to Laccius, a devotion that the dissolution of the world or his body cannot destroy.

4. tetras: from the Greek τετράς used of the four quarters of the moon in Theophr. *Sign.* 5.27.38. Cf. Tert. *Val.* 7, 8; Capel. 7.734. **5. perneverit:** Cf. Mart. 1.89.9: *cum mihi supremos Lachesis perneverit annos.*

Epigram 49

Iambic trimeter. The iamb, the meter of invective, and the meter at which Grannius fails so miserably, is turned against him: Grannius' general incompetence not surprisingly shows up in his compositions. The repetitive use of *facit*, mostly as a line ending, and the variations on the *fraud-* root, coupled with the duplication of *lege* and *miraris* in the same position of different lines, heighten the effect of this poem.

1. sine: creates an anapaest in the third foot.

Epigram 50

Hendecasyllabics. The structure and vocabulary of this poem recall that of Catullus' poem about the couple Septimius and Acme, *c.* 45. There, Septimius wishes that, unless he loves Acme down to his bones forever, he might face a lion in India or some other such fearsome thing. Note the parallels there: *Ni te . . . amo / . . . quantum qui pote . . . | contingant* (subjunctive expressing a wish), and so on.

7. miserrimus malorum: in contrast to *optimus bonorum* in the next line. Muret is not saying that he *is* "the worst of the bad," rather that, if he doesn't keep his promise to love Costecaudus, he *will become* a wretched human being because of the curses he has invoked.

Epigram 51

Muret has in mind Catullus' poem about the castration of Attis (*c.* 63), particularly the ending: *procul a mea tuos sit furor omnis, Era, domo. / alios age incitatos, alios age rabidos* ("May all your madness stay far from my house, Lady; make others frenzied, drive others mad"). In general, the Romans looked with disdain on the castrated priests of Cybele. The point here is that Muret would have his holy men be *real* human beings, afflicted with all the internal struggles and frailties of humanity, than be *semiviri,* men with something less than the full complement of natural impulses and feelings.

6. tibi: Muret purposefully is vague with this pronoun, so as not to appear blasphemous, but one must assume that, since in no case would *sacra* be performed *to* or *for* the priests (why would he suddenly switch to the singular, anyway?), he means to refer to God.

Epigram 52

2. regem: Lycaon, an impious king of Arcadia, who, according to Ovid (*Met.* 1.211–43), tried to feed Jupiter a human child as a test of his divinity. Jupiter became enraged and turned him into a wolf, and then later sent the flood to destroy humanity. **Maenalis ora:** Maenalus was a mountain in Arcadia, sacred to Pan; cf. Ov. *Fast.* 3.84. It receives mention in the Lycaon story (note 2 above) at line 216.

Epigram 53

Corellius is so multi-talented that he should have a large earning potential, but the poet is bewildered that he is squandering it somehow.
6. rem facere: cf. Ter. *Ad.* 2.2.12: *Numquam rem facies* (i.e., "Then you'll never make a fortune").

Epigram 54

Again Lygdus appears in an unfavorable light (see *epig.* 24, 25, and 41 above). Muret notes that his small frame is actually a blessing in disguise: It has helped to lessen the negative impact of his transgressions.
2. hoc ipso: referring back to *corpus* in line 1. **plus satis:** Cic. *Fam.* 4.8.2; Verr. 2.5.46 (123): *plusquam satis est doleo;* Ter. *Phorm.* 5.3.14, *paene plus quam sat erat.*

Epigram 55

Muret's criticism of priests and monks usually centers on their hypocrisy concerning sexual matters. In this vignette, the hostess by chance sees the finery the monk wears beneath his rags and questions him about the apparent incongruity. The monk replies unabashedly that he has a tool that assists him in earning extra income on the side.
1. cordigerum: The Franciscan friars wore a cord around their waist called a "cordon." The cordon had three knots representing the friar's chosen "lot" (the *sorti* of line 6): poverty, chastity, and obedience. **10. fusum:** normally *fusus, -i,* m., but the TLL lists late occurrences of the neuter. The conjunction of *nere* verifies that this is not from *fundere*. Isidore of Seville treats the word as a neuter at *Etym.* 9.19: *Fusum, quod per ipsum fundatur quod netum est.* Perhaps Muret should have written *hic . . . fusus.*

Epigram 56

The poem is somewhat of a puzzle, but the issue seems to be that the dinner host loves to hear himself talk, so much so that he is neglecting the service. Muret would rather have the stuffed pastries than the stuffed sophistry. Moret sees the poem this way:

> *Pour ceux qui demeurent long-temps à table*
>
> A quoy bon ces ragouts? Tu nous les sers en vain?
> Veux-tu que nous mangions; sers nous plûtost la faim.

Leroux has the following:

> *Sur un hôte trop prolixe*
>
> Pourquoi ces tourtes et ces sophismes pour des gens repus?
> Tu veux bien nourrir tes convives? Couple leur faim.

The first edition (1553) reads *plenis* at the end of line 1, though the form as a verb is unattested, unless one considers the archaic form *explenunt* (for *explent*) as mentioned by Festus (*s.v.*) to be a suitable precedent. It is true that *ples* is somewhat unattractive, but it does appear in a fragmentary epistle of Fronto.

Epigram 57

Anne can be likened to precious metals on the outside, but on the inside she conceals something much less shiny and beautiful and much more cold and unbending.

Epigram 58

Poets must drink alcohol to quench the fiery passions within them, lest those passions consume them before their time to die has come.

5. Ante diem: of one's time destined by fate; cf. Ov. *Met.* 6.675: *hic dolor ante diem Pandiona misit ad umbras*; Verg. *Aen.* 4.697: *sed misera ante diem subitoque accensa furore.*

Epigram 59

The conventional epigrammatic and elegiac expectation for eternal fame receives a new twist: if not an enduring monument, then at least an ephemeral *suasoria*.

1. faciles . . . Camenae: Muret has in mind the context of Aus. *Epist.* 8.17–18 (a letter to a friend), where the poet wishes his friend poetic virtuosity in return for the favor of a visit: *sic tibi sint Musae faciles, meditatio prompta / et memor, et liquidi mel fluat eloquii.* **4. tibi scripta . . . nomen erit:** Ovid too claims such power for his poetry (*Am.* 1.10.60–62): *quam volui, nota fit arte mea. / scindentur vestes, gemmae frangentur et aurum; / carmina quam tribuent, fama perennis erit.* **5. verbis et pondus et omen abesto:** as we would say "Knock on wood." Cf. Ov. *Am.* 1.14.41 (*nec tibi vis morbi nocuit—procul omen abesto!*) and 2.14.42 (*et sint ominibus pondera nulla meis!*). **8. animi pignora . . . mei:** a phrase used by Ovid in defense of his loyalty to the emperor as evidenced in his poetry (*Trist.* 2.66, *invenies animi pignora certa mei*).

Epigram 60

The poet combines two oft repeated and compatible sentiments about virtue: 1) Virtue is the surest possession (what Solon calls τὸ ἐμπεδον [Diehl frg. 4]), not subject to the whims of fortune, and 2) Virtue alone immortalizes a human being (*perennibus inserit astris*). Parallels in classical literature abound. Sallust (*BC* 1.4), for example, describes riches and beauty as *fluxa* and *fragilis*, while virtue remains *clara* and *aeterna*. Euripides has Hippolytus (*Hipp.* 426) insisting that only a virtuous heart can endure the buffets of life's battle. The heavenly exaltation of the virtuous is most familiar from Cicero's *Somnium Scipionis.* Cf. also Semonides 1; Theognis 133–142; and Hor. *Carm.* 3.29.49–56.

4. sors inimica: cf. Man. *Astron.* 2.607: *atque hominum gentes inimica sorte feruntur.*

Epigram 61

Ponticus provides no other proof that he is a good poet except the assertion itself. This poem is to be compared with *epig.* 31 above, also about Ponticus (see also *epig.* 30, 43).

Epigram 62

"Lais" is the name of a famous courtesan of Corinth (Ov. *Am.* 1.5.12: *multis Lais amata viris*).

Epigram 63

It is unclear why the woman of this poem should be characterized as *sterilem*, but the title means to keep the reader's attention focused on Avitus. He ordinarily would be expected to give her something in exchange for sex, but does not (*nihil illi donat*). She, after all, is engated in work (*operam*). We might assume that she is a prostitute, therefore, and that *sterilem* describes her contribution to society: she is useless and vile. Or possibly she is a girlfriend who hopes in vain for gifts while Avitus hopes in vain for children. Both are wasting their time.

1. subigat: Adams, 155: "*Subigo* was used of the active role in homosexual or heterosexual intercourse, in which sense it was probably established in ordinary speech." **2. oleum perdat . . . operam:** an allusion to an adage found in Plaut. *Poen.* 322 and Cic. *Fam.* 7.1.3. Erasmus (*Adag.* 1.4.62) explains it to mean wasted expense or time (*oleum*) and wasted effort (*opera*). He derives the imagery of the "oil" from either the oil that athletes rub on their bodies or the oil of lamps.

Epigram 64

While elsewhere Muret praises the role of Lyaeus in the inspiration of poets (see *Od* 5), he also champions moderation, a point that Pontilianus has failed to grasp. Muret plays on the double meaning of *salsa*. Just as 'salty' food is watered down by the addition of too much wine, so 'wit'in poetry is ruined by too much drinking. Pontilianus himself is a stock character of epigram; his character is summed up in an epigram of Martial (12.40), including his penchant for drink and the recitation of bad poetry.

Epigram 65

Glory is to virtue what the body's shadow is to the body itself. For another treatment of the "solidness" of virtue, cf. *epig.* 60 above.

1. corpore constans: for the collocation in the same line position, cf. Man. *Astr.* 2.613. **2. fluxa:** used of beauty and riches at Sallust *BC* 1.4 in contrast to the permanence of virtue.

Epigram 66

Either Lucius has a terrible memory (he used all the skill he had and it still took him three nights to learn a mere three verses), or he has learned elaborate techniques for memorization that are actually hindering him. Given the title, the former interpretation is the most likely.

Epigram 67

Paulus isn't likely to learn anything through his books in bed or at the table, in other words, if he is so quick to indulge bodily appetites. This is what we would call "learning through osmosis."

1. E lecto surgens ad mensam: The philosophizing guest at Trimalchio's party (Pet. *Satyr.* 41) uses this figure for someone who is enjoying life to the fullest: *Dies, inquit, nihil est. Dum versas te, nox fit. Itaque nihil est melius quam de cubiculo recta in triclinium ire.* **4. ut vina catelli:** i.e., he treats his books like dessert.

Epigram 68

Muret alludes to Sen. *Epist.* 107.11: *Ducunt volentem fata, nolentem trahunt.* Cf. Cleanthes, frg. 527.

1. Obsequitor: The future imperative, which is reserved especially for legal language, gives the initial phrase the status of a precept.

Epigram 69

Jokes about large noses abound among the iambic and epigrammatic poets. Catullus (*c.* 13) warns his friend Fabullus that, when he smells the unguents surrounding his dinner party, he will want the gods to make him all nose. Martial (13.2) complains of critics with a nose so large that even Atlas would refuse to hold it up if asked. Here, since Pompilius has such a nose for wine being poured, and the nose itself shows the effects of heavy drinking, the poet, with carnivalesque exaggeration, imagines it as a kind of hovering monster that sucks up wine from everywhere.

2. murus cingit . . . triplex: Cf. Ver. *Aen.* 6.549: *triplici circumdata muro.* On the general significance of the "triple" fortification, see note on *Od* 3.62 below.

Here the sense is merely comic: Pompilius' enormous nose is particularly thick on the sides. **3. turres:** i.e., red bumps resulting from the excessive drinking. **6. calices siccos illius umbra facit:** at least it *seems* that the shadow dries wine goblets, since everytime the nose hovers over a cup (and thereby casts its shadow), the wine disappears.

Epigram 70

Muret inverts the conceit of the previous poem, but with equal exaggeration.

Epigram 71

The work of Christ is compared to the break of day after a night of darkness. Much of the imagery concerning the approaching dawn must have been suggested to Muret from Ov. *Am.* 1.13 (see notes below for some of the more obvious parallels). There Aurora is asked to put off her departure so that the poet's mistress will linger.

1. roscida purpureos ... iugales: In Ovid (*Am.* 1.13.10), the hand of Aurora is crimson and her reins are dewy: *roscida purpurea supprime lora manu!* But cf. *AA* 3.180: *roscida luciferos cum dea iungit equos.* The alliteration of the *r*'s is noteworthy. **3. Noctis aves ... cantu:** In Ovid (*Am.* 1.13.8), the birds signal the dawn with their singing: *et liquidum tenui gutture cantat avis.* **5. flammivomo:** a relatively rare epithet of late Latin derived from *flamma* + *vomere* ("that which vomits flames"). TLL lists two instances in which it describes the sun: Corripus, *De bellis Libycis.* 1.338: *Phaethon ... succenderat omnia curru flammivomis raptus equis;* Arator, *De act. apost.* 2.531: *flammivomo sub sole.*

Epigram 72

Muret was willing to concede to Gaurus a certain amateur status among the poets, but once Gaurus begins to inflate his own worth, Muret withdraws even the concession. Fittingly, "Gaurus" comes from the Greek word meaning "arrogant" (see *epig.* 89).

2. poetastris: a word of late Latin, meaning someone who dabbles feebly in verse.

Epigram 73

Pamphagus means "all-eater" in Greek, the perfect name for a glutton. J. du Bellay includes two poems to the same figure (Gruter, *Delitiae*, vol. 1, 469), with the title, *Pamphagi medici tumulus*. From this we learn that Pamphagus was a physician. The first poem, which also pokes fun at Pamphagus' gluttony, runs as follows:

> Hoc tumulo Tumulus tegitur. miraris? at ipse
>   plus etiam audito nomine credideris.
> Pamphagus heic iaceo, vasta, cui mole gravato
>   pro tumulo venter sesquipedalis erat.
> Somnus et Ingluvies, Bacchusque, Venusque, locusque,
>   numina, dum vixi, sola fuere mihi.
> Cetera quis nescit? fuit ars mihi cura medendi;
>   Maxima ridendi sed mihi cura fuit.
> Tu quoque non lacrimas, sed risum heic solve, viator,
>   Si gratus nostris manibus esse cupis.

Epigram 74

Gallonius, a character taken from Lucilius' satires who typifies the self-indulgent person, enjoys an Epicurean lifestyle, but he has not achieved the *ataraxia* or freedom from disturbance that Epicureans desire (the *constantem animum, mentemque quietam* of line 7). It is noteworthy that Gallonius' name comes up in an Epicurean association in classical literature as well, when Cicero (*Fin.* 2.90), while railing against the "false frugality" of Epicurus, observes, *ad voluptatem omnia referens vivit ut Gallonius, loquitur ut Frugi ille Piso.*

5. temeti: The first two syllables should be long, not short.

Epigram 75

Muret doubts whether Sestius' gifts are given out of genuine affection since he seems so pained to give them. He suspects, therefore, that they come not as presents, but with a price (*vendita*).

4. sic . . . voco: The interlocking word order nicely focuses the attention on the main word: *vendita*.

Epigram 76

The mind is viewed as the helm of a ship that can have either Pleasure as its captain or Reason. The former steers the ship to danger, the latter to safety. In regard to the ship metaphor, clearly Muret has been inspired by the "ship of state" commonplace (e.g., Hor. *Carm.* 1.14). Parallels to the theme of this poem are prevalent. The notion that pleasure is an inadequate guide in life as compared to reason forms the basis of the complaint of the Stoics and other philosophical schools against the Epicureans (see, in particular, the arguments of Cicero's *De finibus*). In the *De senectute* (42) Cicero calls pleasure the enemy of reason and says that it impedes good counsel. Horace (*Epist.* 1.2.55ff.) advises a certain Lollius to spurn pleasures, because they lead to greed and anger (for Muret it is *ambitio, dolus,* and *ira*).

4. Syrtes et vada caeca: reminiscent of the troubles that Aeneas faced when his ships were blown to Libya by the devices of Juno; cf. *Aen.* 1.111 (*in brevia et syrtis urget*) and 1.536 (*in vada caeca tulit*).

Epigram 77

Erasmus (*Adag.* 1.9.47) cites the saying of Jerome that a "rich man is either wicked himself or the heir of a wicked man (*Dives aut iniquus est aut iniqui heres*)." He goes on to compare a passage of Plato's *Laws* (5.743c): "So that there is truth in the current saying, that very rich men are not good men." Solon had already made the observation in an epigram (on this see Plut. *Sol.* 2). Here, Sanso is trying to combine goodness and wealth, but Muret believes, based on the conventional wisdom, that it will be to the detriment of both.

Epigram 78

Otho the glutton is now filling the belly of mother earth.

1. Conditus: echoed in line 3 with *condidit*. **2. justa . . . humus:** The ground is just because it settles accounts by paying back what's due (*officium*). **3. iugera:** metonymy for food.

Epigram 79

Virro exhibits a kind of *furor* that some believe mark him out as a true poet and creative genius. Muret quips ironically that if eccentricities make a poet, then he might as well dispense of the labor and the study (the quills and the books). The portrait of the mad poet comes from Horace's description at *AP* 453ff. There the *vesanus poeta* wanders about (*errat*) and belches forth verses (*versus ructatur*), while the children tease him and grown men flee. Cicero also discusses the matter of frenzied versus deliberate writing at *Div.* 2.111–12.

7. valeant calami: literally, "may quills fare well."

Epigram 80

The bookish Paulus' arcane words obscure his meaning and separate his tone from the easy charm and wit of the epigrammatist.

5. ex libris . . . Sibyllae: The books of the Sibyl, composed in the sixth century BCE and brought into Rome via Cumae during the time of the kings, comprised obscure poems, in Greek hexameters, that gave advice for handling various calamities. These utterances were notoriously difficult to understand and therefore were only consulted by a specially appointed board called, at least in its final form, *quindecimviri sacris faciundis*. **6. Catonis:** Cato the Elder (2nd century BCE) whose Latinity, in comparison with what we think of as the "classical" prose of Rome (Cicero, etc.), is considered archaic, but which itself included archaisms. On Cato's "curious amalgam" of archaisms, colloquialisms, poetic diction, Greek and native rhetorical devices, religious and legalistic formulae, later refined by Cicero and others, see the discussion of L. R. Palmer, *The Latin Language* (London, 1954), 123.

Epigram 81

Muret contemplates becoming a Lucretius (*rerum causas tentare latentes* and *inviaque . . . per loca ferre pedem*) or a Pythagoras (cf. Ov. *Met.* 15.67ff., *magni primordia mundi / et rerum causas, et, quid natura, docebat . . .*). After all, in his preface he promises *seria* for the future, and his conscience is constantly tugging him in that direction (these are *fortia verba*). The power of Cupid, however, is a sure bet to prevail.

3. Erycina: an epithet of Venus derived from the name of the mountain in

Sicily (Eryx) where she had a temple. **longum aeternumque:** Cf. Verg. 11.96–98: *Nos alias hinc ad lacrimas eadem horrida belli / fata vocant: salve aeternum mihi, maxime Palla, / aeternumque vale.* **5. nimium concessimus aevi:** recalling Propertius' complaint against Tullus at 1.6.21: *nam tua non aetas umquam cessavit amori.* **9. contracta fronte:** serious and resolute.

Epigram 82

Everything reminds Pontilianus that *now* is the time for drinking.
  3. esse bibendum: recalling, with the *nunc* of the next line, Hor. *Carm.* 1.37.1: *nunc est bibendum.*

Epigram 83

A propempticon of sorts. Quintius is distressed to be going away, but Muret reminds him that the only way to achieve glory and do good is to go forth into the world.
  1. dea: Fortuna. **8. Dura tulit . . . mari:** more than just Odysseus, we are also to think of Vergil's line about Aeneas at *Aen.* 1.3: *multum ille et terris iactatus et alto.* **10. habet nomen:** The ancients were well aware that heroes who achieve great things still need a chronicler or a "Homer" to be, as Cicero (*Arch.* 10.24) puts it, a herald of their virtue. Both Horace (*Carm.* 4.9.25ff.) and Ovid (*Ex pont.* 4.8.51ff.) use the fame preserved for Agamemnon by the writings of Homer. **11. sors invida:** Fortune is often depicted as jealous of the accomplishments of brave men. See, e.g., Sen. *Herc. fur.* 524: *O Fortuna viris invida fortibus!*

Epigram 84

Muret gives advice to Claude du Bourg, who suffers from melancholy.
  4. nitido . . . ore: a healthy color in the face; cf. Ov. *AA* 3.74: *et perit, in nitido qui fuit ore, colore.*

Epigram 85

On this Catherine and the events mentioned here, see the comments on the next poem.

Epigram 86

The poem, with its address to the traveler, its heroic but deceased subject speaking for herself, the moral lesson drawn from her life, recalls the traditions of *icones, epitaphia,* and hagiographic literature. The specific details of the poem indicate that this refers to St. Catherine of Alexandria, who confronted the Emperor Maxentius, the "tyrant" of *epig.* 85, regarding his violent persecution of Christians. She was of noble birth and well educated, and so outmatched Maxentius in her arguments. He called on scholars and philosophers (Muret's *sophi*), perhaps as many as fifty, to try to refute her arguments, but they failed and became converted to Christianity themselves. Next, Maxentius had her scourged, tortured with fire, and thrown into prison, but still she did not relent. Instead, she so impressed Maxentius' army officers and wife with her endurance and faith, that they too converted. For this they were promptly put to death. Maxentius then asked her to marry him, but she spurned him and declared herself to be the bride of Christ. He ordered that she be put on a torture device that now bears her name: Catherine's Wheel (Muret's *rota*). This contraption used spiked wheels to tear the body of the victim apart. In this case, however, the machine exploded, not harming Catherine, but the executioners instead. The enraged emperor then beheaded her c. 310 CE in Alexandria. The story goes that angels came and carried her body to Mt. Sinai where now stands the church that bears her name. Because of the sharpness and steadfastness of her mind, she became the patron saint of scholars, and her feast day in November attained great popularity in France during the Renaissance.

Epigram 87

Muret is making a play on the mundane and stylistic meanings of *ieiunitas* and *siccitas* (for the latter sense, see the discussion of Cic. *Brutus* 285). A critic accuses him of being "starved" (i.e., jejune, arid, or dull), and that his poems are "dry" (i.e., plain). Using the basic meanings of the same words, Muret retorts that he has noticed that his critic is never dry or starved.

4. Egregia . . . calliditate: or, "with amazing dexterity." **6. semisepultus:** used of bones at Ov. *Her.* 1.55, its only occurrence in classical literature.

Epigram 88

Muret praises the idyllic life of the country and deems it best suited to sharpening the disposition of the poet. Crassus wrongly assumes that refined people live only in the city. For a similar theme, see *eleg.* 3 above and the notes there. The idea behind this and other such poems, both ancient and modern, is that the city, with its noise and constant interruptions, stifles poetic imagination, whereas the countryside fosters harmonious expressions and melodious sounds. The *loc. class.* for these arguments is Horace *Epist.* 2.2.65ff.

1. studiis ... honestis: Muret has in mind Hor. *Epist.* 1.2.32ff., where the poet advises his friend to work on cures for his soul by devoting himself to philosophical study (*rebus honestis,* line 36) and right living (*recte vivendi,* line 41) before it's too late (cf. also Hor. *Epist.* 2.2.141–44). To the person who puts off such endeavors, tellingly, Horace compares the ignorant *rusticus* (line 42) who sits by a river waiting for the water to run out.

Epigram 89

Muret alludes to some sort of calamitous prediction related to poets, but assures Gaurus, who fancies himself a poet, that the prophecy does not apply to him. Gaurus is a stock character taken from Martial (see *epig.* 72 above and note there). Among his many faults, according to Martial, is his propensity for writing bad poetry (see, e.g., 2.89: *carmina quod scribis Musis et Apolline nullo, / laudari debes: hoc Ciceronis habet*).

Epigram 90

Rufinus wants to be a Martial or Catullus by writing *nugae*, but instead of having *sal*, he is witless, and instead of being *doctus,* he dashes off inane verses in incredible number. He produces so many, in fact, that Muret imagines that it would take one hundred days just to get them on paper. The quantity is so massive that the dinner table can barely sustain it. Therefore, despite the fabulous dinners, Muret declines to endure the long torture of listening to Rufinus' recitations.

3. Accubui ... monetque: hendiadys. The guests recline because they have been told that dinner is being served. **7. ab ovo ad mala:** cf. Hor. *Sat.* 1.3.6–7, on a cantor who refuses to quit singing: *si collibuisset, ab ovo / usque ad mala citaret,* "*io Bacche!*"

Epigram 91

It had long become commonplace to bemoan the caprice of Fortune and to portray her as a fickle woman whom only Virtue can disregard (Hor. *Carm.* 3.29.49–56). Pliny the Elder lists most of her standard epithets altogether in one place: *caeca existimata, vaga, inconstans, incerta, varia, indignorumque fautrix.* Other writers add *levis* to the list (e.g., Sen. *Med.* 219; Pub. Syr. *Sent.* 335). Muret creates a tight cohesion and axiomatic tenor in the poem through alliteration (various combinations of t, u, and r) and internal rhyme (*fautura premit* is answered by *nocitura favet*).

Epigram 92

The reader of a book of jurisprudence is taken into confidence in a fashion familiar from the introductory poems of Ovid (e.g., *Tr.* 4.10.132) and Martial (e.g., 1.1), though in this case the book itself must do the speaking because the author is deceased (cf. Mart. 1.70, where the book is sent to perform a *salutatio* on behalf of the author). The long hours that François put into writing the book has hastened his death, but, the book declares, the very same will cause him to live on with abiding fame (cf. Cat. 1.10; Hor. *Carm.* 1.1, 3.30). In the title there is a play on the two meanings of *liber* ("book" and "child"). Because of the date of Connan's death, we can date this poem to the period during or after 1551.
2. patris: the author himself.

Epigram 93

A poet would not normally address the Muse as a sibling, as if she were on equal standing, but the poet does just that, much to the goddess' amusement. The whole poem is a device with which to heap praise upon his mentor.
4. sudum . . . diem: In other words, she cleared his head and release him from his writer's block. **6. Caesar:** Julius Caesar Scaliger.

Epigram 94

Muret picks up a theme from Horace's epistle to Florus (*Epist.* 2.2), with its reproach of the "irritable breed of poets" (*genus irritabile vatum*, 102) who feel they must scribble and recite incessantly to one another. In particular, those who write bad verses (*mala . . . carmina,* 106) are the most likely blissfully and gleefully to inflict compositions on their hapless friends, since to them the writing of poetry is more a parlor trick than a learned enterprise. There is some echo here of Horace's satire on the bore (1.9), who dogged his steps despite his best efforts to shake him. In this poem, the repetition of *huc* and *illuc* at the line ends enhances the feeling of irritation: There is really no escaping this poet.

4. cane . . . peius: cf. Hor. *Ep.* 1.17.30, where the man accustomed to rude and harsh circumstances is said to shun fine clothing "worse than a dog or a snake (*cane peius et angui*). **27. damnata crepuscula:** i.e., far too early; cf. Prop. 4.12.15 (5.11): *damnatae noctes.*

Epigram 95

A play on Paulus' name (meaning "a little"). Paulus gives lettuce for free, but really expects to create obligation. The poet prefers just to go out and pay for the lettuce.

Epigram 96

Muret begins in the first two lines with high praise for the old woman Collina, but we soon find out that her despicable looks and grotesque habits (what the poet sarcastically refers to as her "great grace") provide a somewhat low-brow entertainment. The repellent old woman also allows the poet to exercise his epigrammatic invective (cf. Ov. *Am.* 1.8).

3. anguicomas . . . sorores: the Gorgons; see Ov. *Met.* 4.699: *Gorgonis anguicomae Perseus superator,* and Stat. *Theb.* 12.647: *anguicomae ducunt vexilla sorores.* **7. pompae:** referring to the comic regurgitation to follow. **15. Macte age, macte animo:** The poet eggs on her disgusting display using solemn words usually reserved for encouragement in virtuous living. **18. festiva:** of her looks; cf. Plaut. *Mil. Glor.* 958: *A luculenta et festiva femina.*

Epigram 97

Muret revives the theme that only the wicked can become wealthy (see *epig.* 77 above).

2. **coelo . . . tota via:** cf. Macr. *Sat.* 3.12: *toto coelo errare*, meaning, "to be entirely mistaken."

Epigram 98

A simple joke: The poet encourages Paulus to demonstrate his virtue by giving him a present.
   1. **qui . . . donat:** note the chiasmus, highlighting the contrast between *inferior* and *maior*.

Epigram 99

The ancients often distinguished between scribblers and a learned (*doctus*) poet who hones his craft and labors over every line (cf. Hor. *Epist.* 2.2).
   1. **ex tempore versus:** cf. Cic. *De orat.* 3.194: *solitus est versus hexametros aliosque variis modis atque numeris fundere ex tempore . . .*

Epigram 100

The ancients knew two versions of the myth of Hippolytus and Phaedra, one in which Phaedra confessed her love to Hippolytus and then killed herself out of shame, the other, followed here, in which she falsely accused him and saw his death, whereupon she killed herself.
   5. **terram ore momordit:** as a warrior who falls with a thud to the ground; cf. Verg. *Aen.* 11.418: *procubuit moriens, et humum semel ore momordit.* Also, see Ov. *Met.* 9.61 and Hom. *Il.* 2.418.

Epigram 101

Marcus Iunius Brutus (b. 85 BCE), one of the assassins of Julius Caesar, fell by his own sword after Octavian defeated his army at Philippi in 42 BCE. The Renaissance poets had become interested in historical vignettes of this type and experimented with several genres. Typically, the poet uses the vignette to make some point about virtue or valor, or, as here, to raise broad political issues from the safe distance of history. Muret's primary aim is clear from the two corresponding line endings, lines 4 and 10: "Will I be a slave while you live safe and prosper?" To which comes the adamant reply, in essence, "I will be free, Octavian, against your will."

6. non potuit Patriae: i.e., he would have stabbed Octavian. **7. rutilum:** red from the previous slaughter (line 3 above).

Epigram 102

Phalaecian hendecasyllables. The effect of this poem is satirical. The harmless greeting of line 1, which is echoed with a tone of privileged dismissal in line 17, is overwhelmed and made ridiculous by the immense suffering and poverty of the man described in lines 2–26.

3. recutitus: treated in Roman literature as a mark of shame. See, e.g., Petr. *Satyr.* 68.8: *duo tamen vitia habet, quae si non haberet, esset omnium numerum: recutitus est et stertit.* **5. Orci victima:** that is, he is near death. Muret alludes to the lines of Horace (*Carm.* 2.3.21–28), where the poet laments the fate of every person, rich or poor, as *victima nil miserantis Orci.* **13. harpagare:** "to act like a Harpy," snatching food left over from the day's sacrifices.

Epigram 103

During the Renaissance, the story of the death of Cicero provided much material for poets. The juxtaposition of the final two words suggests that the poet is contemplating the irony occasioned by the simultaneous death of the Republic and its most vocal supporter.

6. te moriente: The antecedent is *libertas.*

Epigram 104

It was customary from Roman days to send gifts to friends on New Year's Day. Poems that accompany such gifts, called *xenia,* are well known from Martial. Muret teases his friend by preempting his objection to his not receiving the customary gift: The poet knows that he loves virtue more than mammon. There may be a touch of sarcasm in Muret's hyperbolic characterization of Lochianus' qualities: *generosas mentes, magnanimi, excelso pectore.*

4. gravis argenti lamina: valuable coins, as opposed to the thinly plated ones mentioned at Ov. *Fast.* 1.209: *et levis argenti lamina crimen erat.*

Epigram 105

A well-worn play on the "poor poet" topos. When Muret digs deep into his purse, the only assets he can extract are his poems. These surpass temporal treasures.
6. Attalicae: Attalus III, king of Pergamon during the 2nd century BCE, proverbial for his wealth (see, e.g., Hor. *Carm.* 2.18.1–8). He is said to have discovered the art of weaving clothes from threads of gold. **8. Pactoli:** a river of Lydia from which much gold was drawn. **9. Quidnam . . . hiatus:** cf. Hor. *AP* 138: *Quid dignum tanto feret hic promissor hiatu?*

Epigram 106

Reminiscent of Hor. *Carm.* 1.9 (note the repeated echo of Horace's *ligna super foco*). There too the suggested cure for the cold is wine.
6. silva . . . opes: used of acorns at Mart. 11.41.3–4; cf. also Sen. *Phaed.* 538–39: *silva nativas opes / et opaca dederant antra nativas domos.* **7. pigro lentescant marmore rivi:** cf. Verg. *Aen.* 7.28: *lento luctantur marmore tonsae.* **13. genio indulgere:** To this phrase cf. *eleg.* 3.35, *genioque litare,* and the note there.

Epigram 107

The book's *sphragis* or seal, nicely concluded with the word *exieris*.
5. Mureti . . . de gente: not a blood relation of Muret, but, as a student of Muret, a literary descendant.

M. ANTONII MURETI EPISTOLARUM LIBELLUS
EPISTLES

1. *Ad Nicolaum Viennensem Epistola*

Inclyta nobilium soboles, Nicolae, parentum,
Qui iam nunc ipso ex aetatis limine signa
Virtutis praebes nobis manifesta futurae,
Nimirum sapis, et rem recte intelligis unus:
Qui, licet antiquis ortus natalibus, haud te 5
Ante tamen ponis reliquis, sed fronte modesta
Alloqueris cunctos vultuque humanus amico,
Non ulli renuis dextram praebere fidelem.
At quidam contra nullis maioribus orti,
Ore tamen tumido voces efflare superbas 10
Aequalesque suos audent contemnere, tanquam
Indignos queis sese aequali foedere iungant.
Quos tu deridens, inter nihil esse, parente
Quo sit quisque creatus, ais, dum sit modo verae
Virtutis studiosus ametque in rebus honestis 15
Ponere labentis fatalia tempora vitae.
Cui non Sicaniae notus dominator opimae,
Qui de figlina est ad regni evectus habenas?
At contra Persei, qui claram rexerat olim
Pallenen, natus, fortunae ludibrium, amplos 20
Inflabat folles, et regis filius, unco
Impositam incudi versabat forcipe massam.
Quid? non et matris captivae abiecta propago,
Cui regni flamma index circum tempora fulsit,
Regali sedit solio? Quid stemmata iactas? 25
Num pueri regum parte enascuntur eadem
Qua mendicorum? nunquid communis utrisque
Materia est? nunquid morbis obnoxius aeque est,
Quem lana Assyrio velat medicata veneno,
Principibus proavis claroque ex sanguine natum, 30
Et sub Aquitanis sordet qui bardocucullis,
De peronato genitus patre? nonne sorores
Noctigenae, vitas hominum quae pollice versant,
Sunt aeque immites generosis vilibus aeque?
Quidnam igitur praestat mendico hic nobilis isti? 35
Aut quid nobilitas tandem est, nisi fumus inanis?
Nam si vim verbi inspicias, et nobile scortum

Epistles

1. *A Letter to Nicolaus de Vienne*

Nicolaus, famous child of noble parents,
who already now, at the very start of your life,
exhibit clear signs to us of your future virtue,
you are very wise, and you alone see clearly how things are:
Although you are the scion of a well-established family, in no way
Do you set yourself before others. Instead, with modesty
you address everyone, and are polite and affable;
you do not refuse to extend a trusty handshake to anyone.
But certain people, by contrast, who have been born into families no greater,
arrogantly blast forth haughty words,
and they dare to hold in contempt even their own equals, as if
they are unworthy of a friendly association.
You scoff at them, and say that it does not matter
who anyone's parents are, so long as he pursues true virtue
and endeavors to spend the last allotted
days of his life in honorable pursuits.
To whom is not known the tyrant of fertile Sicily,
who was elevated to the reins of his kingdom from a lowly station?
But in contrast the son of Perses, who once had ruled famous Pallene,
became the butt of Fortune's joke, and, though a king's son,
was blowing the bellows full, and turning the lump
of metal placed on an anvil with hooked tongs.
What? Has not a slave woman's wretched offspring sat on
a royal throne, while around his temples the flaming
sign of his power gleamed? Why do you boast about lineage?
Sons of kings are begotten in same way as
sons of the poor, right? Their constitution is the same,
isn't it? Is he not equally subject to diseases,
the one born from princely stock and famous blood,
whom wool stained with Tyrian purple covers,
as the filthy fellow under his Aquitanian cagoule,
sired by some country-bumpkin in old leather boots? Surely the night-born
daughters, who turn the lives of men with their thumb,
are just as cruel to the nobles as they are to the low-born?
In regard to what, then, does the well-born surpass the poor?
Or what in the end is nobility but empty smoke?
For if you examine the force of the word, sometimes a slut

Dicitur et latro nonnunquam nobilis; imo
Nomine ita accepto, Pornus quoque nobilis ipse est.
Sed nempe insanit vulgus multoque veratro 40
Indiget, indignos alienis laudibus ornans.
Qui se non ullo deturpat crimine quique
Viribus ingenuas totis amplectitur artes,
Is mihi, sit quamvis genitore creatus egeno,
Nobilis est; at qui, vitiorum mole gravatus, 45
Nil praeter statuas et avorum nomina iactat,
Si verum excutias, longe abiectissimus ille est.

2. *Ad Ianum Antonium Baifium*

Iane, mei cordis longe pars maxima, quocum
Dulce mihi est totos crebro componere soles,
Dum tu aut Niliacae meditaris funera Thisbes,
Inficiens atro candentia poma colore,
Aut opus eximium numeris sublimibus aptas, 5
Syrmate conspicuus picturatoque cothurno;
Carmine nos humili nostros includimus ignes,
Aut brevibus scriptis dulces affamur amicos,
Aut vitiis genuinum infigimus. Omnia nos haec
Parvula inaudaces; tibi fas maiora parare, 10
Cui totus se Helicon totusque recludit Apollo.
Ad vires se quenque suas componere[1] verum est.

3. *Ad Stephanum Iodellum*

Semina sunt quaedam nascentibus insita nobis,
Queis, duce natura, ad varias impellimur artes.
Ille fori rabiem vesanaque iurgia laudat,
Et pavidos grata defendit voce clientes,
Impatiens oti; contra hic sulcare carinis 5
Regna tridentiferi gaudet patris et, trabe vasta,
Visere longinquo terras sub sole iacentes.
Prodigus hic vitae violentis ducitur armis
Gaudet et hostili stagnantes sanguine campos

is called noble, and sometimes a thief. Indeed,
if he takes up the name, Pornus himself is noble.
But to be sure the masses are crazy, in need of strong medicine,
when they honor those who are unworthy of others' praises.
The one who does not taint himself with any sin,
who embraces his natural talents with all his might,
that one, to me, although of lowly birth,
is noble. But the one who, weighed down with vices,
brags constantly about the statues and the renown of his ancestors,
if you want to know the truth, is by far the most wretched.

2. *To Jean Antoine de Baïf*

Jean, by far the greatest part of my heart, with whom
I often like to compare brightly burning suns,
as you meditate the death of Thisbe of the Nile,
staining the white fruit with the blood-red color,
or adapt an exceptional deed to lofty measures,
distinguished, as you are, in the tragic robe and colorful buskin—
I keep my fiery passions in a humble poem,
and address sweet friends in short letters,
or grind my teeth against vices. I am timorous
and so limit myself to these little things; rightly you are intent on greater things,
for to you Helicon and Apollo have revealed themselves whole.
It is fitting that each person adjust himself to his own abilities.

3. *To Étienne Jodelle*

There are certain seeds which are implanted within us at birth,
which, with nature as guide, drive us to various arts.
That one praises the bustle and mad wrangling of the market,
and defends his scared clients with his pleasant voice,
unable to endure leisure. In contrast, this one enjoys cutting the kingdoms
of the trident-bearing father with his keel, and with his huge vessel
to visit lands lying beneath a faraway sun.
This one, careless with his life, is drawn by violent arms
and enjoys seeing the fields covered with the enemy's blood,

Aspicere et litui sonitu recreatur acuto. 10
Ille sui nunquam fines excedere agelli
Ausus, amat tacitis deducere passibus aevum,
Proscindens magnae gremium genitricis et altis
Pinguia Triptolemi committens munera sulcis.
Nos Musae, Iodelle, tenent genitorque Lyaeus, 15
Quem rigidi ambiguo venerantur numine Thraces
Et Nymphae celeres et capripedes Satyrisci.
Nos et luce nova lustrat dum Delius orbem
Et iubar auricomum tremulis dum fluctibus abdit,
Addictos studiis videt intentosque labori. 20
Sed tua te virtus, animi te vividus ardor
Aequales longe ante alios unum abripit; uni
Purpureis dictant Musae tibi talia labris,
Qualia pulchricomus choreas ducentibus ipsis
Cantat et ad numerum simul ipse movetur Apollo. 25
Felix ingenii, viridi cui detur ab aevo
Longaevos aequare senes et carmine dio
Demulcere animos, iam te ipse tumescit alumno
Sequana, iam virides resonant tua nomina ripae.
Perge, agedum, neu te venienti subtrahe famae. 30
Non te Parca feret totum, non totus obibis
Parsque tui effugiet ferales optima flammas.
Musa suos vetat ipsa mori: dat vivere Musa
Perpetuo, et famam memorem per saecla propagat;
Caelo Musa beat. famam tibi Musa perennem 35
Protrahet et caelo te olim, Iodelle, beabit.

33 ipsa 1834, om. 1789

and is refreshed by the piercing sound of the trumpet.
That fellow has never dared leave the borders of his little field,
and loves to pass his life with quiet steps,
trenching the bosom of the great mother and entrusting
the rich gifts of Triptolemus to the deep furrows.
The Muses hold us, Jodelle, and father Lyaeus,
whom the swift nymphs and goat-footed satyrs
venerate along with the twofold divinity of rugged Thrace.
And while he illumines the world with fresh morning light,
and while he tucks away his golden-haired beam in the shimmering waves,
Delian Apollo sees us engrossed in our pursuits, intent on our labor.
But your virtue and the lively enthusiasm of your mind
snatch you away by yourself far beyond your peers.
To you only do the Muses with their deep-red lips communicate such things,
as many things as the lovely-haired Apollo sings to those leading the dances,
while he himself is moved to join them.
Rich in talent, to whom it is granted to equal
long-lived old men in your flourishing days, and to soothe souls
with divine song: Now the Seine itself swells because you
are its child, now its green banks resound with your name.
Continue, carry on, do not shrink from the coming fame.
Fate will not carry you off whole, you will not completely die;
the best part of you will escape the funereal flames.
The Muse does not allow her own to die; she grants them to live
forever, and multiplies their mindful fame throughout the ages;
she blesses them in heaven. For you, Jodellus, the Muse draws forth
eternal fame, and someday she will bless you in heaven.

COMMENTARY ON THE EPISTLES

1. TO NICOLAUS DE VIENNE

The precise identity of this Nicolaus is unknown, though it is clear from the letter itself that he is very young when it is being written (though old enough to extend a handshake) and that he belongs to the nobility (the de Vienne house was quite illustrious). Muret praises the boy for discovering one of the great truths of life, that *true* nobility stems from one's character and accomplishments, and not from one's birth. The *exempla* with which Muret supports his maxim, inasmuch as they are meant to counter those who rest on their social rank, all deal with individuals whose lives have belied their original station. Nicolaus, however, does not fit into this category, since he can claim nobility both by birth and by disposition, a rare combination. The theme of the "nobility of virtue" was a favorite in antiquity (see, e.g., Juv. *Sat.* 8.20: *Nobilitas sola est atque unica virtus*) and even rose to the level of doctrine among the Stoics.

1. Nicolae: At the expense of the scansion, since properly it should be *Nicolae*. **17: dominator:** i.e., Agathocles, Tyrant of Syracuse, in Sicily, from 317 to c. 304, and then after that a self-appointed king. He had been a potter, which was his father's trade, but after distinguishing himself in the army, he seized the government of Syracuse by force. **19–20: Persei . . . natus:** Perses was the last king of Macedonia before it was conquered by Aemilius Paulus in 168 BCE. His son Alexander was carried away as captive to Rome while a child; his younger brother Philip, whom Perses had adopted, also shared his fate (see Livy 40–44; Polyb. 24, 26–27, 29). **Fortunae ludibrium:** or, "a toy of Fortune," borrowed from Cic. *Par. Stoic.* 1.9. **21–22: unco . . . forcipe massam:** For similar phrasing, cf. Verg. *Georg.* 4.175: *Cyclopes versant tenaci forcipe ferrum;* ibid., 2.540: *impositos incudibus ensis;* idem, *Aen.* 8.453: *versantque tenaci forcipe massam;* Cic. *ND* 1.54: *sine follibus et incudibus.* **23. abiecta propago:** i.e., Servius Tullius, who, according to Livy (1.39), was captured at Corniculum and taken back to the king's palace at Rome. Livy relates the story that while the young Servius lay asleep in the palace, his head blazed with fire in the sight of many people. This was taken as a sign that he should be raised as royalty. **29. Assyrio . . . medicata veneno:** Cf. Plin. *NH*

12.15: *Malus Assyria, quam alii Medicam vocant, venenis medetur.* Also, Verg. *Georg.* 2.465 (with the word *lana*). Here, *veneno* does not have a pejorative connotation, but is instead equivalent to *colore* (cf. Festus, p. 516 Lindsay). **31. bardocucullis:** a woolen cowl made in Gaul (Mart. 1.53.5 speaks of its oily fleece that contaminates finer garments). **37. nobile scortum:** Livy's phrase to describe Hispala Faecenia, the prostitute who exposed the Bacchanalia affair (39.9.5; cf. Macrob. *Sat.* 1.10.13). **40. veratro:** hellebore ("Christmas rose"), the roots of which, in small quantities (notice that Muret recommends a strong dose), was thought by the Greeks to cure madness. In Greek mythology, Melampus used hellebore to cure the madness of King Proetus' daughters, who lost their minds and roamed wildly through the mountains and the desert of Tiryns, thinking they were cows. **46. statuas et avorum nomina:** an allusion to Seneca's statement (*Epist.* 44.5) that famous ancestors, even ones worthy of a statue, do not make one noble (on this see *epig.* 29).

2. TO JEAN ANTOINE DE BAÏF

This poem varies the *recusatio* motif, using de Baïf's grander poetic ambitions as a foil to the simpler aims of Muret. To underscore the meagerness of his own efforts he chooses epithets such as "humble" and "short," while contrasting Baïf's interest in epic (the reference to Thisbe makes us think of Ovid's *Metamorphoses*) and drama. The hint of a refusal to scale greater heights, the essence of the *recusatio*, comes at the last few lines of the poem, where Muret says that he has chosen his genre according to the limits of his own disposition. What is curious about this poem is its anticipation of Baïf's career, rather than its reference to published work. To this point, when Muret's book was published, Baïf had published only his *Amours* to Méline (1552), which he then followed with similar sonnets to Francine (1555). In fact, it is truly odd that the genres Baïf pursued later in his career, that is, after the publication of Muret's poetry, receive mention already here, while the sonnets are passed over. For example, Muret attributes to Baïf composition in tragedy, but his work in tragedy (a translation of Sophocles *Antigone* in Alexandrines) was not published until 1572 as part of the *Les Œuvres en rime*. Muret's comments indicate that Baïf was composing such works long before their publication and sharing them with his friends.

2. totos . . . soles: The reference is to the full intensity of the sun on a cloudless day. Cf. Mart. 10.12.7: *i precor et totos avida cute combibe soles.* **componere:** Note its repetition in the same metrical portion of the second and last lines, to draw further attention to the comparison (and thus the difference) between the two men. But at the same time it's a tribute to Muret's poetic abilities.

3. **Thisbes:** Muret is thinking of the story of Pyramus and Thisbe as told by Ov. *Met.* 4.56–116, but how this relates to Baïf is not clear. Leroux believes Muret could have in mind a narrative poem entitled *Meurier,* first published in the *Les Œuvres en rime* mentioned above (but written much earlier). **9. genuinum:** "grinders": cf. Juv. 5.69. **12. Ad vires . . . componere:** an aphorism manifesting itself in many forms in ancient literature, but summed up nicely in Cato's advice (*Disticha* 4.33), *Quod potes id tempta.* Cf. also Hor. *AP* 38–40 for the same guidance.

3. TO ÉTIENNE JODELLE

Another letter of tribute to a member of the Pléiade. Muret begins with the commonplace about the variety of innate impulses within human beings that drive them to choose their path of life. Poets are driven by the Muses and Lyaeus (Bacchus, essentially) to work day and night on their craft, but Jodelle, standing out among the rest, receives special attention from the Muses, who sing to him the secret communications derived from Apollo himself. For his exceptional talent, Jodelle has won for himself a kind of poetic immortality.

14. triptolemi . . . munera: i.e., agriculture. Demeter taught her arts to Triptolemus and commissioned him to ride about the earth teaching all nations. **16. ambiguo . . . numine Thraces:** Silenus, who is "twofold" in the sense that he is always depicted as riding on his ass. **32. Parsque . . . flammas:** The "best part" is one's immortal self that escapes the pyre, be it one's soul or one's name made famous by achievement. Both ideas appear to be in view here, as in the epilogue of Ovid's *Metamorphoses* (15.875–76: *parte tamen meliore mei super alta perennis / astra ferar, nomenque erit indelebile nostrum*). Cf also Hor. *Od.* 3.30.6–7: *non omnis moriar multaque pars mei / vitabit Libitinam;* Ov. *Am.* 1.15.41–2.: *ergo etiam cum me supremus adederit ignis, / vivam, parsque mei multa superstes erit.* In exile, Ovid (*Trist.* 3.3.60) wished for the opposite: *effugiatque avidos pars mihi nulla rogos.* **33. Musa . . . mori:** a play on Hor. *Od.* 4.8.28. Horace affirms the power of the poetic Muse to give eternal fame to worthy heroes, while Muret speaks of the fame of the poet himself.

M. ANTONII MURETI ODAE
ODES

1. *Ad Iohannem Auratum, virum utraque lingua eruditissimum*

Aurate, gentis grande decus meae,
Qui, tensa docta fila legens manu,
Saeclis inexpertum vetustis
Ambrosio iacis ore nectar,
    Quid esse causae suspicer invida 5
Suis quod ortos Gallia finibus
Aut odit aut spernit poëtas,
Usque favens peregrinitati?
    Atqui vetustis temporibus suos
Et fovit Hellas, et Latium suos. 10
Quae pravitas nos mentis unos,
Ne faciamus idem, coërcet?
    Nihil daturum me auribus hic tuis
Velim arbitreris, sim licet et fide
Pridem tibi et communitate 15
Sanguinis et patriae alligatus.
    Nil ista sed me commoveant tamen,
Aurate, palpo percutere inscium,
Ut laudibus te ornare pergam,
Ni tua me prope singularis 20
    Virtus moveret. Nil faciles tibi
Musae negarunt, seu libeat fide
Sacrare Graeca, seu Latina
Nobilium inclyta facta regum.
    Hac arte quondam quas sibi copias 25
Dirces alumnus, quod peperit decus?
Contra, tuos mercede iusta
Quisnam hodie decorat labores?
    Praeiudicatae quod nisi nos premat
Auctoritatis pondus, erit nihil, 30
Cur non, metu plane remoto,
Cedere te inficiemur illi.
    Sed nempe virtus temporibus iacet
Depressa nostris; hinc fit, ut unici
Virtutis altores poetae 35
Clade etiam simili premantur.

1. *To Jean Dorat, a Man Most Learned in Both Greek and Latin*

Dorat, great glory of my clan,
you who, plucking taut strings with learned hand,
utter with ambrosial mouth nectar
previously unknown to the generations of old.
What can explain why grudging
France hates poets sprung from within her own borders,
or spurns them, while constantly favoring the foreign?
In contrast, in ancient days Greece
nurtured her own, Latium hers.
What warped thinking makes only us
not do the same?
Please don't think that I am going
to flatter you, even though I was bound to you
long ago in the bonds of trust
and in the community of blood and country.
In no way do those things sway me
to undertake to extol you with praises—
I am not good at flattering—
but only your near singular
virtue does. The facile Muses deny
nothing to you, whether you desire
to celebrate the famous deeds of noble kings
on Greek or Latin lyre.
By this skill once what riches did the child
of Dirce obtain for himself, what glory?
In contrast, who today honors
your labors with just reward?
But if we are not swayed by presuppositions,
there will be no reason,
once the fear is gone,
not to believe that you are his equal.
But in reality virtue lies suppressed
and silenced these days; hence it happens that the poets,
the only ones who foster virtue,
suffer a similar fate.

2. In discessu Danielis Schleicheri, filii longe dulcissimi

Descende caelo et iam mihi lugubres
Regina dicta Calliope modos,
Quibus furentem, eheu, sub imis
Visceribus retegam dolorem.
    Dic, diva, carmen, quale per herbidi   5
Ripas Caystri candidulum caput
Traiectus immiti sagitta
Voce canit moriente cycnus:
    Aut qualia olim coniuge Thracius
Rapta sacerdos dixerat, ad sonum   10
Quorum et ferae immanes quierunt
Et rabidi posuere venti.
    Ah! unde questus incipiam meos?
Quae prima se vox pectore proferet
Iterque laxabit querelis?   15
Nam meus hinc Daniel recedit.
    Nunquamne posthac, o iuvenum decus,
Quotquot, iugales dum citat aureos
Terramque collustrat iacentem,
Ignivomo videt ore Phoebus,   20
    Nunquamne posthac conspiciam tuos,
Schleichere, vultus? cur igitur moror
Nec tristis invisaeque vitae
Fila ferox inimica rumpo?
    Iam iam valete, o gaudia et o ioci,   25
Et quicquid antehac dulce fuit mihi;
Venite iam fletus perennes
Perpetuique venite planctus.
    Innixa ramis Daulias ut novis,
Cui cautus auceps furtifica manu   30
Pullos tenellos involavit,
Moesta sedet geminatque questus,
    Et se doloris vulnere conficit,
Sic ipse postquam desiero tui
Aspectu amato atque expetito,   35
Posse animum exsatiare vultus,
    Eheu, quibus tunc fluctibus opprimar!

2. On the Departure of Daniel Schleicher, the Sweetest Son by Far

Descend from heaven, Queen Calliope, and dictate now to me
the plaintive strains, with which I may bury
in my guts my raging—ah raging!—grief.
Speak the poem, goddess, the sort the swan sings
with dying voice when pierced
by a cruel arrow in its dear white head
along the banks of the grassy Kara-Su;
or the sort the Thracian priest once spoke,
after his wife was snatched away in death, at the sound
of which the wild spirits of the dead grew quiet,
and the raging winds abated.
Ah! whence shall I begin my complaints?
What first word will spring forth from my heart
and show the way for my plaintive song?
My Daniel has departed.
Never after this, glory of youths—
as many as Phoebus with his fiery face sees,
when he goads on his golden steeds,
and illumines the wide earth—
never after this will I see
your face, Schleicher? Why then do I delay
and not bravely break the cruel threads
of this sad and hated life?
Now farewell, joys and laughter,
and whatever before this was sweet to me;
welcome, endless weeping,
welcome constant tears.
As the nightingale, resting on the young branches,
her tender chicks assailed
by the cautious fowler with his thieving hand,
sits sad, and repeats her complaints,
consuming herself with the wound of grief;
so too I myself,
after I can no longer sate my mind
with the beloved and longed-for sight of your face,
with what floods will I then be overwhelmed!
How many firebrands of grief will I endure!

Quantas dolorum perpetiar faces!
Quam saepe, te ut spectare possim,
Morte mea cupiam pacisci! 40
    Lenito crebris haec mala litteris,
O nate, saltem, neve animo patrem
Depone, qui, dum vivet, unum
Pectore te retinebit arcto.

3. *Ad Claudium Voesium*

    Claudi, integello pectore amabilis,
Qui mente solus disicis a mea
Acerba curarum benignis
Vocibus alloquioque dulci;
    Non sic timenda est in Libyae iugis 5
Quae, matre rupta, vipera nascitur;
Non scorpii cauda minaces,
Non geniti sub aquis chelydri;
    Non herba tetro noxia gramine,
Quamcunque tellus Thessalis educat; 10
Non illa quam stillante rictu
Spuma canis genuit triformis,
    Dira; ut latentis tela Calumniae
Quam Dite tellus sustulit ex patre,
Nefariam insontesque fictis 15
Criminibus premere efficacem.
    Haec conglobatis suspicionibus
Beli nepotem perdidit, haec malae
Adegit ad potum cicutae
Innocuum sophiae parentem. 20
    Dum Phoebus Indos exoriens novo
Afflabit igni, Beticolas cadens,
Non ulla Thesidae modesti
Saecla pudicitiam tacebunt.
    Aggressa blandis hunc sua fraudibus 25
Noverca pellax, quid, iuvenum decus,
Labentis istud ver iuventae
Perdis, ait, tenerumque florem?

How often will I bargain with Death,
just so I can see you!
At least ease these pains by writing often,
child, or don't forget your father,
who, as long as he lives,
will hold you and you alone locked in his heart.

3. *To Claude Voesie*

Claude, worthy of love with your pure heart,
you who alone dispel from my mind
bitter cares with kind
words and sweet address:
Not like this must we fear the vipers born in the hills
of Libya, after bursting from their mother;
not the tail of the menacing scorpion,
nor the serpents born beneath the waters of the sea;
not the harmful herb in the loathsome grass,
whatever the Thessalian earth produces;
not the foam, which the three-headed dog
produces from his drooling jaw;
as we must fear the dire darts of hidden Calumny,
which Earth drew up from father Dis,
depraved and effectual in crushing
the guiltless with invented charges.
She ruined the descendant of Belus
with trumped-up suspicions;
she drove the harmless father of wisdom
to the drink of hemlock.
So long as Phoebus arises and breathes on India
with his fresh fire and sets in Spain,
no generations will be quiet about the chastity
of the son of Theseus. His own deceitful stepmother
addressed him with these coaxing lies: "Why, glory of youths,
do you waste that springtime of passing youth,"
she says, "and the tender flower?"
"Why do you hunt wild beasts that hide in caves

 Cur editorum per iuga montium,
Antris latentes persequeris feras?   30
Tibi absque telis, retibusque
Praeda domi melior parata est.
 Accede, neu te paeniteat mei
Fructus pudoris carpere primulos;
Non me ore natura indecoro   35
Protulit, immeritamve amari.
 Quid vana legum vincula te movent?
Natura nullos concubitus vetat,
Sed compedes vanissima istas
Cura hominum sibi fabricata est.   40
 Nil ille motus, desine vocibus
Tentare mentem spurcidicis meam,
O spurca, et in tauros furenti
Progenies genitrice digna.
 Haec fatus in tesqua et nemorum abditos   45
Abit recessus, gesa manu rotans:
Vadentem odora et vis sagacium
Anteit et sequitur Laconum.
 Quid innocenti sed iuveni tamen
Servasse tanto a crimine profuit   50
Mentem, si apud patrem reversum
Impia plus potuit noverca?
 Cuius querelis ille adeo integer
Per vota patris filius occidit,
Cautes et eliso marinas   55
Imbuit emoriens cerebro.
 Nec me venenis non petiit suis
Illa ipsa mendax anguipedum soror,
Mendaciorum procreatrix,
Perpetua et scelerum architecta,   60
 Sed dexter illi me eripuit deus,
Umbone tanquam me triplici tegens;
Cuius memor nunquam canoris
Versibus hunc celebrare mittam.

along the ridges of high mountains?
Away from your weapons and your traps
a better reward is prepared for you at home.
Come, don't deny me to pluck
the first fruits of your modesty.
Nature has endowed me with a pretty
face, worthy to be loved.
Why do the empty bonds of law influence you?
Nature prohibits no intercourse,
but people's hollow anxiety
has created these shackles for itself."
He was not moved: "Stop tempting
my mind with your foul words, foul woman!
child worthy of your mother
and her taurean passion!"
Once he said this he withdrew into the wild regions
and the hidden retreats of groves, twirling his spear in his hand.
And a pack of keen-scented Spartan hounds
surrounds him as he goes.
But what did it avail this innocent
but young boy to keep his mind from such a great
crime, if with his father, upon his return,
the impious stepmother had more sway?
By her complaints such a chaste son died,
through the vows of his father,
and in his dying stained the rocks
along the shore with his splattered brains.
But that lying sister of the snake-footed giants,
inventor of lies and ever the architect of sin,
did herself assail me with her poison,
yet God looked favorably on me and took me unto himself,
as if covering me with a triple shield.
Ever mindful of him I will never cease
to celebrate him in song.

4. Ad Petrum Ronsardum, Gallicorum poetarum facile principem

Ronsarde, Aonii pectinis arbiter,
Qui princeps resonum solicitas ebur
Ventorumque minas et celeres potens
Lapsus sistere fluminum,
    Quando te reducem Vindocino ex agro   5
Cernemus, veterum turba sodalium?
Quis te, quis niveo vellere conditus,
Nobis restituet dies?
    Qui desiderio perpete nunc tui,
Heu quae non facimus vota? quibus sacros   10
Postes muneribus cingere parcimus?
Quas non concipimus preces?
    O saltem interea, quidquid agis, memor
Nostri vive. ita te curribus aureis
Rumor per liquidum gemmeus aëra,   15
Spectandum populis vehat.

5. Ad Nicolaum Denisotum, comitem Alsinoum

Bacchus poetas et facit et fovet,
Bacchus poetarum ingenia excitat;
Bacchus novem praestat puellis
Et melior potiorque Phoebo est.
    Ter terna quisquis pocula sumpserit   5
Dulcis Falerni sentiet hic sibi
Calere divino furore
Carmina ad eicienda mentem.
    Sic laetus olim vixit Anacreon,
Cinctus virenti tempora pampino,   10
Sic Ennius semper madenti
Gutture carmina funditabat.
    Algentis at quos potus aquae iuvat,
Frigent eorum carmina nec ferunt
Aetatem. Ades mecumque plenis   15
Hic cyathis, Nicolae, certa.

4. To Pierre Ronsard, Easily the Prince of the French Poets

Ronsard, master of the Aonian pecten,
you who best handle the resounding ivory,
who possess the power to calm the menacing winds
and the rushing waterfalls:
When will we, your crowd of old friends, see
you return from the fields of Vendôme?
What day will restore you to us,
what day marked with white wool?
What vows do we not make—
alas!—we who desire you constantly?
What sacred door posts do we neglect to gird with gifts?
What prayers do we not pray?
At least in the meantime, whatever you do,
remember us. It is my wish that studded fame carry
you in a golden chariot through the bright sky
as a spectacle for the people.

5. To Nicolas Denisot, Friend from Alsinois

Bacchus both makes poets and nurtures them;
Bacchus excites the talents of poets.
Bacchus surpasses the nine Muses,
and is better and more powerful than Phoebus.
Whoever takes up three times three cups
of sweet Falernian wine, will feel his mind
growing warm with the divine madness,
ready to issue songs.
Thus Anacreon once lived happily
having encircled his temples with the green vine,
thus Ennius always poured forth songs
from his sodden throat.
But the poems of those who like to drink cold water
are frigid, and they do not have
a long life. Come, Nicolaus,
let's do battle with the ladles.
Each of us will sing songs from our throats bathed in wine

    Miranda seris carmina posteris
Uterque loto gutture concinet.
O dulce tormentum, o gravatis
Certa quies animis, Lyaee!   20
    Quaenam, imperiti, pocula quaerimus
Vocalis undae? quod bifidi duplex
Montis cacumen somniamus?
Quam petimus, fatui, Hippocrenen?
    Haec Hippocrene est, unicus hic liquor   25
Vates stupendos efficere evalet.
En, par pari gratus repende:
Hoc ego te cyatho saluto.

6. *Ad Ianum Tilium Paraeneticon*

    Modus tenellis quis tibi ab unguibus
Vitae tenendus, Iane, sit accipe,
Benigna quem Natura finxit
Ingenio puerum sequaci.
    Primum ergo amorem numinis intimo   5
Serva usque fixum pectore et illius
Ad iussa te compone: nulla est
Sors nocitura deum colenti.
    Fac et parentes sis pius in tuos
Honore et illos promerito colas: 10
Impune nunquam sprevit ullus,
A quibus ortus erat, parentes.
    Fas et magistris, sint licet asperi
Nonnunquam, honorem reddere debitum.
Si quando te obiurgent, id illos,   15
Te quod ament, facere arbitrator.
    Nam primula aetas innumeris rapi
Affectionum turbinibus solet;
Frenari eam quare et magistri
Assiduo imperio necesse est.   20
    Nil turpe factu dicere fas puta:
Quae quisque gaudet dicere, eis quoque
Gaudere patrandis putatur.

that later generations must marvel over.
Sweet torture, sure rest
for heavy minds, Lyaeus!
What cups of a song-inspiring spring,
you half-wits, do we desire?
Of what cloven mount's twin peak do we dream?
What Hippocrene, you simpletons, do we seek?
This is our Hippocrene; this liquid alone
has the ability to inspire sacred poets.
Look, return the favor as a grateful equal to an equal:
I salute you with this ladle of wine.

6. *Exhortation to Jan Tilius*

Hear, Jan, what mode of life you should uphold
from the earliest days of your life,
you whom kindly Nature fashioned
as a youth with an inquisitive spirit.
First, keep the love of God
fixed deep within your heart,
and obey his commands.
No turn of fortune will harm
the one who worships God.
Be pious to your parents and
honor them as they deserve;
no one spurns his
birth parents with impunity.
Likewise give due respect to your teachers,
though they are sometimes harsh.
If ever they rebuke you, understand
that they do it because they love you.
For frequently youthful age is caught up
in the innumerable whirlwinds of the affections;
it's up to teachers, therefore,
to constantly rein it in.
Consider it wrong to say what is indecent to do.
What one enjoys saying, people figure

Indicium sua cuique lingua est.
   Disce et sodales quos tibi debeas 25
Parare, nam omnes consimiles fere
Evadere illis assolemus,
Queiscum agimus; neque pestilenti
   Si quis frequenter vixerit in domo,
Nec si in malorum coetibus, ut sibi 30
Contagio nil obsit, unquam
Arte cavere valebit ulla.
   Vide ergo, ut illos, Iane, pares tibi,
Queis esse te olim consimilem voles.
At immodestos, quos videbis, 35
Et cane peius et angue vita.
   Laborem amato, dum iuvenis viges,
Ut otieris, cum senium premet;
Laboris osores nec ulla
Laus sequitur neque splendor ullus. 40
   Haec si sub imo pectore clauseris
Praecepta, Tili, spes bona nos tenet,
Tuis fore ut maioribus te
Persimilem videamus olim.

that one enjoys doing as well.
One's tongue is one's informant.
Learn too what kind of friends you should
obtain. For we usually turn out like the ones
we spend time with.
If anyone lives for a long time in an unhealthy home,
or in the company of unwholesome people,
in no way can he avoid becoming contaminated from them.
See to it, therefore, Jan, that you acquire those friends
whom you wish to be like.
But the immodest people that you see,
avoid worse than a dog or a snake.
Work hard while you are young
so that you can enjoy leisure when old age
weighs down on you.
No praise or glory
comes to those who hate work.
If you will shut these precepts deep into your heart,
Tilius, we have good hope
that one day you will be
very much like your parents.

Commentary on the Odes

1. Ode to Jean Dorat
Alcaic Strophe

Muret complains that France has not suitably recognized and honored its poets, particularly Jean Dorat (Latinized as "Auratus" from the alternate spelling "Daurat"), whom he considers the equal or better of any poet of Greece or Rome. This is a topic that Muret touches on in his preface as well. There he singles out Dorat as the teacher of many of the great vernacular poets and members of the Pléiade, Ronsard, de Baïf, du Bellay, and so on, while noting that Dorat himself has yet to publish his own Greek and Latin poems (presumably because France does not value poetry originating from within its own borders). If he were to publish them, Muret asserts, he "would make it so that France would not begrudge Italy her Pontanos, Sannazaros, Molzas, and Flaminios." For more on Dorat, see "Names" above.

1. gentis grande decus meae: cf. Hor. *Carm.* 2.17.3–4, *Maecenas, mearum / grande decus columenque rerum,* and Mart. 9.1.8, *Flaviae decus gentis.* The precise nature of the relationship between Dorat and Muret is not known. **2. tensa ... fila:** i.e., of the lyre. **3. Saeclis inexpertum vetustis:** Although *inexpertum* can be active, here it is used in a passive sense: This nectar has never been tasted or tried in previous generations. So Statius (4.5.10–11) describes the songs of young birds in the springtime: *nunc volucrum novi / questus inexpertumque carmen.* **4. Ambrosio ... ore:** i.e., having a divine quality about it; cf. Vergil's *ambrosiae comae* (*Aen.* 1.403). **nectar:** For this figurative sense (= sweet poetry), see Pers. prol. 14: *cantare credas Pegaseium nectar.* Other poets refer to their own melodies as "nectar"; see Pindar *Ol.* 7.7ff.; Theocritus *Id.* 7.82. **13. daturum ... auribus:** For the idiom (with the sense of "to deceive you by speaking words you want to hear"), cf. Cic. *Fam.* 12.16.1 (Trebonius writing): *Noli putare, mi Cicero, me hoc auribus tuis dare.* **18. palpo percutere:** "to flatter"; cf. Plaut. *Am.* 526; *Merc.* 153. **26. Dirces alumnus:** i.e., Pindar, whom Horace (*Carm.* 4.2.25) calls *Dircaeum cycnum.* "Dirce" was the name given to a spring near Thebes and by extension refers to the whole region (cf. Verg. *Ecl.* 2.24). **29–30. Praeiudicatae ... :** weight of authority prohibits us [i.e., Muret] from sorting out good arguments from bad ones. After expressing his disapproval of the Pythagorean reliance on the **Auctoritatis pondus:** Muret alludes to Cicero's rebuttal to those who seek to learn his personal dogmas at *DND* 1.10: For dependence on the authority of Pythagoras (*ipse dixit*), Cicero concludes, *tantum opinio praeiudicata poterat, ut etiam sine ratione valeret auctoritas.* **32. inficiemur:** from *infitiari.*

2. ODE TO DANIEL SCHLEICHER
ALCAIC STROPHE

The affectionate tone that Muret takes toward this student or companion exemplifies what Dejob (53) calls the "moeurs faciles" that so often provoked suspicions of sodomy. In his poem, *Triple amour* (1584) Jean-Edouard du Monin describes Muret's affection for Schleicher with a touch of irony.[1]

> En tel miroir jadis, le pudique Platon
> Mira l'eternal beau au beau fils d'Agathon.
> Je croy que Scalichier fut en telle lunette
> Pour aider à voir Dieu à la muse Murette.

> As if in a mirror once modest Plato marveled at eternal beauty in the beautiful son of Agathon. I believe that Scalichier was like a pair of eyeglasses that help us see God in the Muse of Muret.

Truly there was much suspicion surrounding Muret, but from where did it originate? Giovanni Dall'Orto, in his article on Muret in *Who's Who in Gay and Lesbian History,*[2] points to this ode of Muret as proof that the rumors of sodomy were true and calls Schleicher one of the humanist's lovers, but the poem itself cannot lead us definitively to that conclusion. Dejob (p. 55), as Dall'Orto indicates, mentions a seventeenth-century *Apologia pro Mureto criminis sodomiae postulato* written by J. Voigt (neither Dejob nor Dall'Orto saw it),[3] which is likely to be a response to attacks appearing in Protestant literature. For example, Théodore de Bèze, who faced similar charges, ridicules Muret for his immorality in this regard,

---

1. Colletet, who cites this poem (p. 281), identifies "Scalichier" as Schleicher, and "Murette" as Muret.
2. Edd. R. Aldrich and G. Wotherspoon, vol. 1 (London and New York, 2001): 320–21
3. Appearing in *Apparatus societatis colligentium,* 1: 93–616.

or rather, ridicules Rome for accepting and honoring the man that France and Venice rejected (*Poemata* [Geneva, 1599], 74–75). Regardless, such condemnation only surfaced in the literature when Muret became a priest in 1576. It seems clear that Muret's rapport and interaction with his students, the camaraderie itself, aroused feelings of mistrust and apprehension in the parents and close observers. Significantly, though, we have no record of the students themselves complaining about their teacher.

In antiquity, the lyric ode did not typically serve as a vehicle for complaint or lament for a lost loved one; that was more often the function of elegy. Here, at first glance, by virtue of the compounding of death imagery, Muret gives the impression that he is lamenting the deceased and departed Schleicher—the swan dies, Orpheus descends into the underworld, the poet despairs of seeing him again and contemplates death—but as the poem progresses we discover that his friend has just moved away and, in fact, can ease the pain by writing.

1–2. Descende caelo . . . modos: from Hor. *Carm.* 3.4.1–2: *Descende caelo et dic age tibia / regina longum Calliope melos.* **regina . . . Calliope:** Hesiod (*Theog.* 79) says that she is the most excellent of all the Muses: ἣ δὴ προφερεστάτη ἐστὶν ἁπασῶν. **6. Caystri:** or "Caystros," a river in Lydia celebrated for its abundance of swans. **8. Voce canit moriente cycnus:** Muret is making a variation on Sen. *Phaed.* 302: *dulcior vocem moriente cycno.* The sad song that the swan sings at death was proverbial; see esp. Mart. 13.77: *Dulcia defecta modulatur carmina lingua / cantator cycnus funeris ipse sui.* See also *id.* 5.37.1 and Ov. *Her.* 7.1–2. **9–10. Thracius . . . sacerdos:** Orpheus, husband of Eurydice. **12. posuere venti:** cf. Verg. *Aen.* 7.27–28: *cum venti posuere, omnisque repente resedit / flatus.* **17. o iuvenum decus:** cf. *Carm.* 1.1. above and 3.26 below. Also, cf. Vergil speaking of Turnus, *Aen.* 7.473: *decus . . . iuventae.* **29. Daulias:** a reference to the transformed Philomela, a story told at Ov. *Met.* 6.424ff. See also Cat. 65.14, where she is described as *gemens.* **30. furtifica manu:** *Furtific-* is found only in Roman comedy; cf. Plaut. *Ps.* 887: *ut praerodatis vostras furtificas manus.* **37. fluctibus opprimar:** i.e., a flood of tears, but reminiscent of Vergil's depiction of the drowned Trojans (*Aen.* 1.128–129): *disiectam Aeneae toto videt aequore classem, / fluctibus oppressos Troas caelique ruina.*

3. Ode to Claudius Voesius
Alcaic Strophe

One can only assume that the "calumny" of which Muret speaks in this poem relates to the charge of "penchants antiphysiques" already discussed in the introduction above and in the notes on the second ode. This must be the accusation he faced while at Paris, since the problem at Toulouse was with Frémiot, not Voesie. It is by no means clear, however, in what way the Daniel Schleicher of the previous ode fits into the picture, other than giving an indication of the behavioral pattern that brought suspicion on Muret. But even given the tender language with which Muret addresses his students (if, indeed, we are talking about a student here), a language that he is not afraid to use in the poem itself, we cannot make the assumption that something sinister lies beneath the words. The charges against him, personified here by the goddess Calumny, once made, "crush the guiltless," an insistence upon his own innocence that comes right on the heels of an admission of strong affection. With that point made, Muret uses historical and mythological exempla to illustrate the ruinous effects of calumny, in each case choosing characters who were exonerated only after suffering the consequences of the accusation.

6. matre rupta, vipera nascitur: The widely-held belief that vipers are born by bursting from the mother (Plin. 10.82) generated a number of emblems on the subject during the Renaissance. For example, Théodore de Bèze uses the imagery in his emblem entitled, *Vipera ex utero matris rupto erumpens* (xviii in the 1599 ed. of his poetry) to illustrate the point that sometimes the Church's enemies come from within herself. **8. geniti sub aquis chelydri:** not "sea turtles," as one would expect at first glance, since they would hardly fit into a list of sinister creatures. For χέλυδρος as an amphibious serpent see Nicander *Ther.* 411 (see the notes of Gow-Scholfield *ad loc.*) and Verg. *Georg.* 2.214, where likewise the turtle would be out of place. **9–10: herba ... Thessalis:** Thessaly was proverbially the land of black magic and witches. The cult of Hecate thrived there as well. **13. Calumniae:** The earliest known personification of "Slander" occurs in a painting of the famous Greek artist Apelles after a rival slandered him to his patron, Ptolemy IV Philopator, king of Egypt. His allegorical representation is itself lost, but Lucian provides a detailed description of the painting in his *De calumnia* 5 that inspired Botticelli's "The Calumny of Apelles." For a discussion of the influence of Lucian's description on the Renaissance, see Rudolph Altrocchi, "The Calumny of Apelles in the Literature of the Quattrocento," *PMLA* 36 (1921): 454–91. **18. Beli nepotem:** a rather oblique reference to the story of Leucothoë and the Sun-god, as told by Ov. *Met.* 4.190ff. (see esp. line 213, where her father is described as "seventh in line from old Belus"). Clytie slanders Leucothoë and as a result she is buried alive. **20. sophiae parentem:** Socrates. **23. Thesidae:** The story of Phaedra's attempted seduction of Hippolytus, son of Theseus, now follows at some length. **45. genitrice:** an allusion to the story of Pasiphae's lust for the bull that resulted in the birth of the Minotaur. **46. gesa:** i.e., *gaesa*, a kind of Greek spear (cf. Stat. *Theb.* 4.64, *pars gaesa manu*). **47. odora et vis sagacium:** a transferred epithet; cf. Verg. *Aen.* 4.132: *odora canum vis*. **58. soror:** i.e., Calumny, who sprang from the earth as did the giants. **62. Umbone . . . triplici:** When defenses are tripled they are considered particularly strong. Vergil (*Aen.* 6.549) describes Tartarus as "surrounded by a triple wall" (*triplici circumdata muro*). We are to marvel that Aeneas is so powerful that he can drive his spear through Mezentius' shield of triple bronze to wound him (*Aen.* 10.784).

4. ODE TO RONSARD
SECOND ASCLEPIADEAN STROPHE

Muret's relationship to Ronsard, "prince of the French poets," is well known (see introduction and "Names") and his respect for his accomplishments is apparent from the commentary on the *Amours*. Ronsard's own book of odes (in the vernacular) was first published in 1550, and so appropriately Muret chooses it as the medium for expressing his affections for him.

1. Aonii pectinis: The word "pecten" can refer to the pick used to strike the strings of a lyre, to the song played on the lyre, or to the lyre itself. Vergil (*Aen.* 6.647) has Orpheus in the underworld striking the seven lyre strings "with an ivory pecten" (*pectine pulsat eburno*), the image Muret himself has in mind as indicated by the mention of ivory in the next line. "Aonian" is an epithet of the Muses and is applied to anything within their purview, particularly the lyre (cf. Ov. *Am.* 1.1.12 and Prop. 1.2.27–8). **3–4: potens . . . sistere:** Orpheus is commonly attributed with the power to calm winds, move rocks, and tame wild beasts with his music. See, e.g., Ov. *AA* 3.321; *Trist.* 4.1.17–18; Hor. *AP* 392–93, etc. **5. Vindocino ex agro:** Ronsard was born at Château de la Possonnière near Vendôme. **7–8. quis . . . dies:** The "day stored up in white fleece" alludes to a passage of Statius' well-known epithalamium (1.2.24–25), where the poet refers to a supremely happy day as *Parcarum conditus albo / vellere*. In spinning the threads of life the Fates mark happy days with white wool, unhappy days with black (and see Hor. *Carm.* 2.3.15–16 concerning death: *sororum / fila trium patiuntur atra*). For *niveo vellere*, cf. Tib. 1.6.77. **11. postes:** i.e., of temples, where one might properly hang up votive offerings. **13–14. memor / Nostri vive:** echoing the dying wish of Canace at Ov. *Her.* 11.125: *vive memor nostri, lacrimasque in vulnera funde.* **ita:** introducing an emphatic wish. **15. Rumor . . . gemmeus:** taken from Mart. 10.3.10, speaking of the fame of his books: *quos rumor alba gemmeus vehit pinna.* Muret wishes that Ronsard find fame through his writing.

5. ODE TO DENISOT
ALCAIC STROPHE

Picking up a topos already developed in Horace's epistle to Maecenas (*Epist.* 1.19), Muret extols the role that Dionysus (i.e., wine) plays in poetic inspiration. For his part, Horace denies that poems written by "water-drinkers" (*aquae potoribus*) could ever be pleasing, while at the same time asserting that the Muses themselves take to hard drinking and often smack of wine in the morning. Cratinus and Homer, he says, also taught that poets should be drinkers. Muret agrees, adding that wine has always been a secret subsitute for the traditional sacred springs that supposedly have inspired poets from Hesiod onward.

3. novem . . . puellis: the nine Muses, who would be the usual inspiration for poets. **14–15. ferunt / aetatem:** for the phrasing cf. Cic. *Sen.* 6; Petr. *Satyr.* 43.7; Macr. *Sat.* 2.3.1 (*bibite Falernum hoc, annorum quadraginta est: bene, inquit, aetatem fert*). **9. Anacreon:** Greek lyric poet from Teos in Asia Minor, died c. 490 BCE. For most of his career he was a court poet of Polycrates of Samos. After the latter's death he moved to Athens. To posterity Anacreon was famed for his drunkenness. His statue on the acropolis in Athens shows him inebriated and singing, with one shoe missing and the other loose (G. Richter, *The Portraits of the Greeks*, 3 vols. [London, 1965], 1: 75–78, figs. 271–98; cf. *A.P.* 16.306). A Hellenistic epigram (*A.P.* 7.24) describes him as φιλάκρατος and οἰνοβαρής i.e., "fond of neat wine" and "heavy with wine." **11. Ennius:** Roman poet who wrote the *Annales*, d. 169 BCE. Horace (*Epist.* 1.19.7–8) claims that Ennius never wrote epic without first having a drink: *Ennius ipse pater numquam nisi potus ad arma prosiluit dicenda*. This explains Ennius' own statement (*Sat.* 64) that he never composes poetry unless he has the gout: *numquam poetor nisi si podager*. **19. dulce tormentum:** an oxymoronic mental state induced by the wine; cf. Hor. 3.21.13: *Tu lene tormentum ingenio admoves*. **22. vocalis undae:** cf. Stat. *Silv.* 1.2.6: *de Pieriis vocalis fontibus unda;* id. ib. 5.5.2: *Castaliae vocales undae*. The reference is to a spring frequented by the Muses. **21. imperiti:** Cicero (*Pro Val. Flac.* 16) defines *homines imperiti* as *rerum omnium rudes ignarique*, i.e., "inexperienced and uninstructed." Cf. Liv. 1.19.4, *multitudo imperita et rudis*. Muret addresses his remarks to those uninitiated who expect their poets to draw inspiration from sacred springs and the gift of the Muses and are shocked to find them with a bottle instead. The same are called *fatui* in line 24. **22–23. bifidi duplex / Montis cacumen:** Mt. Parnassus, haunt of Apollo and the Muses. Its two peaks (Tithorea and Lycorea) are often alluded to; see, e.g., Ov. *Met.* 1.316–17: *mons ibi verticibus petit arduus astra duobus, / nomine Parnasus*. . . . Here, between the Nauplia and Hyamplia cliffs of Lycorea flows the Castalian spring. Persius

(*Prol.* 2) claims not to remember sleepng on double-peaked Parnassus (*bicipiti . . . Parnaso*) to obtain his inspiration, but to have been driven by necessity alone to exercise his talents. **24. fatui:** recalling the first words that the Muses spoke to Hesiod (*Theog.* 26): Ποιμένες ἄγραυλοι, κάκ' ἐλέγχεα, γαστέρες οἶον.

6. ODE TO JAN TILIUS
ALCAIC STROPHE

Muret uses the paraenesis form (exhortation or entreaty to becoming conduct), to commend the young Jan Tilius to the love of God, parents, and teachers. His inspiration comes not so much from classical sources as from the New Testament and the ecclesiastical tradition, where paraenesis finds its fullest expression (e.g., I Thess. 4:13–18; 5:1–11; I Cor. 5–15).

1. **tenellis . . . ab unguibus:** Muret uses the same idiom in the preface: *a teneris, ut Graeci dicunt, unguiculis.* **21. Nil turpe factu dicere fas puta:** Théodore de Bèze, in the preface of the second edition of his poetry (1569), cites a similar verse from his own poetry: *Quae fecisse nefas, fingere facta nefas.* The verse does not appear among the extant poems of Bèze, however (on this see *Correspondance de Théodore de Bèze,* vol. X [Geneva, 1980], 92). For comparable wording but a somewhat different thrust, cf. Tac. *Dial. de orat.* 28.4: *coram qua neque dicere fas erat quod turpe dictu neque facere quod inhonestum factu videretur.*

INDEX

The following list includes only names and subjects of special interest. Modern authors and scholars have been excluded altogether. References to names and subjects are tied only to the English translation of the poems, preface, and the commentary, as well as to the introduction. If reference is made to a theme, motif, or proper name in the poems, the reader should assume that the same is discussed in the commentary and need not be doubly referenced here.

Achilles, 29
Adagia (Erasmus), 4 n2, 10n1, 45, 141, 149, 160, 164
adultery, 55, 59
Aeolus, 45, 71, 93, 139, 152
Aethra, 71, 138
Agen, xiii, xv, xliii, xliv, 145
Alciato, xxiii, xxxv, xxxxi, xxxviii, 64
Alexandrianism, xvii, 42
Alis, Étienne, 105
Alisius, Stephanus. *See* Alis, Étienne
Alsinous, Comes. *See* Denisot, Nicolas
Anacreon, 197, 208
androgyny, 50
Aonian pectin, 207
Apella, 95, 152
Apelles, 206
Apollo, 31, 46, 47, 48, 49, 57, 64, 97, 135, 138, 145, 153, 179, 181, 185, 208
apotropaic phrases, 42, 43
Arcadia, 103, 156
Archilochus: attack on Lycambes, 59, 65

Aristotle, xx, xxii, xxiv
Armagnac, Cardinal d', xvi
Asclepius, 49
Auch, xv–xvi
Augustus, 13, 47, 129
Auratus. *See* Dorat
Aurora, 69, 111, 138, 139, 162
Aurunca, 55
Ausonius, xxv, 13
Avitus, 107, 160

Bacchus, 42, 109, 152, 163, 185, 197.
 See also Lyaeus
Baïf, Jean Antoine de, 3, 5, 11, 15, 44, 179, 184–85, 203
Balbus, 55
Baldus de Ubaldis, 39, 51
Baluze, E., xxv
Bellay, Joachim du, xiii, xxxiv, 11
Bellerophon, 25
Belus, 181
Benci, F., xix, xxiv
Bèze, Théodore de, xxii, xxv–xxvi, xliv,

211

42, 47, 48, 140, 204, 206, 209
Bordeaux, xv–xvi, 29
Boug, 29
Bourbon, Nicolas, xxv–xxvi
Bourg, Claude du, 119, 166
Brinon, Jean de, xliii, 9, 11, 15
Briseis, 29
Brutus, 57, 129, 171–72
Buchanan, George, xiii, xx, 1 n1
Burge, Claude, xlii

cabalistic imagery, xxv
Cairiechius, François Laccius, 101
Caliantheus, Charles, x, 83, 146–47
Callée, Antoine, xlii
Calumny: personified, 193, 206
carpe diem, 43, 141
Castalian spring, 69, 208
Catherine of Alexandria, St., 119, 121, 166–67
Cato, 95, 117, 153, 165, 185
Catullus, xiii, xvi–xx, xxv, 13; castration of Attis (*c.* 63), 156; inversion of *c.* 16; laments his brother, 45; language imitated, 141, 150, 156 (*c.* 45); scorns the old, 44; variation on *c.* 32; writes naughty poetry
cena. *See* dinner invitation
Chaos, 101
Charles IX, xxiii
Charon, 31, 48, 81, 131, 145
Chesneau, Louis, 15
Chiron, 31
choragus, 64
Christ, 55, 57, 111
Church Fathers, xxiv
Cicero, xiv, xvi, xxi, xxiii, 131
Clain, 29
Clio, 35
Colet de Rumilly en Champagne, Claude, 99
Coletus Campanus. *See* Colet de Rumilly

Collaeus, Antoine. *See* Collet, Antoine
Collège de Boncourt, xvi
Collège de Guyenne, xvi
Collège du Cardinal Lemoine, xvi
College of Sainte-Marthe, xv
Colletet, xx n14
Collina, xlii, 127, 170
Colloquy of Poissy, xxii
Condom, Rudolphe, 83
Connan, François de, 123
Connanus, Franciscus. *See* Connan, François de
Cordus, 59, 65
Corellius, 103, 157
Corinna, 42, 57, 64
Costecandus, Jean, 101, 156
Costecaudus. *See* Costecandus
Crassus, 121, 168
Croesus, 99
Crouzeil, Pierre, xli, 31, 48–49
Crucius, Marius, 85, 107
Crucius, Sanso, 115
Cruselius, P. *See* Crouzeil, Pierre
Cujas, Jacques, xxiii
Cumae, 27
Cupid (Love), ix, 19, 21, 31, 33, 87, 89, 97, 117, 137; band of Erotes, 69; Eros and Anteros, 150
Cynthia (Propertius' girlfriend), 63, 138

Daphne, 48–49, 97, 153
Daurat. *See* Dorat
death, 23, 101, 123
Délian, Jean, 105
Denisot, Nicolas, 3, 5, 15, 197, 208
dinner invitation, 83, 85, 123
Dis, 193
Dorat, Jean, xiii, xxv, xxxvii, xl, 2–3, 11, 13; as master of both Greek and Latin, 189, 203
doves: as erotic symbols, 45; term of endearment, 75
dream motif, 73
drunkenness, 105, 107, 109, 113, 117,

121
Duchat, François le, xiii

Electra, 25
elegy: the "elegiac life," 51; its roots, 47; nature of, 158
emblematic imagery, xxv, 64, 206
Ennius, 150, 197, 208
Epicureanism, 64, 97, 149, 154, 163–64
epigrams: carnivalesque exaggeration in, 161; nature of, 69, 89, 137, 150, 158, 161, 170
Erebus, 27, 69, 139
Erycina, 117, 165. *See also* Venus
Este, Ippolito d', xiii, xxi–xxii, xxiii n18
Este, Louis d', xxiii n18
Estes, Alphonse II d', xxiii
Estienne, Robert, xxiv n19
Eteocles, 19
Étoile, Pierre de l', xxxviii
evil leaders, 103. *See also* poor, abuse of
extravagance, 57

Falernian wine, 29, 197
false learning, 109
fame, 166, 169, 181, 195, 197
Fates, 21, 31, 83, 101, 109, 119
Ferrara, xxi
Ferri, Girolamo, xxi
fidelity, 27
Flaminio, Marcantonio, xxxvii, 13
Fortune, 86, 107, 119, 123, 166, 169, 183
Francis I, xl, 151
Frémiot, Luc-Menge (or Memmius), xx, 135, 148, 206
friendship, 201
Frogs (Aristophanes), 153
Furies, 27, 127

Galatea, 48
Galla, 79, 81, 145
Gallonius, 113, 163
Garonne river, 47

Gaurus, 111, 121, 162, 168
Gellia, 99, 154
gift-giving, 113, 127, 129, 131, 133
gluttony, 113, 115, 121
golden mean, 154
Gorgons, 170
Goudimel, Claude, xiii
Gouvéa (or Govéa), Antoine de, 69
Grannius, 101, 155
greed, 97
Grévin, J., xvi n 8

Harpy, 172
Helen, 27, 47
Helicon, 179
hellebore, 184
Henri II, 13
Hercules, 55
Hermaphroditus, 49–50
hieroglyphic tradition, xxv
Hippocrates, 31
Hippocrene, 199
Hippolytus, 129, 159, 171, 206
Homer, 95, 119
hope, 25, 27
Horace, xxi–xxii, 13, 169–70 (satire on the bore); contempt for riches, 44; on philosophical study, 168; on satire, 65; on wine, 173, 208
Horapollo, xxv
Hymen, 19
hypocrisy, 55, 59

icy fire motif, 35. *See also* Petrarch
India, 193
insomnia, 97, 143
Iris, 99
iuvenilia, meaning of the term, xxv–xxvi, 3, 15, 19, 21

Jodelle, Étienne, xiii, xxxviii, 1 n1, 7, 15, 181, 185
Jodellus, Stephanus, *see* Jodelle
Julius Caesar, 129, 137–38, 171

Juno, 71, 85, 152, 164
Jupiter, 19, 25, 57, 69, 71, 103
Justinian, 39
Juvenal, xxv, 63

Kara-Su, 191
kisses, 23, 29, 73, 75, 77; as ambrosia, 49

Lais, 107
Lambin, Denys, xiii, xxi–xxii, xxxix
language: 93, 95; jejune and dry, 167; unclean, 101
Latium, 95
law, 51, 123
Leucothoë, 206
Limoges, xiii, xv, xxv
Limousin, xl
Linocier, Guillaume, xl
Lochianus, Michel, 131
Lombardy, xx
Loménie, François de. *See* Lomenius, F. Gratus
Lomenius, F. Gratus, xxxviii, 87, 93
Lomenius, F. Verus, xxxviii, 35
Lorraine, Cardinal de, xxxvii
love: attempts to conceal, 87; bestial appetites, 85; lovesickness, 31; paradoxical nature of, 141; as reciprocity, 79, 81; as soldiery, 19; as surrender, 144; union of souls, 23, 33
lover as hunter, 153
Lucilius, 63
Lucius, xlii, 109
Lucretius, 57, 139, 149, 165
Lyaeus, 93, 152, 160, 181, 185, 199
Lycaon, 156
Lycinna, 55
Lydia, 154, 173, 205
Lygdus, xlii, 85, 95, 103

Macrin, Jean Salmon, xiii, xxxviii–xxxix, 13
magnet, 73

Manutius, Paulus, xiii, xvi, xx
Manuzio, Paolo. *See* Manutius
Marc Antony, 63
Marcus Brutus, 129
Marguerite, xlii, 19, 27, 29, 33, 35, 37, 69, 79, 129, 131
Marot, xxvi
Martial, xvii, xix, xxv, 168; language imitated, 150
masking, 99, 154
Melampus, 184
Memmius. *See* Frémiot, Luc-Menge
Midas, 64
Molza, Francesco Maria, xxxix, 13
Moncaudus, François, xxxix
Monin, Jean-Edouard du, 204
Montaigne, xiii, xv–xvi
Montausier, Charles de, xxxix, 91, 93
Montbas, Guillaume de. *See* Montbasius
Montbasius, Guillelmus, xxxix
Morin, Pierre, xxi
Morrison, M., xvi
Muret, Marc-Antoine: birth and early career, xv–xvi; and the Calvinists, xxii; Catullus lectures and commentaries, xvi–xviii; contamination of Christian piety and classicizing humanism, xiii–xv; death, xxiv; and homosexuality (*penchants antiphysiques*), xx–xxi, 192–94; the *Iulius Caesar,* xv–xvi; *De laudibus literarum,* xiv–xv, xxi; library, present location, xxiv; *mos docendi gallicus,* xxiii; plagiarism, xxii; poetry creates "flashes of glory," xiv–xviii; religious poems and hymns, xxiv; retirement, xxiv; *Variae Lectiones,* xxii
Muses, 19, 21, 35, 83, 105, 125, 135, 137–38, 145–46, 181, 185, 189, 197, 205–209; Aonian cohort, 81; Calliope addressed, 191-205; *ferox,* 65

Nature: personified, 103

nautical metaphor, 164
Navarre, Marguerite de, 91, 93
Nicolas de Vienne, 177, 183
Nicolaus of Vienna. *See* Nicolas de
 Vienne
Nicolay, Antoine, xxxvii
Noallius, xxxix, 95
nobile scortum, 184
noble ancestry, 87, 179, 184
nugae, 137, 168
Numa, 57
nymphs, 181
Nyx, 27, 69

Odysseus. *See* Ulysses
Oeagrus, 19
Oenone, 27
Ogerie, Anne, xlii
old age, 131
old woman, 127
Orcus, 131
Orestes, 25
Orpheus (Thracian priest), xv, 42, 205, 207
Otho, xlii, 115
otium: among poets, 37, 39; vs.
 negotium, 137
outbidding formula, 138, 153
Ovid, xxv

Padua, xxi–xxii, xxiv
Pamphagus, xlii, 113
Pandects, xxiii
Parcae. *See* Fates
Paris (of Troy), 27
Paris, xvi, xix–xx, xxiv n19
Paroemiographi (Diogenianus), 10 n1
Pasiphae, 206
Paul, 55
Paula, xlii
Paulus, xlii, 109, 111, 127, 129
peacock, 147
Penelope, 29
Persephone, 25, 31

Perses, 201
Petrarch, xxvi; and the "icy fire" motif, 50, 71
Phaedra, 129, 171, 206
pheasant, 147
Philomela, 205
philosophy, 146–47
Phoebus. *See* Apollo
Phyllis, xlii, 83
Picton, 29
Pindar, 203
Plato, xiii, xiv, xxiii–xxiv
Plautus, xix
pleasure: vs. reason, 113; vanity of sensual pleasure, 140
Pléiade, xvi, 11, 185, 203
Po, 29
poetry, 89, 95, 111; critics and criticism, 43, 89, 101, 121, 125, 129; enduring, 105, 107, 209; figuratively called nectar, 203; in France, 11, 13, 189, 203; golden, 89; in Greece and Rome, 189; and madness, 105, 115, 197; as a means of complaint, 205; and memorization, 109; as a mirror, 42; obscurity of, 115, 117; and riches, 133
poets: *doctus,* 168, 171; as liars, 143; poverty of, 173; and wine, 158, 185, 187
poison, 181
Poitiers, xiii, xv
Poland, xxiv
Poliziano, xxv
Polyneices, 19
Polyphemus, 48
Pompilius, xlii, 109
Pontano, Giovanni. *See* Pontanus
Pontanus, Joannes Jovianus, xxv, xxxix, 13
Ponticus, xlii, 89, 97, 107
Pontilianus, xlii, 107, 117
poor: abuse of, 55, 59
Pope Paul IV, xxii

Pope Pius IV, xxii
Pope Pius V, xiii, xxiii
Porna, xlii, 87
Pornus, 203
Priapus, 91
priests: criticism of, 59, 103
prodigiousness, 97
Proetus, 184
propempticon, 166
Propertius, xxi, 39; diatribe against cosmetics, 154
prostitution, 57, 107
Pythagoras, 204

Querculus, Ludovicus. *See* Chesnau, Louis
quintessence, 77
Quintius, Pierre, xl, 119

Ramus, xxii
recusatio, 19, 93, 145, 184
Romanus, xlii, 99
Rome, xxi–xxii
Ronsard, Pierre, xiii, xvi, xx n13, xl, 11, 44, 197, 203, 207
Roussanes. *See* Roux, Pierre le
Roux, Pierre le, 53, 57
Rufa, 99
Rufinus, xlii, 123
Rufus, Petrus. *See* Roux, Pierre le
rustic simplicity, 23, 37, 121, 133

sadness, 119
Sammarthanus, Scaevola, xxv
Sannazaro, Jacopo, xl, 13
satire: as uncontrollable indignation, 55, 59
satyrs, 205
Scaliger, Joseph, xvi, xix n12
Scaliger, Julius Caesar, xiii, xvi, xl–xli, 69, 81, 83, 93, 125; his genius, 91
Schleicher, Daniel, xli, 59, 191, 204–206
Secundus, xxv; borrowings from, 141
Seine, 181

separation, 25, 29, 45, 47, 77, 179, 205
Sestius, xlii, 113
Sigismond of Poland, xxiii
Silenus, 185
slothfulness, 113
Socrates, 206
sodomy, 148, 155
sophistry, 105
soul: address to, 71; as a runaway slave and an army deserter, 139
Spain, 193
sparrow: term of endearment, 75
sphragis, 173
Stentor, 55
Studium Sapientiae. *See* University of Rome
Styx, 99, 127, 129
Sybaritic poets, 91
Symposium (Plato), 49. *See also* Plato

Tacitus, xiii
Terence, xvi, xxi
Theseus, 27
Thisbe, 179, 184–85
Thrace, 181
Tibullus, xxi, 39
Tilius, Janus. *See* Tillet, Jean du
Tillet, Jean du, 199, 201, 209
time: perception of, 146
Titan, 83, 117
Tithonius, 139
Torannus, 55
Toulouse, xiii, xx
Tournon, Cardinal de, xxi–xxii
Trinquet, xvi
Triptolemus, 181, 185
Troy, 19, 25

Ulysses, 29, 119
University of Paris, xxii
University of Rome, xviii, xxii, xxiv

Valeriano, Pierio, xviii
Valesius, Louis, xli, 135

Vendôme, 197, 207
Venice, xiii, xiv, xvii, xxi, xxiv n19
Venus, 19, 21, 77, 79, 91. *See also* Erycina
Vergil, 95; use of language, 139
Vermélian d'Ussel, Jan. *See* Vermelianus
Vermelianus, Janus, xli, 1 n1, 105
Virro, xlii
virtue, 107, 119, 159–60, 171–72, 177, 181, 183, 189, 201; and glory, 109, 160; lack of, 61, 177; and wealth, 115, 127, xxv, 181
Voesie, Claude, xxv, 181

Voesius, Claudius. *See* Voesie, Claude
vows: instability of lovers', 46
Vulcan, 93

winds, 71
word play, 41, 48, 148, 152, 169, 170

Xenia (Martial), 172

youth: exhortations to, 209; the springtime of life, 21,193; untainted time of life, 59

www.ingramcontent.com/pod-product-compliance
Lightning Source LLC
Chambersburg PA
CBHW020944230426
43666CB00005B/168